DEVELOPMENTAL NEUROPSYCHOLOGY, 28(2
Copyright © 2005, Lawrence Erlbaum Associates, In

The Measurement of Executive Function in Early Childhood

Clancy Blair, Philip David Zelazo, and Mark T. Greenberg

Department of Human Development and Family Studies
Pennsylvania State University
Department of Psychology
University of Toronto

During the past decade there has been increasing interest in aspects of the broad construct of executive function (EF) in childhood. This construct, which has long been linked to cortical networks involving prefrontal cortex (PFC; e.g., Luria, 1973), includes a number of cognitive processes that are integral to the emerging self-regulation of behavior and developing social and cognitive competence in young children. These cognitive processes include the maintenance of information in working memory, the inhibition of prepotent responding, and the appropriate shifting and sustaining of attention for the purposes of goal-directed action.

Interest in the early development of EF has grown in part because of research showing that the development of EF, like the development of PFC, is particularly rapid during early childhood (for reviews, see Diamond, 2002; Zelazo & Müller, 2002) and in part because of research indicating that EF is implicated in a variety of developmental disorders and early developing psychopathologies (e.g., Barkley, 1997; Diamond, Prevor, Callendar, & Druin, 1997; McLean & Hitch, 1999; Pennington & Ozonoff, 1996). The healthy development of EF also appears to play a key role in children's developing social competence (Hughes, 1998; Hughes, Dunn, & White, 1998) and academic and social readiness to attend school (Blair, 2002; Blair, Granger, & Razza, 2005; Riggs, Blair, & Greenberg, 2004).

Although there has been great interest in and growing research on EF in early childhood, work on the early development of EF has been limited by the lack of

Correspondence should be addressed to Clancy Blair, Department of Human Development and Family Studies, Pennsylvania State University, 110 Henderson South, University Park, PA 16802. E-mail: cbb11@psu.edu

suitable measures for assessing specific aspects of EF in young children. Greater precision in the measurement of EF in young children may prove valuable for both basic and clinical science work on children's development. To begin, it has the potential to help clarify the construct of EF—for example, by allowing researchers to address ongoing questions about the relations among specific aspects of EF. In addition, however, it may contribute substantially to our understanding of developing brain–behavior relations, how these relations are affected by genetic and environmental influences, and how these relations result in specific developmental outcomes.

The purpose of this special issue, which arose from a 1-day symposium held at Pennsylvania State University on March 1, 2004, is to highlight some key issues in the measurement of EF in early childhood and to add to the corpus of reliable measures of EF that are suitable for use with young children. As demonstrated by the articles in this special issue, many issues in the definition and measurement of the construct remain. These include

- The scalability of various measures of EF in preschool children.
- The extent to which various EF tasks provide evidence for a primarily unified construct or a diverse, moderately interrelated set of constructs in early childhood.
- The role of inhibitory control in EF tasks requiring attention shifting relative to those that require only the inhibition or suppression of a given response.
- The extent to which change in EF is a cause or a consequence of other cognitive and behavioral changes, such as changes in children's theory of mind.
- The extent to which distinct processes and brain systems are at work in EF tasks that present some level of emotional arousal or appetitive or aversive contingency versus those that are emotionally neutral.
- The extent to which the characteristics of measurement stimuli are a determinant of performance in tasks requiring attention shifting.

Each of these definitional and measurement issues in the study of EF has been addressed in one form or another with older children and adults. What is of particular interest in the following articles is their examination in populations of very young children. By examining these issues in young children, each of the articles presents data on new or newly adapted measures of EF appropriate for children as young as 2 years of age and, by doing so, provides data on the emergence of EF. As the reader will find, this set of articles raises valuable questions and new directions for research on the construct and its development.

For example, Carlson's (this issue) findings provide much needed information on relations among and developmental trends in EF tasks in ages 2 through 6 years, and they demonstrate the utility of scoring tasks as pass/fail for analysis. Furthermore, with an unprecedented volume of data, a sample size of 602 and 20 EF tasks,

Carlson is able to provide an analysis of developmental trends in task performance and scalability of various tasks at various ages. Such an analysis can do much to advance understanding of the development of EF but has not been previously available. Thus, the data she describes provide a very useful first step toward the creation of a reliable and valid battery for the measurement of EF across the early childhood years. Given the proliferation of research on EF and the growing number of similar yet distinct tasks utilized in various studies, Carlson's data provide the first sound basis for estimating the expected probability of success on a given task at a given age. As such, Carlson's analysis works to provide for the measurement of EF what Wellman and Liu (2004) recently provided for the measurement of theory of mind. Although Carlson's analysis does not specifically address the unity versus diversity of EF, it does provide the basis for further work to examine whether there may be scalable tasks to assess distinct processes of working memory, attention shifting, and inhibitory control. In this way, Carlson's article adds substantial new knowledge on the basic developmental course of EF and suggests an important direction for future research.

As with Carlson, Espy and Bull (this issue) identify some of the dimensions along which future studies may examine the unity and diversity of EF in young children. By utilizing a between-groups approach, a design applied frequently in the study of working memory in adults, the authors identify groups of preschool children characterized by high versus low memory span. Controlling for working memory capacity in this way, the authors present data concerning the extent to which differences between the groups are observed in tasks primarily characterized by response suppression as opposed to those that demand the suppression of an internally represented rule or previously active response set. As expected, no differences were observed between the memory span groups on tasks characterized by response suppression. However, differences were observed on tasks that required the appropriate shifting of attention. Espy and Bull's results suggest that response suppression is distinct from and developmentally in advance of attention control. In addition, their findings provide evidence in preschool children for distinctions between response suppression and attention shifting that have been observed previously in older children and adults in both neuropsychological and brain-imaging research (e.g., Casey, Thomas, Davidson, Kunz, & Franzen, 2002; Ridderinkhof, Wildenberg, Segalowitz, & Carter, 2004).

In their article, Hughes and Ensor (this issue) introduce several new tasks of EF appropriate for 2-year-olds and provide evidence for a relation between EF and two newly developed measures of theory of mind in a sample of children from low-income families in the United Kingdom. In their analysis, Hughes and Ensor demonstrate moderate internal consistency among their EF tasks, utilizing an aggregate score for analyses rather than attempting to isolate distinct working memory, attention shifting, or inhibitory control subcomponent processes of EF. As a consequence, their results do not address the issue of the unity versus diversity of

EF but do provide the clear indication that individual differences in EF and theory of mind are meaningfully related in children as young as 2 years of age. Also of particular interest, there is further indication in their data of the advisability of utilizing a pass/fail approach to the measurement of EF in which the binomial theorem is utilized to determine criteria for success.

The contribution of Diamond, Carlson, and Beck (this issue) also demonstrates the utility, if not necessity, of scoring tasks as pass/fail with young children in the investigation of the role of attentional inertia, or the inability to shift attention from a previously attended dimension, in performance on tasks examining EF. Working from the perspective that a characteristic of cognition is to bind stimulus properties, the data of Diamond et al. suggest that improvements in performance on attention shifting tasks between ages 2½ to 3½ years of age can be understood to occur as a function of the extent to which the young child can unbind stimulus characteristics. By varying the degree to which stimulus characteristics are bound, the authors present developmental evidence indicating that young children are better at making an attention shift in a dimensional change task when the to-be-inhibited dimension of the task is a property of the background rather than the shape itself. As with previous work by the authors and others, Diamond et al. once again demonstrates the role of context and support as a determinant of EF task performance. The manipulation of stimulus properties in their study provides a highly illuminating example of the ways in which this type of experimental control works to advance understanding of developmental change in EF task performance.

In their article, Hongwanishkul, Happaney, Lee, and Zelazo (this issue) point to recent work in cognitive neuroscience to support a distinction between two aspects of EF, the relatively "hot" affective aspects associated more with ventromedial regions of PFC and the more purely cognitive, "cool" aspects associated with dorsolateral PFC. By distinguishing between hot and cool EF, these authors address the question of the unity versus diversity of EF in a different way: The same basic control processes may operate differently depending on whether one is in a situation that has some appetitive or aversive component. Their finding that hot EF demonstrated age-related changes but was generally unrelated to other aspects of child functioning to which cool EF was related raises several interesting questions. For example, is hot EF more contextually bound than cool EF? How do levels of child arousal or arousability within a task setting influence task performance? Another question concerns a possible need for further measurement development and theorizing about hot EF and its relation to cool EF and to aspects of child social and cognitive functioning. At a minimum, the findings of Hongwanishkul et al. suggest an exciting new direction in work on EF that may serve as an example of the type of work that can help to expand the definition and scope of the construct and ultimately lead to a more holistic and integrated model of cognitive and social development.

In their article, Rueda, Posner, and Rothbart (this issue) examine relations between the emerging control of attention and the emerging self-regulation of behavior from psychological, neurological, and temperamental perspectives. Of particular interest in their contribution is an articulation of the integrated and reciprocal nature of relations among different influences on EF, including those at the genetic level. In essence, Rueda and colleagues consider EF from a developmental systems perspective and provide a conceptual and empirical framework within which advances in the control of attention contribute to and are supported by advances in the self-regulation of behavior. This developmental systems approach to the study of EF provides an important foundation for understanding ways in which the executive control of attention serves to integrate social and cognitive domains of functioning. When considering the whole child and the relation of specific cognitive processes to the regulation of ongoing behavior, the roles of emotional arousal and reactivity become prominent and need to be accounted for in a comprehensive understanding of behavior. Similarly, as shown in the contribution by Rueda and colleagues, training studies of executive attention and influences of training-related advances in executive attention on behavior provide a valuable means for studying EF and its role in emerging self-regulation early in development.

THE MEASUREMENT OF EF IN YOUNG CHILDREN: ASSESSMENT OF A UNIQUE ASPECT OF CHILD FUNCTIONING

One of the overarching themes of this special issue is that continued work of the measurement of EF in early childhood is essential for the advancement of the study of developing self-regulation. EF characterizes dimensions of cognition and social–emotional functioning that are not captured by previous constructs. For example, although the brain structures and neural interconnectivity that support cognitive processes representative of EF overlap considerably with those associated with general intelligence (Braver et al., 1997; Duncan, 2001; Duncan et al., 2000; Gray, Chabris, & Braver, 2003; Prabhakaran, Smith, Desmond, Glover, & Gabrieli, 1997; Thompson et al., 2001), EF is distinct from general intelligence. Specifically, as seen in a wide variety of work ranging from studies on rising mean IQ (Flynn, 1999), to clinical neuropsychological work on individuals sustaining damage to specific areas of the PFC (Waltz et al., 1999), to work on a number of early developing psychopathologies and developmental disorders (Pennington, 1997; Pennington & Ozonoff, 1996), EF plays a unique role in human development (see Blair, in press, for review). It may be that the distinction between EF and general intelligence is especially true of the more affective, hot aspects of EF (Hongwanishkul et al., this issue), and it is hoped that advances in the measurement of both hot and cool EF can help to provide increased specificity to the distinction between EF and general intelligence.

Some of the most pressing evidence concerning the unique role of EF in human development and the need for increased precision in its measurement is found in the study of cognitive impairment among individuals with specific developmental disorders (Zelazo & Müller, 2002). Studies examining cognition in children with attention deficit hyperactivity disorder, early and continuously treated phenylketonuria, and specific learning disabilities indicate impaired performance on measures of EF but general intelligence in the normal range (Barkley, 1997; Berlin, 2003; Diamond et al., 1997; McLean & Hitch, 1999; Stanovich, Siegel, & Gottardo, 1997; Swanson, 1999). From an individual differences perspective, work on EF in the study of disorders of early childhood highlights the need for reliable and valid normative data on EF in preschool children. Given the presence of fluid skills deficits in a number of developmental and learning disorders, increased attention to the measurement of EF is a high priority. It may be that identification of EF deficits in the presence of otherwise typically developing cognitive abilities could prove to be an indicator of increased risk for early developing psychopathology or learning disorder in very young children (Riggs, Blair, & Greenberg, 2003).

A DEVELOPMENTAL NEUROSCIENCE PERSPECTIVE ON THE MEASUREMENT OF EF IN YOUNG CHILDREN

Further valuable insight into the unique role of EF in the self-regulation of behavior and need for increased precision in its measurement in young children is gained from a developmental neuroscience approach to the study of human cognitive abilities. Given that aspects of EF have been localized primarily to cortical networks associated with the PFC and anterior cingulate cortex (ACC; see Casey et al. 1997; Durston et al., 2000, for evidence in children), it is of interest to note that these brain areas known to be important for performance of executive functions (Braver et al., 1997; Duncan et al., 2000; Gray et al., 2003; Prabhakaran, Narayanan, Zhao, & Gabrieli, 2000) are extensively and reciprocally interconnected with limbic and brainstem structures associated with emotional reactivity, the stress response, and autonomic function (Allman, Hakeem, Erwin, Nimchinsky, & Hof, 2001; Bush, Luu, & Posner, 2000; Drevets & Raichle, 1998; LeDoux, 1995; Paus, 2001; see edited volume by Uylings, Van Eden, de Bruin, Feenstra, & Pennartz, 2000). For example, the ACC contains affective and cognitive divisions associated with the processing of emotional and cognitive information. Brain-imaging studies of the processing of attention- and emotion-related information in adults indicate the integrated and reciprocal relation between affect and cognition in the brain. Distinct regions of the ACC are activated in response to cognitive tasks and to stimuli eliciting emotional arousal (Bush et al., 2000; Drevets & Raichle, 1998). Similarly, examinations of intentional reappraisal of emotional arousal and of changes in emotional state associated with emotionally arousing stimuli have indicated reciprocal prefrontal cortical-limbic activation (Mayberg et al., 1999; Ochsner, Bunge, Gross, & Gabrieli, 2002). With reappraisal of negative emotion and recovery from sadness and depression, prefrontal and cognitive ACC activation is increased and limbic and emotional ACC activation is decreased. During periods of negative affect without reappraisal, however, limbic and emotional ACC activation is increased and prefrontal and cognitive ACC activation is decreased.

Examination of the interplay of cognition and emotion in ongoing work on the measurement of EF in very young children would seem to be an important and challenging direction for future work. As prefrontal, limbic, and brainstem structures integrate cognitive, emotional, and autonomic responses to stimulation, a primary implication is that prefrontally mediated executive cognitive processes directly influence and are influenced by emotional and autonomic responses to stimulation (de Kloet, Oitzl, & Joels, 1999; Erickson, Drevets, & Schulkin, 2003; Groenewegen & Uylings, 2000; Kaufman & Charney, 2001). This reciprocal interconnectivity of emotion and cognition is highly consistent with the idea that EF is goal directed. Working memory, attention shifting, and inhibitory control processes are utilized in the service of specific goals such as problem solving and the regulation of behavior. However, at high levels of emotional arousal, these executive cognitive functions are likely to be inhibited. In the study of the development of problems with the self-regulation of behavior, increased precision in the measurement of EF can provide valuable diagnostic information to assist with the identification and remediation of deficits in self-regulation skills.

Advances in the measurement of EF early in the life course will also enable researchers to begin to address central developmental questions about the role of emotional reactivity in cognitive development and the role of emerging cognition in advances in social–emotional competence. Such an integrative approach to relations between emotional and cognitive development has been of interest for some time (Cicchetti & Schneider-Rosen, 1984; Lamb, 1982). It is expected that advances in the measurement of early developing EF will provide indicators of specific cognitive skills through which continued empirical validation of this integrative framework can be realized. The prefrontal cortical structures associated with EF exhibit considerable growth during early childhood (Gogtay et al., 2004). The functional implications of these structural changes are only starting to be understood, but knowledge of the role of experience in brain development suggests that advances in the measurement of EF in young children can provide some indication of the extent to which different types of early caregiving experiences may foster or hinder the emergence of EF. As noted in several of the articles in this special issue, emotional reactivity can have a substantial effect on the performance of EF skills. Although research on hot or emotionally laden versus cool or emotionally neutral EF is in an early stage in children, it is increasingly clear that improvements in the measurement of developmental change in EF are needed to address questions about the ways in which early emotional experience might impact cognition and the extent to which specific developmental pathways within diverse contexts may be characterized by relatively greater problems with hot or cool EF (Hongwanishkul et al., this issue; Zelazo & Müller, 2002). This may be especially relevant to specific behavior problems, such as aggression, that have the potential to interfere with children's school performance. Many children exhibit potentially problematic behavior in early childhood (e.g., Tremblay et al., 2004). However, most of them learn to inhibit these behaviors. Failure to do so may be tied to atypical development of EF.

CONCLUSION

The articles in this special issue help to advance understanding of the development of EF in young children. They also provide for an increased understanding of the challenges researchers face when attempting to characterize an aspect of cognition in very young children that is in a process of rapid development and that is central to emerging self-regulation. However, it is hoped that by adding to the knowledge base on various aspects of the study of EF, the articles serve to spur further work on the construct and its relations with developing competence in young children. A central concern of work on EF is an interest in how children come to adapt to developmental demands for the regulation of behavior. Whether this concerns the control of emotional arousal, the inhibition of desire, the control of impulsive behavior, the maintenance of peer relations, or the control of attention in school settings, it is likely that advances in the measurement of EF in young children can ultimately enhance understanding of the myriad ways in which children come to exhibit age-appropriate levels of social and cognitive competence.

ACKNOWLEDGMENTS

The scholarly activities of Clancy Blair and Mark T. Greenberg are supported by the National Institute of Child Health and Human Development Grant P01 HD39667 and those of Philip David Zelazo by grants from the Natural Sciences and Engineering Research Council of Canada and the Canada Research Chairs program.

We thank the Penn State University Children, Youth, and Families Consortium and the Prevention Research Center for the Promotion of Human Development of the Department of Human Development and Family Studies at Penn State University for their generous support for the symposium from which the articles in this special issue originated.

REFERENCES

Allman, J. M., Hakeem, A., Erwin, J., Nimchinsky, E., & Hof, P. (2001). The anterior cingulate cortex: The evolution of an interface between emotion and cognition. *Annals of the New York Academy of Sciences, 935,* 107–117.

Barkley, R. A. (1997). Behavioral inhibition, sustained attention, and executive function: Constructing a unifying theory of ADHD. *Psychological Bulletin, 121,* 65–94.

Berlin, L. (2003). *The role of inhibitory control and executive functioning in hyperactivity/ADHD.* Comprehensive summaries of Uppsala dissertations from the faculty of social sciences 120. Uppsala, Sweden: Acta Universitatis Upsaliensis.

Blair, C. (2002). School readiness: Integrating cognition and emotion in a neurobiological conceptualization of child functioning at school entry. *American Psychologist, 57,* 111–127.

Blair, C. (in press). How similar are fluid cognition and general intelligence? A developmental neuroscience perspective on fluid cognition as an aspect of human cognitive ability. *Behavioral and Brain Sciences.*

Blair, C., Granger, D., & Razza, R. P. (2005). Cortisol reactivity is positively related to executive function in preschool children attending Head Start. *Child Development, 76,* 554–567.

Braver, T. S., Cohen, J. D., Nystrom, L. E., Jonides, J., Smith, E. E., & Noll, D. C. (1997). A parametric study of prefrontal cortex involvement in human working memory. *Neuroimage, 5,* 49–62.

Bush, G., Luu, P., & Posner, M. I. (2000). Cognitive and emotional influences in the anterior cingulate cortex. *Trends in Cognitive Sciences, 4,* 215–222.

Carlson, S. M. (2005/this issue). Developmentally sensitive measures of executive function in preschool children. *Developmental Neuopsychology, 28,* 595–616.

Casey, B. J., Thomas, K. M., Davidson, M. C., Kunz, K., & Franzen, P. L. (2002). Dissociating striatal and hippocampal function developmentally with a stimulus response compatability task. *Journal of Neuroscience, 22,* 8647–8652.

Casey, B. J., Trainor, R., Giedd, J., Vauss, Y., Vaituzis, C. K., Hamburger, S., et al. (1997). The role of the anterior cingulate in automatic and controlled processes: A developmental neuroanatomical study. *Developmental Psychobiology, 30,* 61–69.

Cicchetti, D., & Schneider-Rosen, K. (1984). Theoretical and empirical considerations in the investigation of the relationship between affect and cognition in atypical populations of infants. In C. Izard, J. Kagan, & R. Zajonc (Eds.), *Emotions, cognition, and behavior* (pp. 366–406). New York: Cambridge University Press.

de Kloet, E. R., Oitzl, M. S., & Joels, M. (1999). Stress and cognition: Are corticosteroids good or bad guys? *Trends in Neuroscience, 22,* 422–426.

Diamond, A. (2002). Normal development of prefrontal cortex from birth to young adulthood: Cognitive functions, anatomy, and biochemistry. In D. Stuss & R. Knight (Eds.), *Principles of frontal lobe function* (pp. 466–503). New York: Oxford University Press.

Diamond, A., Carlson, S. M., & Beck, D. M. (2005/this issue). Preschool children's performance in task switching on the Dimensional Change Card Sort Task: Separating the dimensions aids the ability to switch. *Developmental Neuropsychology, 28,* 689–729.

Diamond, A., Prevor, M. B., Callendar, G., & Druin, D. P. (1997). Prefrontal cognitive deficits in children treated early and continuously for PKU. *Monographs of the Society for Research in Child Development, 62*(4, Serial No. 252).

Drevets, W. C., & Raichle, M. E. (1998). Reciprocal suppression of regional cerebral blood flow during emotional versus higher cognitive processes: Implications for interactions between emotion and cognition. *Cognition and Emotion, 12,* 353–385.

Duncan, J. (2001). An adaptive coding model of neural function in the prefrontal cortex. *Nature Reviews: Neuroscience, 2,* 820–829.

Duncan, J., Seitz, R. J., Kolodny, J., Bor, D., Herzog, H., Ahmed, A., et al. (2000). A neural basis for general intelligence. *Science, 289,* 457–460.

Durston, S., Thomas, K. M., Yang, Y., Ulug, A. M., Zimmerman, R. D., & Casey, B. J. (2000). A neural basis for the development of inhibitory control. *Developmental Science, 5,* F9–F16.

Erickson, K., Drevets, W., & Schulkin, J. (2003). Glucocorticoid regulation of diverse cognitive functions in normal and pathological emotional states. *Neuroscience and Biobehavioral Reviews, 27,* 233–246.

Espy, K. A., & Bull, R. (2005/this issue). Inhibitory processes in young children and individual variation in short-term memory. *Developmental Neuropsychology, 28,* 669–688.

Flynn, J. R. (1999). Searching for justice: the discovery of IQ gains over time. *American Psychologist, 54,* 5–20.

Gogtay, N., Giedd, J. N., Lusk, L., Hayashi, K.M., Greenstein, D., Vaituzis, A. C., et al. (2004). Dynamic mapping of human cortical development during childhood through early adulthood. *Proceedings of the National Academy of Sciences, USA, 101,* 8174–8179.

Gray, J. R., Chabris, C. F., & Braver, T. S. (2003) Neural mechanisms of general fluid intelligence. *Nature Neuroscience, 6,* 316–322.

Groenewegen, H. J., & Uylings, H. B. M. (2000). The prefrontal cortex and the integration of sensory, limbic, and autonomic information. In H. Uylings, C. Van Eden, J. De Bruin, M. Feenstra, & C. Pennartz (Eds.), *Progress in brain research, Vol. 126, Cognition, emotion and autonomic responses: The integrative role of the prefrontal cortex and limbic structures* (pp. 3–28). Amsterdam: Elsevier.

Hongwanishkul, D., Happaney, K. R., Lee, W. S. C., & Zelazo, P. D. (2005/this issue). Assessment of hot and cool executive function in young children: Age-related changes and individual differences. *Developmental Neuropsychology, 28,* 617–644.

Hughes, C. (1998). Executive function in preschoolers: Links with theory of mind and verbal ability. *British Journal of Developmental Psychology, 16,* 233–253.

Hughes, C., Dunn, J., & White, A. (1998). Trick or treat?: Uneven understanding of mind and emotion and executive dysfunction in "hard-to-manage" preschoolers. *Journal of Child Psychology and Psychiatry, 39,* 981–994.

Kaufman, J., & Charney, D. (2001). Effects of early stress on brain structure and function: Implications for understanding the relationship between child maltreatment and depression. *Development and Psychopathology, 13,* 451–471.

Lamb, M. E. (1982). Individual differences in infant sociability: Their origins and implications for cognitive development. In H. Reese & L. Lipsitt (Eds.), *Advances in child development and behavior, Volume 16* (pp. 213–239). New York: Academic.

LeDoux, J. (1995). Emotion: Clues from the brain. *Annual Review of Psychology, 46,* 209–235.

Luria, A. R. (1973). *The working brain: An introduction to neuropsychology* (B. Haigh, trans.). New York: Basic Books.

Mayberg, H. S., Liotti, M., Brannan, S. K., McGinnis, S., Mahurin, R. K., et al. (1999). Reciprocal limbic-cortical function and negative mood: Converging PET findings in depression and normal sadness. *American Journal of Psychiatry, 156,* 675–682.

McLean, J. F., & Hitch, G. J. (1999). Working memory impairments in children with specific arithmetic learning difficulties. *Journal of Experimental Child Psychology, 74,* 240–260.

Ochsner, K. N., Bunge, S. A., Gross, J. J., & Gabrieli, J. D. E. (2002). Rethinking feelings: An fMRI study of the cognitive regulation of emotion. *Journal of Cognitive Neuroscience, 14,* 1215–1229.

Paus, T. (2001). Primate anterior cingulate cortex: where motor control, drive, and cognition interface. *Nature Reviews: Neuroscience, 2,* 417–424.

Pennington, B. F. (1997). Dimensions of executive functions in normal and abnormal development. In N. Krasnegor, R. Lyon, & P. Goldman-Rakic (Eds.), *Development of the prefrontal cortex: Evolution, neurobiology, and behavior* (pp. 265–281). Baltimore: Brookes.

Pennington, B. F., & Ozonoff, S. (1996). Executive functions and developmental psychopathology. *Journal of Child Psychology and Psychiatry, 37,* 51–87.

Prabhakaran, V., Narayanan, K., Zhao, Z., & Gabrieli, J. D. E. (2000). Integration of diverse information in working memory within the frontal lobe. *Nature Neuroscience, 3,* 85–90.

Prabhakaran, V., Smith, J. A. L., Desmond, J. E., Glover, G. H., & Gabrieli, J. D. E. (1997). Neural substrates of fluid reasoning: An fMRI study of neocortical activation during performance of the Raven's Progressive Matrices Test. *Cognitive Psychology, 33,* 43–63.

Ridderinkhof, K. R., van den Wildenberg, W. P., Segalowitz, S. J., & Carter, C. S. (2004). Neurocognitive mechanisms of cognitive control: The role of prefrontal cortex in action selection, response inhibition, performance monitoring, and reward-based learning. *Brain and Cognition, 56,* 129–140.

Riggs, N., Blair, C., & Greenberg, M. (2003). Concurrent and 2-year longitudinal relations between executive function and the behavior of 1st and 2nd grade children. *Child Neuropsychology, 9,* 267–276.

Rueda, M. R., Posner, M. I., & Rothbart, M. K. (2005/this issue). The development of executive attention: Contributions to the emergence of self-regulation. *Developmental Neuropsychology, 28,* 573–594.

Stanovich, K. E., Siegel, L. S., & Gottardo, A. (1997). Converging evidence for phonological and surface subtypes of reading disability. *Journal of Educational Psychology, 89,* 114–127.

Swanson, H. L. (1999). Reading comprehension and working memory in learning-disabled readers: Is the phonological loop more important than the executive system? *Journal of Experimental Child Psychology, 72,* 1–31.

Thompson, P., Cannon, T., Narr, K., van Erp, T., Poutanen, V., Huttunen, M., et al. (2001). Genetic influences on brain structure. *Nature Neuroscience, 4,* 1253–1258.

Tremblay, R. E., Nagin, D. S., Seguin, J. R., Zoccolillo, M., Zelazo, P. D., Boivin, M., et al. (2004). Physical aggression during early childhood: trajectories and predictors. *Pediatrics, 114,* e43–50.

Uylings, H., Van Eden, C., de Bruin, J., Feenstra, M., & Pennartz, C. (Eds.). (2000). *Progress in brain research, Vol. 126, Cognition, emotion and autonomic responses: The integrative role of the prefrontal cortex and limbic structures.* Amsterdam: Elsevier.

Waltz, J. A., Knowlton, B. J., Holyoak, K. J., Boone, K. B., Mishkin, F. S., Santos, M., et al. (1999). A system for relation reasoning in the human prefrontal cortex. *Psychological Science, 10,* 119–125.

Wellman, H., & Liu, D. (2004). Scaling of theory of mind tasks. *Child Development, 75,* 523–541.

Zelazo, P. D., & Müller, U. (2002). Executive function in typical and atypical development. In U. Goswami (Ed.), *Handbook of childhood cognitive development* (pp. 445–469). Oxford, England: Blackwell.

DEVELOPMENTAL NEUROPSYCHOLOGY, 28(2), 573–594

The Development of Executive Attention: Contributions to the Emergence of Self-Regulation

M. Rosario Rueda

Departamento de Psicología Experimental
Universidad de Granada, Spain

Michael I. Posner and Mary K. Rothbart

Department of Psychology
University of Oregon

Over the past decade, developmental studies have established connections between executive attention, as studied in neurocognitive models, and effortful control, a temperament system supporting the emergence of self-regulation. Functions associated with the executive attention network overlap with the more general domain of executive function in childhood, which also includes working memory, planning, switching, and inhibitory control (Welch, 2001). Cognitive tasks used with adults to study executive attention can be adapted to children and used with questionnaires to trace the role of attention and effortful control in the development of self-regulation. In this article we focus on the monitoring and control functions of attention and discuss its contributions to self-regulation from cognitive, temperamental, and biological perspectives.

Self-Regulation refers to the many processes by which the human psyche exercises control over its functions, states, and inner processes. It is an important key to how the self is put together. Most broadly, it is essential for transforming the inner animal nature into a civilized human being. (Vohs & Baumeister, 2004, p. 1)

The ability to control one's behavior plays an important role in the development of personality and the socialization of the child. Self-regulation has been related to

---

Correspondence should be addressed to M. Rosario Rueda, Departamento de Psicología Experimental, Universidad de Granada, Campus de Cartuja s/n, 18071 Granada, Spain. E-mail: rorueda@ugr.es

emotionality, delay of gratification, compliance, moral development, social competence, empathy, adjustment, and cognitive and academic performance (Eisenberg, Smith, Sadovsky, & Spinrad, 2004). In addition, self-regulation is thought to be the key mediator between genetic predispositions, early experience, and adult functioning (Fonagy & Target, 2002).

Over the past decade, studies have attempted to integrate the study of attention and self-regulation (Posner & Rothbart, 1992, 1998). During the 1st year of life, attentional orienting appears to act as a distress regulator (Harman, Rothbart, & Posner, 1997). In successive months, infants experience a transition from a more reactive or stimulus-driven form of attentional selection toward more controlled attention (Rothbart, Posner, & Boylan, 1990). This transition supports the voluntary control of action needed to regulate one's behavior (Posner & Rothbart, 1998). Although attention and self-regulation have been studied within two very different research traditions, we have made an effort to integrate these bodies of literature by considering hypotheses about the specific neural mechanisms involved in self-regulation and their connection to executive attention and effortful control (Rueda, Posner, & Rothbart, 2004). In this article, we analyze the cognitive, temperamental, and biological systems supporting attentional control and its contributions to the emergence of self-regulation. In addition, we report our recent efforts to trace and foster the development of this aspect of attention in young children.

EFFORTFUL CONTROL

Links between attention and self-regulation have been found in temperament research. In these studies, individual differences are commonly measured using temperament or personality questionnaires. Effortful control consistently emerges from factorial analysis of temperament questionnaires, with temperament scales loading on the factor including shifting and focusing attention, inhibitory control, perceptual sensitivity, and low-intensity pleasure. Effortful control allows individuals to regulate their behavior in relation to current and future needs, as in situations that involve coping with immediate punishment or avoiding instant reward in the face of a more rewarding situation in the future.

Rothbart, Ahadi, and Hershey (1994) showed that 6- and 7-year-olds high in effortful control were high in empathy and guilt/shame and low in aggressiveness. Eisenberg and her colleagues found that 4- to 6-year old boys with good attentional control tend to deal with anger by using nonhostile verbal methods rather than overt aggressive methods (Eisenberg, Fabes, Nyman, Bernzweig, & Pinulas, 1994). In line with these data, the work by Kochanska and colleagues over the past decade has shown that effortful control plays an important role in the development of conscience. In studies of temperament and conscience, the early internalization of moral principles appears to be facilitated in fearful preschool-age children, especially when their mothers use gentle discipline (see Kochanska, 1991, 1995, 1997). In addition, internalized control is greater in children who are high in effortful control (Kochanska, Murray, & Harlan, 2000; Kochanska, Murray, Jacques, Koenig, & Vandegeest, 1996).

Individual differences in effortful control are also related to aspects of meta-cognitive knowledge, such as theory of mind (i.e., knowing that people's behavior is guided by their beliefs, desires, and other mental states; Carlson & Moses, 2001). Tasks that require inhibitory control are correlated with performance on theory of mind tasks even when other factors such as age, planning skills, and re-ceptive vocabulary are factored out (Carlson, Moses, & Claxton, 2004).

All these data point to the idea that effortful control serves as the basis for the development from more reactive to more self-regulative behavior. Systems of effortful control may contribute to this development by providing the attentional flexibility required to manage negative affect, consider potential actions in light of moral principles, and coordinate reactions that are under voluntary control (Rothbart & Rueda, 2005).

VOLUNTARY CONTROL OF ACTION

Selecting information and controlling thoughts and actions have been a major function of attention from the earliest theoretical models (Broadbent, 1958; James, 1890). Attentional selection has an important adaptive role in individuals' interac-tions with the environment. Even simple behaviors (e.g., reaching for a pencil ly-ing on a table among other objects) require selecting the stimulus toward which the action is directed. Orienting attention over a scene and selecting the object or loca-tion to attend to is necessary for carrying out desired actions. Likewise, attention can be directed internally to coordinate memories, thoughts, and emotions.

The attentional system exerts its influence by modulating the functioning of sys-tems involved in information processing. Many of the studies of the regulatory as-pect of attention involve modulation of sensory systems. Studies using functional magnetic resonance imaging (fMRI) and cellular recording have demonstrated that a number of brain areas such as the superior parietal lobe and temporal parietal junc-tion play a key role in modulating activity within primary and extrastriate visual sys-tems when attentional orienting occurs (Corbetta & Shulman, 2002; Desimone & Duncan, 1995). In addition, other neuroimaging studies have suggested that the reg-ulatory effects of attention apply just as well to brain areas involved in processing the semantics of words, storing information in memory, and generating emotions such as fear and sadness (Posner & Raichle, 1994, 1998).

Attention can be automatically driven by external stimulation or endogenously controlled by the goals and wishes of the individual. Norman and Shallice (1986) developed a cognitive model for distinguishing between automatic and controlled processes. According to their model, psychological-processing systems rely on a number of hierarchically organized schemas of action and thought used for routine actions. These schemas are automatically triggered and contain well-learned responses or sequences of actions. However, a different mode of operation involving the Supervisory Attention System is required when situations call for more carefully elaborated responses. These are situations that involve (a) novelty, (b) error correction or troubleshooting, (c) some degree of danger or difficulty, or (d) overcoming strong habitual responses or tendencies.

Data from multiple domains have supported the existence of three brain networks that contribute to attention (Posner & Dehaene, 1994; Posner & Petersen, 1990). These networks carry out the functions of alerting, orienting, and executive control. Alerting is the most elementary aspect of attention and describes the state of wakefulness and arousal of an organism; orienting is the selection of information from sensory input; and executive control involves the mechanisms for resolving conflict among thoughts, feelings, and responses. The three brain networks have been shown to differ in their functional anatomy, the circuitry of their component operations, and the neurochemical modulators that influence their efficiency (Posner & Fan, in press). Among these networks, executive control is the network involved in the volitional and controlled aspect of the attentional system. Its functions include resolving into appropriate actions the kinds of situations described by Norman and Shallice as requiring cognitive control (Posner & DiGirolamo, 1998).

What are the cognitive mechanisms by which the voluntary control of behavior is achieved, and how is the study of these mechanisms approached in cognitive neuroscience? We address these questions in the next sections.

MECHANISMS OF CONTROL

Conscious Detection

According to Posner and Raichle (1994), the executive attention network serves the function of

> bringing an object into conscious awareness. … [Detection is further defined as] more than the conscious recognition that an object is present. It may also include recognition of the object's identity and the realization that the object fulfills a sought-after goal … . In this sense, detection is the conscious execution of an instruction. (pp. 168–169)

Conscious detection plays a special role in selecting a target stimulus from among alternatives and engages attention in a way that resists interference by other signals. One way to study detection is by presenting target stimuli among distractors. Imaging studies have shown that, independent of the type of target stimulus (color, motion, form, etc.), particular brain areas are specifically activated by detected targets as contrasted to passive viewing of the same type of stimuli (Corbetta & Shulman, 2002).

A type of detection particularly interesting for action monitoring is the detection of erroneous responses. Detecting errors is one of the functions attributed to the Supervisory Attention System in the Norman and Shallice's (1986) model. A behavioral indicator of error detection and correction is the slowing of reaction time immediately following the commission of an error. An electrophysiological component, the error-related negativity (ERN), is also consistently recorded following the participant's detection of an error (Gehring, Gross, Coles, Meyer, & Donchin, 1993). Further, the distribution of the activity associated with the ERN on the scalp has been linked to activity originating in the anterior cingulate cortex (ACC; van Veen & Carter, 2002), a brain region that, as we discuss later, is related to executive attention.

Inhibition

Inhibitory mechanisms have been widely discussed in cognitive psychology as involved in attention, memory, and language processes (Dagenbach & Carr, 1994). In the attentional domain, inhibition has been studied in connection to both the orienting and the executive functions of attention (Fuentes, 2004) and therefore appears to be essential to attentional selection and executive control. The negative priming phenomenon—increased reaction time to stimuli that have been previously ignored—is an example of the influence of inhibitory processes on attentional selection. In a widely accepted interpretation of negative priming, the effect is accounted for by an inhibitory process that acts on the representation of the ignored information, allowing the system to focus on information relevant for current action (Houghton & Tipper, 1994).

Inhibition is also required for withholding responses that, although prompted by current stimulation, might not be appropriate. The most common way to measure response inhibition is by using tasks in which participants respond to one stimulus but are required to inhibit their response when a related stimulus is presented (Go/No-Go tasks). Under Go/No-Go instructions, promptness to respond can be manipulated by varying the proportion of Go trials or by presenting a No-Go signal at varying time intervals after the Go stimulus (the Stop-signal Paradigm). The efficiency of inhibition is measured behaviorally by the number of omissions and false alarms, but it can be also measured using physiological indices, such as muscular preparation or brain activity.

Conflict Resolution

Monitoring and resolving conflict between incompatible responses also requires voluntary and attentive control of action (Posner & DiGirolamo, 1998). Conflict resolution involves selecting a subdominant object or response in the presence of a competing dominant object or response. Cognitive tasks involving conflict have been used extensively to measure the efficiency with which control of action is exerted (Botvinick, Braver, Barch, Carter, & Cohen, 2001).

Conflict can be induced in many ways. A very popular way is the Stroop task. The original form of this task required participants to report the color of ink in which a word was written, when the color word (e. g., *red*) might conflict with the color of ink (e.g., blue). In general, Stroop-like tasks induce conflict by requiring a response to a stimulus that is incongruent with the one suggested by the stimulus. For example, in the Spatial Conflict task (Gerardi-Caulton, 2000), the requirement is to respond to the identity of a stimulus regardless of its spatial compatibility with the matching response key. The Flanker task (Eriksen & Eriksen, 1974), another widely used task for studying executive attention, induces conflict by presenting additional stimulation in the display, suggesting a response incompatible with the correct one. A recent study carried out by Fan, Flombaum, McCandliss, Thomas, and Posner (2003) showed that these three types of tasks (Stroop color, Spatial Conflict, and Flanker task) activate a common set of brain regions (although to different extents) as well as areas unique to each task, suggesting a common underlying process implemented according to the specific requirements of the task.

THE NEURAL SYSTEM FOR ATTENTIONAL CONTROL

Anatomy and Circuitry

 Many of the tasks described earlier have been used together with neuroimaging techniques to localize the brain regions related to executive attention. Data from many studies have shown that situations requiring attentional control activate a neural network including the ACC and lateral prefrontal areas (Posner & Fan, in press). Other studies have attempted to dissociate different operations involved in the control of action, identifying brain areas within the executive network responsible for these operations (Casey, Durston, & Fossella, 2001). In fMRI studies, the ACC was found to be involved in the detection and monitoring of conflict, whereas lateral prefrontal areas were shown to be mainly related to processes required to resolve the conflict (Botvinick, Nystrom, Fissell, Carter, & Cohen, 1999). Detection and resolution of conflict have also been anatomically dissociated from selection of the relevant information, which involves areas of the superior parietal cortex and superior frontal gyrus (Casey et al., 2000).

The main node of the executive attention network, the ACC, is part of the limbic system and is strongly connected to structures involved in processing emotions. In a meta-analysis of imaging studies, the dorsal section of the anterior cingulate was found to be activated in cognitive conflict tasks such as variants of the Stroop task (Bush, Luu, & Posner, 2000). An adjacent area of the anterior cingulate was found to be activated by emotional tasks and emotional states. The two divisions also seem to interact, so that when the cognitive division was activated, the affective division tended to be deactivated and vice versa, suggesting the possibility of reciprocal effortful and emotional controls of attention (Bush et al., 2000). Cingulate activity as shown by fMRI was also found to be related to the instruction of regulating sexual arousal induced by watching videos (Beauregard, Levesque, & Bourgouin, 2001). In a different study, cognitive reappraisal of photographs producing negative affect showed a correlation between extent of cingulate activity and the reduction in negative affect (Ochsner, Bunge, Gross, & Gabrieli, 2002). These results show a role for this anatomical structure in regulating limbic activity related to emotion and provide evidence for a role of the cingulate as a part of the network controlling affect.

A number of studies have used the high temporal resolution of event-related potentials (ERPs) to assess the timing of action-monitoring processes with adults. One of the ERP indexes associated with executive control, the N2, is a preresponse negative deflection in the ERP at around 300 msec poststimulus, which appears to be larger (more negative) for trials involving more conflict. The N2 is observed over parietal and frontal leads and has been obtained with both flanker (Kopp, Rist, & Mattler, 1996; van Veen & Carter, 2002) and Go/No-Go tasks (Jackson, Jackson, & Roberts, 1999). In both situations, the N2 has been associated with the withholding of a prepotent, but inappropriate, response. In a recent ERP study with a Flanker task, van Veen and Carter (2002) linked the scalp distribution of activity associated with the N2 to a source of activation originating at the caudal portion of the ACC, supporting a connection between this electrophysiological index and the executive attention network.

Neurochemistry

The ventral tegmental area, a source of dopamine (DA) neurons, strongly projects to the brain areas involved in executive attention. In addition, all types of DA receptors are expressed within the cingulate cortex. DA appears to be an important modulator of performance on tasks that entail executive functions and involve dorsolateral prefrontal cortex (Diamond & Goldman-Rakic, 1989). Some studies have shown evidence of DA modulation of prefrontal function in the rat (Seamas, Floresco, & Phillips, 1998). In addition, administering DA D_1 receptor agonists and antagonists appears to respectively enhance and impair the accuracy level of performance of rats in a task that requires detecting brief visual targets (Granon et al., 2000). In humans, tasks that involve conflict and require inhibition also appear to be more sensitive to DA levels than tasks with a stronger working memory component, although both types of tasks rely on lateral prefrontal structures (Diamond, Briand, Fossella, & Gehlbach, 2004).

Genetics

Links between the anatomy of executive attention and the chemical modulators involved in its functioning have provided a tool for studying the genetic basis of this network. Pioneering studies following this approach have shown attentional processes related to cognitive control to be determined in part by the biological processes expressed through particular dopamine-related genes (Goldberg & Weinberger, 2004).

Recently, Fan, McCandliss, Sommer, Raz, and Posner (2002) developed the Attention Network Test (ANT). This task provides a measure for each of the three anatomically defined attention networks: alerting, orienting, and executive attention. The ANT can be used as a phenotype of the efficiency of the attentional functions. In a small-scale twin study using the ANT, the executive network showed high-enough heritability (0.89) to justify the search for specific genes (Fan, Wu, Fossella, & Posner, 2001). In a second study, DNA from cheek swabs of participants who performed the ANT was used to examine candidate differences in gene polymorphisms related to dopamine. This process showed at least two candidate genes that were related to the executive network to a greater degree than to overall performance as measured by RT and accuracy (Fossella, Posner, Fan, Swanson, & Pfaff, 2002). One of these genes was the dopamine D4 receptor gene, widely reported to be associated with attention deficit hyperactivity disorder (ADHD) and with the personality trait of sensation seeking (Swanson et al., 2000). The other was the Monoamine oxidase A gene, related to both dopamine and norepinepherine. In a third study, Fan, Fossella, Sommer, and Posner (2003) showed that these two genes were also related to differences in brain activation within the anterior cingulate gyrus while performing a conflict task.

The Catechol-O-Methyltransferase (COMT) gene, involved in the degradation of dopamine, has also been related to prefrontal executive processes (Egan et al., 2001). A particular variant of the COMT gene (the Met-Met genotype) results in greater levels of dopamine at the synapse due to a lower degradation rate. Some studies have found the Met-Met COMT gene variant to relate to better performance in the Wisconsin Card Sorting Test (Egan et al., 2001; Joober et al., 2002). Diamond et al. (2004) found that children with the Met-Met variant performed better in a conflict task than age-matched children with different polymorphisms of the COMT gene. It is of interest that this genotype did not differentiate between the groups in another task that relied more on working-memory processes.

NEUROCOGNITIVE DEVELOPMENT
OF EXECUTIVE ATTENTION

So far we have discussed temperamental, cognitive, and biological aspects that play a role in the development of self-regulation. Different assessment tools can be used to investigate the development of these aspects. Individual differences in the efficiency with which effortful control is exerted in daily life can be assessed using temperament questionnaires. Laboratory tasks from adult studies that have been adapted to children can be used to isolate specific measures of executive attention. In addition, these cognitive tasks can be used online with techniques for brain function assessment to study the biological processes supporting behavioral maturation. At the Attention and Temperament Laboratory in the University of Oregon, we have followed this approach to trace the development of executive attention.

Developmental studies have stressed the relative lack of executive control in infants (Ruff & Rothbart, 1996). However, a sign of the control of cognitive conflict is found at the end of the 1st year of life. Infants younger than 12 months fail to search for an object hidden in a location when previously trained to reach for the object in a different location. After the 1st year, children develop the ability to inhibit the prepotent response toward the trained location and successfully reach for the object in the new location (Diamond, 1991).

At 2 years of age and older, children are able to perform simple tasks in which their reaction time can be measured. In one study, toddlers were asked to perform a task that induces conflict between the identity and the location of an object (Spatial Conflict task; Gerardi-Caulton, 2000). Between 2 and 4 years of age, children progressed from an almost complete inability to carry out the task to relatively good performance. Although 2-year-old children tended to perseverate on a single response, 3-year-olds performed at high accuracy levels, although, like adults, they responded more slowly and with reduced accuracy to incompatible trials. In this study, performance of children in the Spatial Conflict task was related to temperament as reported by parents. Consistent with a similar study conducted with adults (Derryberry & Reed, 1998) where high performance was associated with self-reported attentional control, and low trait anxiety, children who performed well were also described by their parents as more skilled at attentional shifting and focusing, less impulsive, and less prone to frustration reactions. These findings are also consistent with the idea that effortful attention, as measured through questionnaire or laboratory methods, may help individuals constrain negative forms of emotion.

The Visual Sequence Learning (VSL) task can be used to assess implicit and attentional forms of learning in children as young as a few months. In the VSL task, a series of cartoons are presented on three different computer monitors in a predictable sequence. In unambiguous sequences, each location is followed by one and only one subsequent location (e.g., 123123 ... , with numbers referring to the monitor in which the stimulus appears). Ambiguous associations refer to sequences where a location is followed by one of two or more different locations, the particular location depending on its place within the sequence (e.g., 121312 …). Learning of ambiguous sequences requires the monitoring of context and, in adult studies, has been shown to depend on lateral prefrontal cortex (Keele, Ivry, Mayr, Hazeltine, & Heuer, 2003). Previous studies showed that ambiguous associations within sequences of events are not acquired at above-chance levels until about 2 years of age (Clohessy, Posner, & Rothbart, 2001).

We recently conducted a study using the VSL task to further explore the relation between cognitive and temperamental measures of executive control in 2- to 3-year-old children (Rothbart, Ellis, Rueda, & Posner, 2003). In this study, we also used a touch screen version of the Spatial Conflict task and asked the parents to complete the Children's Behavior Questionnaire (CBQ; Rothbart, Ahadi, Hershey, & Fisher, 2001). Children were divided into three groups according to their age: 24–25 months, 30–31 months, and 36–37 months. In consonance with previous data, children in all three groups were able to anticipate the correct locations above chance in ambiguous sequences of the VSL task, therefore demonstrating learning of this type of sequence. In addition, we found a great increase in the ability to perform the Spatial Conflict task between the 2- and 3-year-old groups (see upper part of Table 1). At 30 months, when toddlers were able to perform the Spatial Conflict task more successfully, we found that performance on this task was significantly related to the toddlers' ability to learn ambiguous associations in the VSL paradigm. In addition, in two of the groups, interference in the Spatial Conflict task correlated negatively with temperamental effortful control. For the youngest group, effortful control was also related to the percentage of completed trials, and children in the group that did not complete the task were significantly lower in effortful control and higher in negative affect than those completing sufficient trials for analysis (Rothbart et al., 2003). Altogether these data support the existence of a link between attentional efficiency as evaluated by cognitive tasks and parent-reported measures of effortful control.

Another form of action monitoring is the detection and correction of errors. In our study, reaction times following an error in the Spatial Conflict task were 200 msec longer than those following a correct trial for 30-month-old children, and over 500 msec longer at 36 months, indicating that children were noticing their errors and using them to guide performance in the next trial. However, no evidence of slowing following an error was found at 24 months (Rothbart et al., 2003). A similar result with a different time frame was found when using a version of the Simple Simon game. In this task, children are asked to execute a response when a command is given by one stuffed animal while inhibiting responses commanded by a second animal (Jones, Rothbart, & Posner, 2003). Children of 36 to 38 months were unable to inhibit their response and showed no slowing following an error, but at 39 to 41 months, children showed both an ability to inhibit and a slowing of

TABLE 1
Development of Conflict Resolution Assessed With Different Conflict Tasks

Age	Task	Congruent Trials		Incongruent Trials		Conflict Effect		Study Reference
		RT	% Correct	RT	% Correct	RT	% Correct	
2	Spatial conflict	3,476	69.1	3,378	53.9	−98	−15.2	Rothbart, Ellis, Rueda, and Posner (2003)
2½	Spatial conflict	2,489	80.8	3,045	57.8	556	−23.0	Rothbart, Ellis, Rueda, and Posner (2003)
3	Spatial conflict	2,465	90.1	3,072	80.3	607	−9.8	Rothbart, Ellis, Rueda, and Posner (2003)
4	Flanker (child ANT)[a]	1,490	89.4	1,913	77.1	424	−13.0	Rueda, Posner, Rothbart, and Davis-Stober (2004)
6	Flanker (child ANT)	890	92.0	1,005	76.4	115	−15.6	Rueda, Fan, et al. (2004)
7	Flanker (child ANT)	828	94.6	891	93.9	63	−0.7	Rueda, Fan, et al. (2004)
8	Flanker (child ANT)	791	95.0	862	95.3	71	0.3	Rueda, Fan, et al. (2004)
9	Flanker (child ANT)	724	98.1	791	96.5	67	−1.6	Rueda, Fan, et al. (2004)
10	Flanker (child ANT)	624	98.7	693	96.6	69	−2.1	Rueda, Fan, et al. (2004)
Adults	Flanker (child ANT)	473	99.5	534	97.9	61	−1.6	Rueda, Fan, et al. (2004)

Note. Conflict effects are calculated by subtracting congruent from incongruent conditions. In all the studies, RT data are the means (across participants) of the median RT (per participant, in milliseconds).

[a]The stimuli used in this study were larger than in the Rueda, Fan, et al. (2004) study also using the child ANT, resulting in slightly smaller conflict scores.

reaction time following an error. These results suggest that between 30 and 39 months, children greatly develop their ability to detect and correct erroneous responses and that this ability may relate to the development of inhibitory control.

As discussed earlier, resolving conflict from competing stimulation also requires attentional control. We have recently adapted the ANT (Fan et al., 2002) for use with children as young as 4 years of age (Rueda, Fan, et al., 2004; see Figure 1). In this task, a row of five fish appears in the center of the screen, and the child's job is to help in "feeding" the middle fish by pressing the key corresponding to the direction in which the middle fish is pointing. On half the trials, the flanker fish are pointing in the same direction as the middle fish (congruent trials); on the other half, the flanker fish are pointing in the opposite direction (incongruent trials). The time to resolve conflict, calculated by subtracting the reaction time for congruent trials from the reaction time for incongruent trials, is a measure of conflict resolution. In a series of studies using this task, we have observed considerable development of conflict resolution between 4 and 7 years of age, but a striking consistency in performance after age 7 to adulthood (see Table 1).

To examine the brain mechanisms underlying differences in conflict resolution between children and adults, we have recently conducted an ERP study in which we used the fish flanker task with 4-year-old children and adults (Rueda, Posner,

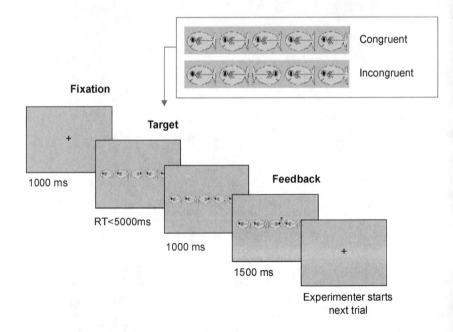

FIGURE 1   Schematic representation of the Flanker task in the Child ANT.

Rothbart, & Davis-Stober, 2004). Characteristics of the ERP make this technique amenable to children of all ages. In our study, we used a high-density system of electroencephalography (Tucker, 1993). This procedure allows evaluation of differences between children and adults in the time course of brain activations related to the task and provides a wide sampling of the distribution of activation over the scalp. As expected, we found the N2 effect for adults over the mid-frontal leads. The children's data also showed a larger negative deflection for the incongruent condition at the mid-frontal electrodes. Compared to adults, this effect had a larger size, had greater amplitude, and was extended over a longer period of time (see Figure 2).

Differences between children and adults in ERP amplitude have been related to brain size and skull thickening. Differences in the latency of components, however, may be related more to the large differences between adults and children in reaction time (431 msec vs. 1,614 msec) and conflict resolution times (30 msec vs. 424 msec). Whereas the frontal effect was evident for adults at around 300 msec posttarget, children did not show any effect until approximately 550 msec after the target. In addition, the effect was sustained over a period of 500 msec before the

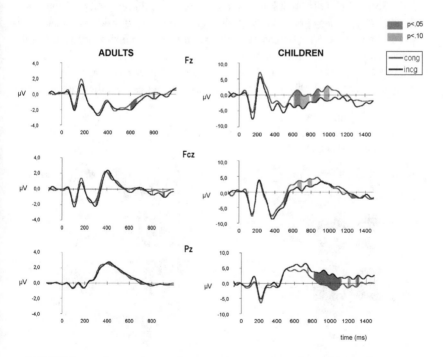

FIGURE 2   Adults' and 4-year-old children's ERPs obtained with the Child ANT at frontal (Fz), frontal-central (Fcz) and parietal (Pz) leads. Notice adult versus child differences in the scale of the graphs.

children's responses, in contrast with only 50 msec in the case of adults. The differences observed between children and adults over the frontal channels differed from other components observed at mid-parietal channels. For both children and adults, we found a greater positivity for incongruent trials over mid-parietal leads. For adults, this effect was observed at approximately 400 msec posttarget, in the time window of the P300, whereas it was more delayed in the case of children (between 800 and 1,100 msec posttarget). The P300 is thought to be an index of stimulus evaluation (Coles, Gratton, Bashore, Ericksen, & Donchin, 1985). This parietal effect could reflect developmental differences in the difficulty of evaluating the display depending on the congruence of surrounding flankers, whereas the frontal effect could reveal differences in the time course of conflict resolution.

Another important difference between 4-year-old children and adults was the distribution of effects over the scalp (see Figure 3). In adults, the frontal effects appear to be focalized on the midline, whereas in children the effects were observed mostly at prefrontal sites and in a broader number of channels, including the midline and lateral areas. In addition, the effect on the P3 appears to be left-lateralized in the adult data but lateralized to the right side in the children. The focalization of signals in adults as compared to children is consistent with neuroimaging studies conducted with older children, where children appear to activate the same network of areas as adults when performing similar tasks, but the average volume of activation appears to be remarkably greater in children compared to adults (Casey, Thomas, Davidson, Kunz, & Franzen, 2002; Casey et al., 1997; Durston et al., 2002). Altogether, these data suggest that the brain circuitry

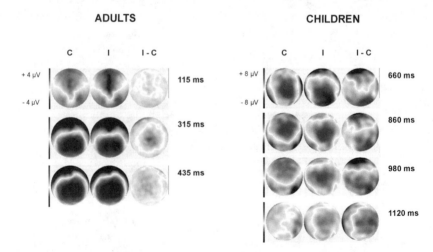

FIGURE 3   Adults and children's scalp topographic distributions of ERPs associated with congruent (C) and incongruent (I) conditions, and the conflict effect (I-C) at time points when significant effects (see Figure 2) were found.

underlying executive functions becomes more focal and refined as it gains in efficiency. This maturational process involves not only greater anatomical specialization but also reducing the time these systems need to resolve each of the processes implicated in the task.

PLASTICITY

Connections between self-regulation and the executive attention network place some emphasis on the biological processes underpinning the efficiency of control systems. However, the role of experience in brain development is not to be neglected (Bavelier & Neville, 2002; Neville & Bavelier, 1999). Examples of brain plasticity as shown by training-induced increases in performance can be found in both children and adults. Several training oriented programs have resulted in improved executive control in patients with specific brain injury. The use of Attention Process Training (APT) has led to specific improvements in executive attention in tasks quite remote from those that have undergone training (Sohlberg, McLaughlin, Pavese, Heidrich, & Posner, 2000). Other studies suggest that the effects of training may depend on first establishing a minimum level of alerting and orienting capacities (Sturm, Willmes, Orgass, & Hartje, 1997). The APT has also proven successful in training attentional abilities in children with ADHD (Kerns, Esso, & Thompson, 1999; Semrud-Clikeman, Nielsen, & Clinton, 1999). With normal adults, training with video games has been shown to produce better performance on a range of visual attention tasks (Green & Bavelier, 2003).

We have tested whether specific attention training during the development of executive attention in 4 year olds can influence the efficiency with which this network is activated (Rueda, Rothbart, McCandliss, Saccamono, & Posner, 2005). We have designed a set of computerized training exercises to help preschool children develop their executive attention skills. The program begins with training the child to control the movement of an animated cat on a computer screen by using a joystick. Other exercises involve prediction of where an animated figure will move given its initial trajectory, retention of information for a matching to sample task, and the resolution of conflict. The exercises were designed to be completed in five 45-min sessions conducted over a 2- to 3-week period. Behavioral and electrophysiological measures of executive attention (Child ANT; Rueda, Fan, et al., 2004), general intelligence (Kaufman Brief Intelligence Test [K-BIT]; Kaufman & Kaufman, 1990), and temperament (CBQ; Rothbart et al., 2001) were used in assessment sessions conducted before and after training. Children were randomly assigned to an experimental group that underwent training or to a control group that did not. The experimental group showed more adultlike conflict scores following training than did the control group. Although some or all of this effect might have been due to differences in the pretest, we also found that following training, the experimental group was the only group showing a pattern in the N2 component of the ERPs similar to the one shown by adults (see Figure 4; Rueda et al., 2005).

The training also produced significant increases in overall IQ, mostly due to increasing the score in the Visual Matrices scale measured by the K-BIT. Other forms of attention training for children with ADHD have also improved performance on abstract reasoning as measured by Raven's Progressive Matrices (Klingsberg, Forssberg, & Westerberg, 2002), suggesting that training of attention may benefit cognitive functioning extending over a range of tasks. The fact that training on executive attention may result in improvement of general intelligence is not very surprising, considering their common anatomies (Duncan et al., 2000).

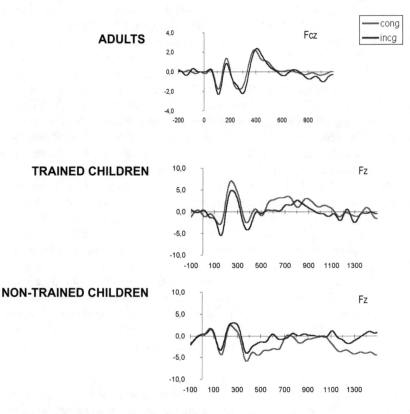

FIGURE 4   Comparison of the ERPs of adults and the trained and control (nontrained) groups of 4-year-old children involved in the attention training study. All ERPs were obtained while participants were performing the Child ANT. Notice adult versus child differences in the scale of the graphs.

Although these results need to be replicated and extended, they suggest that the brain mechanisms associated with attentional control can be improved by training and that this improvement produces a benefit in behavioral measures of competence. Given the connection between attention and self-regulation, plasticity of the neural system underlying executive attention opens a window for fostering self-regulation in young children. In our study, the short time period elapsing between the pre- and postassessment sessions did not allow for examining changes in reported temperament scores related to effortful control. Studies specifically testing the benefits of training of attention on the ability of children to control their behavior remain to be done.

CONCLUSION

In cognitive models, attention has been traditionally involved in the control of intended actions. In this sense, attentional control has been identified as an important domain in self-regulation (Posner & Rothbart, 1998; Rueda, Posner, & Rothbart, 2004). With the emergence of cognitive neuroscience, numerous studies have combined the use of simple but theoretically grounded cognitive tasks with neuroimaging techniques and have greatly extended our understanding of the neural system supporting attentional control. Conflict tasks (e.g., Flanker, Stroop, and Spatial Conflict tasks) have been widely used to study this form of control. A network of brain areas, referred to as the executive attention network, is primarily active in tasks that involve conflict resolution. This network includes the ACC and lateral prefrontal cortex.

We have used conflict tasks adapted to children to study the development of executive attention. In our studies, we have combined the use of laboratory tasks with parent-reported questionnaires and with techniques for assessment of brain function amenable to young children. The ability to deal with conflict in young children appears to relate to parent-reported measures of effortful control, supporting the connection between executive attention and self-control skills. We have found considerable improvement in the ability to resolve conflict between 2 and 5 years of age, and continuous improvement up to 7 years, when children appear to reach the adult level of performance, at least when using the Child ANT (see Table 1). Consistent with the much greater difficulty for children to resolve conflict, we have found longer latencies and sustained conflict effects on children's evoked potentials compared to adults. It is of interest that the pattern of electrophysiological activity seems to be susceptible to modulation through attention training. This result shows the potential of cognitive and behavioral training for fostering brain processes related to attentional control. Considering executive attention as a system for the voluntary control of action, the benefits of training attention could extend to greater cognitive and emotional regulation of children's behavior.

ACKNOWLEDGMENTS

Most of the research conducted by the Attention and Temperament Laboratory, at the University of Oregon, was supported by Grant JSMF20002075 from the James S. McDonnell Foundation and by a National Institutes of Health Grant #MH43361. Dr Rueda's work was partially supported by a grant from La Caixa Foundation—U.S. Program.

REFERENCES

Bavelier, D., & Neville, H. J. (2002). Cross-modal plasticity: Where and how? *Nature Reviews Neuroscience, 3,* 443–452.

Beauregard, M., Levesque, J., & Bourgouin, P. (2001). Neural correlates of conscious self-regulation of emotion. *Journal of Neuroscience, 21,* 6993–7000.

Botvinick, M. M., Braver, T. S., Barch, D. M., Carter, C. S., & Cohen, J. D. (2001). Conflict monitoring and cognitive control. *Psychological Review, 108,* 624–652.

Botvinick, M., Nystrom, L. E., Fissell, K., Carter, C. S., & Cohen, J. D. (1999). Conflict monitoring versus selection-for-action in anterior cingulate cortex. *Nature, 402,* 179–181.

Broadbent, D. E. (1958). *Perception and communication.* London: Pergamon.

Bush, G., Luu, P., & Posner, M. I. (2000). Cognitive and emotional influences in the anterior cingulate cortex. *Trends in Cognitive Science, 4/6,* 215–222.

Carlson, S. T., & Moses, L. J. (2001). Individual differences in inhibitory control in children's theory of mind. *Child Development, 72,* 1032–1053.

Carlson, S. M., Moses, L. J., & Claxton, L. J. (2004). Individual differences in executive functioning and theory of mind: An investigation of inhibitory control and planning ability. *Journal of Experimental Child Psychology, 87,* 299–319.

Casey, B. J., Durston, S., & Fossella, J. A. (2001). Evidence for a mechanistic model of cognitive control. *Clinical Neuroscience Research, 1,* 267–282.

Casey, B. J., Thomas, K. M., Welsh, T. F., Badgaiyan, R. D., Eccard, C. H., Jennings, J. R., et al. (2000). Dissociation of response conflict, attentional selection, and expectancy with functional magnetic resonance imaging. *Proceeding of the National Academy of Sciences, USA, 97,* 8728–8733.

Casey, B. J., Thomas, K. M., Davidson, M. C., Kunz, K., & Franzen, P. L. (2002). Dissociating striatal and hippocampal function developmentally with a Stimulus-Response compatibility task. *Journal of Neuroscience, 22,* 8647–8652.

Casey, B. J., Trainor, R. J., Orendi, J. L., Schubert, A. B., Nystrom, L. E., Giedd, J. N., et al. (1997). A developmental functional MRI study of prefrontal activation during performance of a go-no-go task. *Journal of Cognitive Neuroscience, 9,* 835–847.

Clohessy, A. B., Posner, M. I., & Rothbart, M. K. (2001). Development of the functional visual field. *Acta Psychologica, 106,* 51–68.

Coles, M. G. H., Gratton, G., Bashore, T. R., Ericksen, C. W., & Donchin E. (1985). A psychopsysiologicl investigation of the continuous flow model of human information processing. *Journal of Experimental Psychology: Human, Perception & Performance, 11,* 529–553.

Corbetta, M., & Shulman, G. L. (2002). Control of goal-directed and stimulus-driven attention in the brain. *Nature Neuroscience Reviews, 3,* 201–215.

Dagenbach, D., & Carr, T. H. (Eds.). (1994). *Inhibitory processes in attention, memory, and language.* San Diego, CA: Academic.

Derryberry, D., & Reed, M. A. (1998). Anxiety and attentional focusing: Trait, state and hemispheric influences. *Personality & Individual Differences, 25,* 745–761.

Desimone, R., & Duncan, J. (1995). Neural mechanisms of selective visual attention. *Annual Review of Neuroscience, 18,* 193–222.

Diamond, A. (1991). Neuropsychological insights into the meaning of object concept development. In S. Carey & R. Gelman (Eds.), *The epigenesis of mind: Essays on biology and cognition* (pp. 67–110). Hillsdale, NJ: Lawrence Erlbaum Associates, Inc.

Diamond, A., Briand, L., Fossella, J., & Gehlbach, L. (2004). Genetic and neurochemical modulation of prefrontal cognitive functions in children. *American Journal of Psychiatry, 161,* 125–132.

Diamond, A., & Goldman-Rakic, P. S. (1989). Comparison of human infants and rhesus monkeys on Piaget's A-not-B task: Evidence for dependence on dorsolateral prefrontal cortex. *Experimental Brain Research, 74,* 24–40.

Duncan, J., Seitz, R. J., Kolodny, J., Bor, D., Herzog, H., Ahmed, A., et al. (2000). A neural basis for general intelligence. *Science, 289,* 457–460.

Durston, S., Thomas, K. M., Yang, Y., Ulug, A. M., Zimmerman, R. D., & Casey, B. J. (2002). A neural basis for the development of inhibitory control. *Developmental Science, 5,* F9–F16.

Egan, M. F., Goldberg, T. E., Kolachana, B. S., Callicott, J. H., Mazzanti, C. M., Straub, R. E., et al. (2001). Effect of COMT val[108/158] met genotype of frontal lobe function and risk for schizophrenia. *Proceedings of the National Academy of Sciences, USA, 98,* 6917–6922.

Eisenberg, N., Fabes, R. A., Nyman, M., Bernzweig, J., & Pinulas, A. (1994). The relations of emotionality and regulation to children's anger-related reactions. *Child Development, 65,* 109–128.

Eisenberg, N., Smith, C. L., Sadovsky, A., & Spinrad, T. L. (2004). Effortful control: Relations with emotion regulation, adjustment, and socialization in childhood. In R. F. Baumeister & K. D. Vohs (Eds.), *Handbook of self regulation: Research, theory, and applications* (pp. 259–282). New York: Guilford.

Eriksen, B. A., & Eriksen, C. W. (1974). Effects of noise letters upon the identification of a target letter in a nonsearch task. *Perception & Psychophysics, 16,* 143–149.

Fan, J., Flombaum, J. I., McCandliss, B. D., Thomas, K. M., & Posner, M. I. (2003). Cognitive and brain consequences of conflict. *NeuroImage, 18,* 42–57.

Fan, J., Fossella, J. A., Sommer, T., & Posner, M. I. (2003). Mapping the genetic variation of executive attention onto brain activity. *Proceedings of the National Academy of Sciences, USA, 100,* 7406–7411.

Fan, J., McCandliss, B. D., Sommer, T., Raz, M., & Posner, M. I. (2002). Testing the efficiency and independence of attentional networks. *Journal of Cognitive Neuroscience, 340,* 340–347.

Fan, J., Wu, Y., Fossella, J., & Posner, M. I. (2001). Assessing the heritability of attentional networks. *BioMed Central Neuroscience, 2,* 14.

Fonagy, P., & Target, M. (2002). Early intervention and the development of self-regulation. *Psychoanalytic Quarterly, 22,* 307–335.

Fossella, J., Posner, M. I., Fan, J., Swanson, J. M., & Pfaff, D. M. (2002). Attentional phenotypes for the analysis of higher mental function. *The Scientific World Journal, 2,* 217–223.

Fuentes, J. J. (2004). Inhibitory processing in the attentional networks. In M. I. Posner (Ed.), *Cognitive neuroscience of attention* (pp.45–55). New York: Guilford.

Gehring, W. J., Gross, B., Coles, M. G. H., Meyer, D. E., & Donchin, E. (1993). A neural system for error detection and compensation. *Psychological Science, 4,* 385–390.

Gerardi-Caulton, G. (2000). Sensitivity to spatial conflict and the development of self-regulation in children 24–36 months of age. *Developmental Science, 3/4,* 397–404.

Goldberg, T. E., & Weinberger, D.R. (2004). Genes and the parsing of cognitive processes. *Trends in Cognitive Science, 8,* 325–335.

Granon, S., Passetti, F., Thomas, K. L., Dalley, J. W., Everitt, B. J., & Robbins, T. W. (2000). Enhanced and impaired attentional performance after infusion of D1 dopaminergic receptor agents into rat prefrontal cortex. *Journal of Neuroscience, 20,* 1208–1215.

Green, C. S., & Bavelier, D. (2003). Action video game modifies visual selective attention. *Nature, 423,* 534–537.

Harman, C., Rothbart, M. K., & Posner, M. I. (1997). Distress and attention interactions in early infancy. *Motivation and Emotion, 21,* 27–43.

Houghton, G., & Tipper, S. P. (1994). A model of inhibitory mechanisms in selective attention. In D. Dagenbach & T. Carr (Eds.), *Inhibitory mechanisms in attention, memory, and language* (pp. 53–112). Orlando, FL: Academic.

Jackson, S. R., Jackson, G. M., & Roberts, M. (1999). The selection and suppression of action: ERP correlates of executive control in humans. *NeuroReport, 10,* 861–865.

James, W. (1890). *The principles of psychology.* New York: Holt.

Jones, L. B., Rothbart, M. K., & Posner, M. I. (2003). Development of executive attention in preschool children. *Developmental Science, 6,* 498–504.

Joober, R., Gauthier, J., Lal, S., Bloom, D., Lalonde, P., Rouleau, G., et al. (2002). Catechol-O-methyltransferase Val-108/158-Met gene variants associated with performance on the Wisconsin Card Sorting Test. *Archives of General Psychiatry, 59,* 662–663.

Kaufman, A. S., & Kaufman, N. L. (1990). *Kaufman Brief Intelligence Test–Manual.* Circle Pines, MN: American Guidance Service.

Keele, S. W., Ivry, R., Mayr, U., Hazeltine, E., & Heuer, H. (2003). The cognitive and neural architecture of sequence representation. *Psychological Review, 110,* 316–339.

Kerns, K. A., Esso, K., & Thompson, J. (1999). Investigation of a direct intervention for improving attention in young children with ADHD. *Developmental Neuropsychology, 16,* 273–295.

Klingsberg, T., Forssberg, H., & Westerberg, H. (2002). Training of working memory in children with ADHD. *Journal of Clinical and Experimental Neuropsychology, 24,* 781–791.

Kochanska, G. (1991). Socialization and temperament in the development of guilt and conscience. *Child Development, 62,* 1379–1392.

Kochanska, G. (1995). Children's temperament, mothers' discipline, and security of attachment: Multiple pathways to emerging internalization. *Child Development, 66,* 597–615.

Kochanska, G. (1997). Multiple pathways to conscience for children with different temperaments from toddlerhood to age 5. *Developmental Psychology, 3,* 228–240.

Kochanska, G., Murray, K. T., & Harlan, E. T. (2000). Effortful control in early childhood: Continuity and change, antecedents, and implications for social development. *Developmental Psychology, 36,* 220–232.

Kochanska, G., Murray, K., Jacques, T. Y., Koenig, A. L., & Vandegeest, K. A. (1996). Inhibitory control in young children and its role in emerging internationalization. *Child Development, 67,* 490–507.

Kopp, B., Rist, F., & Mattler, U. (1996). N200 in the flanker task as a neurobehavioral tool for investigating executive control. *Psychophysiology, 33,* 282–294.

Neville, H. J., & Bavelier, D. (1999). Specificity and plasticity in neurocognitive development in humans. In M. Gazzaniga (Ed.), *The cognitive neurosciences* (2nd ed., pp. 83–98). Cambridge, MA: MIT Press.

Norman, D. A., & Shallice, T. (1986). Attention to action: Willed and automatic control of behavior. In R. J. Davidson, C. E. Schwartz, & D. Shapiro (Eds.), *Consciousness and self-regulation* (pp. 1–18). New York: Plenum.

Ochsner, K. N., Bunge, S. A., Gross, J. J., & Gabrieli, J. D. E. (2002). Rethinking feelings: An fMRI study of the cognitive regulation of emotion. *Journal of Cognitive Neuroscience, 14,* 1215–1229.

Posner, M. I., & Dehaene, S. (1994). Attentional networks. *Trends in Neuroscience, 7,* 75–79.

Posner, M. I., & DiGirolamo, G. J. (1998) Executive attention: Conflict, target detection, and cognitive control. In R. Parasuraman (Ed.), *The attentive brain* (pp. 401–423). Cambridge, MA: MIT Press.

Posner, M. I., & Fan, J. (in press). Attention as an organ system. In J. Pomerantz (Ed.), *Neurobiology of perception and communication: From synapse to society. The IVth De Lange Conference.* Cambridge, England: Cambridge University Press.

Posner, M. I., & Petersen, S. E. (1990). The attention system of the human brain. *Annual Review of Neuroscience, 13,* 25–42.

Posner, M. I., & Raichle, M. E. (1994). *Images of mind.* New York: Scientific American Books.

Posner, M. I., & Raichle, M. E. (Eds.). (1998). Overview: The neuroimaging of human brain function. *Proceedings of the National Academy of Sciences, USA, 95,* 763–764.

Posner, M. I., & Rothbart, M. K. (1992). Attention and conscious experience. In A. D. Milner & M. D. Rugg (Eds.), *The neuropsychology of consciousness* (pp. 91–112). London: Academic.

Posner, M. I., & Rothbart, M. K. (1998). Attention, self-regulation, and consciousness. *Philosophical Transactions of the Royal Society of London, B, 353,* 1915–1927.

Rothbart, M. K., Ahadi, S. A., & Hershey, K. L. (1994). Temperament and social behavior in childhood. *Merrill-Palmer Quarterly, 40,* 21–39.

Rothbart, M. K., Ahadi, S. A., Hershey, K., & Fisher, P. (2001). Investigations of temperament at three to seven years: The Children's Behavior Questionnaire. *Child Development, 72,* 1394–1408.

Rothbart, M. K., Ellis, L. K., Rueda, M. R., & Posner, M. I. (2003). Developing mechanisms of conflict resolution. *Journal of Personality, 71,* 1113–1143.

Rothbart, M. K., Posner, M. I., & Boylan, A. (1990). Regulatory mechanisms in infant development. In J. Enns (Ed.), *The development of attention: Research and theory* (pp. 139–160). Amsterdam: Elsevier.

Rothbart, M. K., & Rueda, M. R. (2005). The development of effortful control. In U. Mayr, E. Awh, & S. W. Keele (Eds.), *Developing individuality in the human brain: A tribute to Michael I. Posner* (pp. 167–188). Washington, DC: American Psychological Association.

Rueda, M. R., Fan, J., McCandliss, B., Halparin, J. D., Gruber, D. B., Pappert, L., et al. (2004). Development of attentional networks in childhood. *Neuropsychologia, 42,* 1029–1040.

Rueda, M. R., Posner, M. I., & Rothbart, M. K. (2004). Attentional control and self regulation. In R. F. Baumeister & K. D. Vohs (Eds.), *Handbook of self regulation: Research, theory, and applications* (pp. 283–300). New York: Guilford.

Rueda, M. R., Posner, M. I., Rothbart, M. K., & Davis-Stober, C. P. (2004). Development of the time course for processing conflict. An ERP study with 4 year olds and adults. *BMC Neuroscience, 5,* 39.

Rueda, M. R., Rothbart, M. K., McCandliss, B. D., Saccamono, L., & Posner, M. I. (2005). *Relative influences of training, maturation and genetic differences in the development of executive attention.* Manuscript submitted for publication.

Ruff, H. A., & Rothbart, M. K. (1996). *Attention in early development: Themes and variations.* New York: Oxford University Press.

Seamas, J. K., Floresco, S. B., & Phillips, A. G. (1998). D_1 receptor modulation of hippocampal-prefrontal cortical circuits integrating spatial memory with executive functions in the rat. *Journal of Neuroscience, 18,* 1613–1621.

Semrud-Clikeman, M., Nielsen, K. H., & Clinton, A. (1999). An intervention approach for children with teacher and parent-identified attentional difficulties. *Journal of Learning Disabilities, 32,* 581–589.

Sohlberg, M. M., McLaughlin, K. A., Pavese, A., Heidrich, A., & Posner, M. I. (2000). Evaluation of attention process therapy training in persons with acquired brain injury. *Journal of Clinical and Experimental Neuropsychology, 22,* 656–676.

Sturm, W., Willmes, K., Orgass, B., & Hartje, W. (1997). Do specific attention deficits need specific training? *Neuropsychological Rehabilitation, 7,* 81–103.

Swanson, J., Oosterlaan, J., Murias, M., Moyzis, R., Schuck, S., Mann, M., et al. (2000). ADHD children with 7-repeat allele of the DRD4 gene have extreme behavior but normal performance on critical neuropsychological tests of attention. *Proceedings of the National Academy of Sciences, USA, 97,* 4754–4759.

Tucker, D. M. (1993). Spatial sampling of head electrical fields: The geodesic sensor net. *Electroencephalography and Clinical Neurophysiology: Evoked Potentials, 87,* 154–163.

van Veen, V., & Carter, C. S. (2002). The timing of action-monitoring processes in the anterior cingulate cortex. *Journal of Cognitive Neuroscience, 14,* 593–602.

Vohs, K. D., & Baumeister, R. F. (2004). *Handbook of self regulation: Research, theory, and applications.* New York: Guilford.

Welch, M. C. (2001). The prefrontal cortex and the development of the executive function in childhood. In A. F. Kalverboer & A. Gramsbergen (Eds.), *Handbook of brain and behavior in human development* (pp. 767–790). Dordrecht, The Netherlands: Kluwer Academic.

DEVELOPMENTAL NEUROPSYCHOLOGY, 28(2), 595–616
Copyright © 2005, Lawrence Erlbaum Associates, Inc.

Developmentally Sensitive Measures of Executive Function in Preschool Children

Stephanie M. Carlson
Department of Psychology
University of Washington

Changes in executive functioning in the preschool years are recognized as playing a critical role in cognitive and social development, yet comprehensive data and recommendations about measurement of these changes are lacking. The performance of 602 preschool children on several executive function tasks was analyzed and reported as (a) age trends in performance and (b) task difficulty scales at 2, 3, 4, and 5 to 6 years of age. This analysis informs theories of executive function development and offers researchers an evidence-based guide to task selection and design.

Executive functioning (EF) refers to higher order, self-regulatory, cognitive processes that aid in the monitoring and control of thought and action. These skills include inhibitory control, planning, attentional flexibility, error correction and detection, and resistance to interference (Dempster, 1992; Welsh, Pennington, & Groisser, 1991; Zelazo, Carter, Reznick, & Frye, 1997). EF is often assessed using neurocognitive tasks that have been adapted for young children. For example, Hughes (1998) adapted Luria's Hand Game (Luria, Pribram, & Homskaya, 1964), in which preschoolers were asked first to imitate the hand gestures of an experimenter and then to make an opposite gesture (e.g., if the experimenter points a finger, the child must make a fist, and vice versa). These anti-imitation trials are considerably more difficult for young children and for adults with prefrontal brain lesions. Performance on EF tasks may be moderated by working memory capacity (Engle, 2002; Roberts & Pennington, 1996). For example, in Luria's Hand Game, the ability to hold the rules in mind is critical to task success. As both working

---

Correspondence should be addressed to Stephanie M. Carlson, Department of Psychology, University of Washington, Seattle, WA 98195–1525. E-mail: carlsons@u.washington.edu

memory and inhibition improve in the preschool years, so does performance on this and similar tasks.

Historically, EF has been considered in neuropsychology to be interchangeable with frontal lobe function. Accordingly the initial wave of research on EF in children tended to focus on executive dysfunction in atypical participant populations, including children with traumatic head injury (Dennis, Barnes, Donnelly, Wilkinson, & Humphreys, 1996; Levin et al., 1996), early hydrocephalus (Fletcher et al., 1996), Tourette's syndrome (Denckla, 1996), attention deficit hyperactivity disorder (Barkley, 1997; Denckla, 1996), neurofibromatosis (Denckla, 1996), meningitis (Taylor, Schatschneider, Petrill, Barry, & Owens, 1996), premature birth (Espy et al., 2002), lead exposure (Canfield, Kreher, Cornwell, & Henderson, 2003), phenylketonuria (Diamond, Prevor, Callender, & Druin, 1997), and autism (e.g., Ozonoff, Pennington, & Rogers, 1991; Zelazo, Jacques, Burack, & Frye, 2002). Much of this cited work appeared in a past special issue of *Developmental Neuropsychology* on EF in children, where Fletcher (1996) drew three main conclusions about the topic. First, EFs reflect such a broad array of cognitive functions that they are difficult to define. He pointed to the need for careful operationalization of the term. Second, EFs are factorially complex, that is, EF tasks often measure multiple aspects of attention and memory that may be separable (see also Miyake et al., 2000). Finally, he emphasized the importance of measuring EF in children for understanding childhood disorders and of further developing measurement tools that are based on the cognitive development of children rather than relying exclusively on models of brain damage in adults.

A more recent special issue of *Developmental Neuropsychology* on executive control marks major advances in this field, such as decomposing the relative contributions of inhibitory control and working memory to certain problem-solving tasks (Espy et al., 2004; Senn, Espy, & Kaufmann, 2004; see also Beveridge, Jarrold, & Pettit, 2002; Carlson, Moses, & Breton, 2002), and expanding assessment tools, such as a questionnaire measure for parents and teachers (Isquith, Gioia, & Espy, 2004). However, there continues to be no consensus on the definition of the term. Therefore, the need for careful operationalization of EF persists. In the absence of a concise definition, do we at least "know it when we see it?"

Behavioral assessment of EF in young children is especially important to examine because there is a surge of interest in the role that EF plays in normative cognitive and social development (e.g., Blair, 2002; Carlson & Moses, 2001; Hughes, 1998; Kochanska, Murray, & Harlan, 2000). A notable difference from Fletcher's (1996) observations is that more recent investigations have shown that individual variation within the normal range can be meaningful and predictive. For example, Hughes (1998; Hughes & Ensor, this issue) and Carlson (Carlson, Mandell, & Williams, 2004; Carlson & Moses, 2001) have found that individual differences in EF skills were significantly related to children's theory of mind (i.e., the ability to reason about mental states of self and others) both concurrently and longitudinally in the preschool years. In turn, self-regulation and theory of mind are implicated in older children's social competence (e.g., Bosacki & Astington, 1999). Similarly, Kochanska and colleagues found that early differences in attention and effortful control predicted later social functioning including moral conduct (Kochanska et al., 2000; Kochanska, Murray, Jacques, Koenig, & Vandegeest, 1996).

There has also been a recent shift toward greater consideration of the affective components of EF in addition to the traditional cognitive model of prefrontal cortical functions (i.e., "cool" EF). "Hot" EF refers to flexible representation and control over appetitive reward systems (Hongwanishkul, Happaney, Lee, & Zelazo, this issue; Zelazo & Müller, 2002). It is associated with orbitofrontal cortex, which has close connections with the limbic system. Damage to this region often results in inappropriate social and/or emotional behavior. Recent investigations of hot EF in preschoolers utilized the Children's Gambling Task (Kerr & Zelazo, 2004) and the Less is More task (Carlson, Davis, & Leach, 2005), where children need to defer short-term gains to receive a larger, long-term reward outcome. Although hot EF and cool EF are believed to interact as part of a single coordinated system, they may be separable both behaviorally and neuroanatomically (see Hongwanishkul et al., this issue; Zelazo & Müller, 2002).

With such wide-ranging conceptualizations of EF and recent research implicating it in a broad array of cognitive and social developmental phenomena, it is especially crucial that adequate measurement tools be available to further advance early childhood EF research. Several investigators have designed or adapted innovative and effective measures of EF for children. Recent years have seen a shift away from downward extension of tests used with adult frontal patients and toward more developmentally sensitive measures for young children. A coherent overview of measures used with typically developing preschoolers is lacking. There is little consensus or guidance in the EF literature as to which measures are appropriate for a given age range or ability level. To begin to address this need, we conducted an analysis of 602 children's EF task performance in our laboratory and attempted to answer the following questions: Which measures are sensitive to age changes across this period? What is the relative difficulty level of tasks administered at a given age?

The data included in this analysis were obtained from nine studies conducted in our laboratory. Eight of these studies were designed to assess the relation between individual differences in EF and other aspects of cognitive development (theory of mind, pretend play, and language). They included batteries of 3 to 11 EF tasks, administered one on one by a researcher in a fixed order across one or two 60-min sessions. (The other study included just 1 EF task.) We combined this information into one database and conducted preliminary analyses to ensure there were no significant sampling differences for EF tasks administered in more than one study. Then we proceeded with the analyses of age trends in performance and task difficulty.

METHOD

Participants

Children ranged in age from 22 to 83 months. They included 118 two-year-olds (M = 24 months, SD = 1.34; 60 boys and 58 girls), 207 three-year-olds (M = 42 months, SD = 2.89; 106 boys and 101 girls), 194 four-year-olds (M = 53 months, SD = 3.51; 94 boys and 100 girls), and 83 five- and six-year-olds (M = 70 months, SD = 5.6; 43 boys and 40 girls), for a total of 602 children (50% female). Eighty-one of the 2-year-olds in a longitudinal sample also were tested at age 3 on a different set of EF tasks. Families were recruited from a university database of parents interested in being contacted about developmental research and from flyers posted in schools. Ethnicity and income information were not requested of all parents, but the majority of children in the recruitment populations were White and middle class. One exception is the 5- to 6-year-old sample, which was 15% Hispanic and bilingual. Table 1 summarizes the age range and number of EF tasks for each study sample included in the analyses.

Measures

The EF measures we administered are described briefly next and summarized in Table 2 in terms of the prepotent (i.e., dominant, canonical) response and the correct response for each task. All sessions were scored from videotape after interrater reliability was established. Each task took approximately 5 min to administer, with the exception of Spatial Conflict, a computerized game that took 15 to 20 min. Task protocols are available from the author.

TABLE 1
Study Samples Included in the Analyses

Study	Reference	Age Range (Months)	Mean Age	n	No. of Executive Function Tasks
1	Unpublished data	58–83	72	50	3
2	Carlson and Moses (2001)	39–59	47	107	11
3	Unpublished data	39–60	48	104	9
4	Unpublished data	51–72	61	40	4
5	Carlson, Davis, and Leach (2005)	36–49	44	44	1
6	Unpublished data	39–54	48	43	4
7	Carlson, Moses, and Claxton (2004)	38–59	48	49	3
8	Carlson, Mandell, and Williams (2004a)	22–40	24; 39	118; 81	5; 8
9	Carlson, Moses, and Breton (2002)	40–66	55	47	5

Preschool Executive Function Task Summary

Task	Reference	Prepotent Response	Correct Response
Reverse Categorization	Carlson, Mandell, and Williams (2004)	"Mommy" animals → Mommy bucket "Baby" animals → Baby bucket	"Mommy" animals → Baby bucket "Baby" animals → Mommy bucket
Snack Delay	Kochanska et al. (2000)	Retrieve treat from under cup now	Wait until E rings bell (5–20 sec)
Multilocation Search	Zelazo et al. (1998)	Search for treat in previously rewarded location	Search in new location (after delay)
Shape Stroop	Kochanska et al. (2000)	Point to large shape	Point to smaller shape embedded
Gift Delay (bow)	Kochanska et al. (2000)	Open gift now	Wait until E returns with bow (3 min)
Day/Night	Gerstadt et al. (1994)	Say "day" for sun Say "night" for moon/stars	Say "night" for sun Say "day" for moon/stars
Grass/Snow	Carlson and Moses (2001)	"Grass" point to green "Snow" point to white	"Grass" point to white "Snow" point to green
Bear/Dragon	Reed et al. (1984)	Do all commanded actions	Do what bear says, not dragon
Hand Game	Hughes (1998), based on Luria et al. (1964)	Imitate E's hand gesture	Make opposite gesture to E
Spatial Conflict	Gerardi-Caulton (2000)	Press key on same side as target picture	Press key on opposite side
Whisper	Kochanska et al. (1996)	Blurt out names of familiar characters	Whisper all names
Tower	Kochanska et al. (1996)	Place all blocks oneself	Take turns with E
Delay of Gratification	Mischel et al. (1989)	Eat snack now	Wait until E returns (1 min, 5 min)
Gift Delay (wrap)	Kochanska et al. (1996)	Peek at gift	Do not peek while E wraps gift (60 sec)
Pinball	Reed et al. (1984)	Release plunger now	Wait until E says "Go!"
Motor Sequencing	Carlson and Moses (2001), based on Welsh et al. (1991)	Press the same key repeatedly	Press keys in sequence for 10 sec
Count and Label	Gordon and Olson (1998)	"One is a [label], one is a [label]"	Interleave counting and labeling
Backward Digit Span	Davis and Pratt (1996)	Repeat digits in forward order	Reverse order of digits
Standard DCCS	Frye et al. (1995, Exp. 2), see also Zelazo et al. (2003)	Sort cards according to previous dimension	Sort according to new dimension
Less is More	Carlson, Davis, and Leach (2005)	Select larger amount of treats	Point to smaller amount
Simon Says	Strommen (1973)	Do all commanded actions	Do only if E says "Simon says …"
KRISP	Carlson and Moses (2001), based on Wright (1971)	Select first similar drawing found	Examine all drawings to find match
Forbidden Toy	Adapted from Lewis et al. (1989)	Touch attractive toy	Do not touch toy until E returns (5 min)
Disappointing Gift	Saarni (1984)	Express disappointment with unattractive toy	Suppress disappointment

Note. E = experimenter; KRISP = Kansas Reflection-Impulsivity Scale for Preschoolers.

Toddler Tasks

Reverse Categorization (Carlson, Mandell, & Williams, 2004).   Children were introduced to two buckets and asked to help the experimenter sort big blocks into the "big" bucket and little blocks into the "little" bucket (24 months) or mommy animals into a "mommy" bucket and baby animals into a "baby" bucket (3 years). Then the experimenter suggested they play a "silly game" and reverse this categorization scheme. There were 12 test trials, with a rule reminder on every trial (24 months) or midway through (3 years). Scores were the number of correct responses out of 12.

Snack Delay (Kochanska et al., 2000).   The experimenter placed a gold-fish cracker under a clear cup and told children to wait until she rang a bell before getting the treat. After a brief demonstration, there were four trials with delays of 5, 10, 15, and 20 sec. Children were reminded of the rule on every trial. Scores were the number of trials with a full wait.

Multilocation Search (Zelazo, Reznick, & Spinazolla, 1998).   The experimenter presented a set of wooden drawers connected side by side. Three drawers had strings with symbols (e.g., a green circle) attached. Children were shown how to pull the string to open a drawer. Following a brief warm-up, the experimenter placed a candy treat inside one drawer and asked children to go get it. After three consecutively correct retrievals at this location, the experimenter visibly switched the hiding place to a different drawer (having a different symbol attached) and imposed a 10-sec delay before inviting children to get the treat. Perseveration on the switch trial (searching incorrectly in the previously rewarded location) was scored as failing.

Shape Stroop (Kochanska et al., 2000).   Children were shown cards depicting three fruits (both a large and small version of each). The experimenter labeled the sizes and asked children to identify each fruit. Next, she presented three cards each having a small fruit embedded in a drawing of a large, different fruit (e.g., a small banana inside a large apple next to a small orange inside a large banana) and asked children to identify the small fruit (e.g., "show me the *little* banana"). There were three trials, each scored as correct (e.g., pointing to the little banana) or incorrect (e.g., pointing to the big banana).

Gift Delay (bow; Kochanska et al., 2000).   The experimenter praised children for doing such a good job and announced she had a present for them (producing a large gift bag with a wrapped gift inside). Then she said she forgot to put a bow on the gift and asked children to wait until she returned with a bow before opening it. The experimenter left the room for 3 min, returned with a bow, and invited children to open the gift (if they had not done so already). Peeking was scored as a fail.

Preschooler Tasks

Day/Night (Gerstadt, Hong, & Diamond, 1994). The experimenter engaged children in a conversation about when the sun comes up (in the day) and when the moon and stars come out (in the night). She then presented a white card with a yellow sun drawing on it and a black card with a white moon and stars on it. Children were instructed that in this game they were to say *night* for the sun card and *day* for the moon/stars card. After a brief warm-up, there were 16 test trials with each card presented (from beneath the table) in a fixed, pseudorandom order. There were no breaks or rule reminders. Accuracy (number correct out of 16) was recorded.

Grass/Snow (Carlson & Moses, 2001). Children were asked to place their hands on top of two child-size, felt hand shapes centered beneath a white card and a green card on the table. Similar to the Day/Night task, the experimenter asked children to name the color of grass (green) and snow (white). Then she explained that in this silly game they should point to the white card when the experimenter says *grass* and point to the green card when she says *snow*. Following practice, there were 16 test trials presented consecutively. Accuracy was recorded. (In both Day/Night and Grass/Snow, children's first responses were scored, even if they changed their minds and self-corrected.)

Bear/Dragon (Reed, Pien, & Rothbart, 1984). The experimenter introduced children to a "nice" bear puppet (using a soft, high-pitched voice) and a "naughty" dragon puppet (using a gruff, low-pitched voice). She explained that in this game they are to do what the bear asks them to do (e.g., touch your nose) but *not* to do what the dragon asks. After practicing, there were 10 test trials with the bear and dragon commands in alternating order. Children were seated at a table throughout the task, and all actions involved hand movements. Performance on dragon trials was taken as an index of self-control (0 = movement, 1 = no movement, scored individually for each trial).

Hand Game (Hughes, 1998). Children were instructed to make the same hand motion as the experimenter (fist or pointed finger). After reaching a criterion of 6 correct trials, the experimenter explained that children were to make a gesture opposite to the one he made (e.g., children should point a finger when he makes a fist). Fifteen of these anti-imitation test trials followed after a brief practice. Scores were the number of correct trials out of 15.

Spatial Conflict (Gerardi-Caulton, 2000).   Children were trained on a computer game in which they press down on a picture to their left or right that corresponds to a picture appearing on the screen, using their left or right hand, accordingly. For example, if a rabbit picture appears on the screen, they need to press a rabbit button but not the duck button. After a brief warm-up, test trials followed in which spatial conflict was induced when the target appears on the opposite side of the screen to the correct button. Test trials consisted of four blocks of 8 trials each. Identity and location were incompatible for half the trials. Scores were recorded as the number of correct incompatible trials out of 16. (Reaction time difference scores also were recorded, but the results were similar using accuracy in the present analyses.)

Whisper (Kochanska et al., 1996).   The experimenter asked children if they could whisper their names and then presented a series of 10 cards depicting cartoon characters (6 familiar, 4 unfamiliar to most preschoolers). Children were told to whisper the names of each character and that it was okay if they did not know all of them. On each trial they received a score of 0 if they blurted out the name or used a normal voice and a score of 1 if they whispered. Unfamiliar characters were included so that children would be more excited upon seeing a familiar one (and more likely to shout out the name); "don't know" trials were unscored.

Tower (Kochanska et al., 1996).   Children were invited to help the experimenter build a tower with wooden blocks on the floor. The experimenter said they would take turns and demonstrated turn taking (repeating, "now I go, and then you go"). After this brief practice, the experimenter placed the first block (the largest one) and told children it was their turn to go next. Thereafter, for the 20 remaining blocks, the experimenter did not remind children of the turn-taking rule. Instead, he or she waited for an explicit signal from the children to take a turn (e.g., they handed the experimenter a block or said it was his or her turn). The proportion of blocks placed by the experimenter was recorded (ideally, .5, or 10 blocks).

Delay of Gratification (Mischel, Shoda, & Rodriguez, 1989).   The experimenter presented a choice of snack treats and allowed children to taste each (e.g., fruit-flavored cereal, chocolate chips). After children made a selection, the experimenter placed 2 of the treats in a shallow bowl and 10 of the treats in another identical bowl and asked them which bowl they preferred. (All selected the larger amount with little or no coaching.) He explained that he had to leave the room to do some work but that if the children waited until he returned on his own they could have the larger amount. However, if they did not want to wait so long, they could ring a bell (placed directly in front of them, centered between the two bowls). In this case, the experimenter would return right away, but they could only receive the smaller amount of treats. After a verbal rule check, the experimenter exited the room. Children were observed through a one-way mirror, and the experimenter returned when they rang the bell or began eating the snacks (score = 0) or after the waiting period had passed (score = 1; delay of 1 min for a sample of 39-month-olds; 5 min for 3- and 4-year-olds).

Gift Delay (wrap; Kochanska et al., 1996).   Children were told they had done a great job and that they were going to receive a prize. However, the experimenter "forgot" to wrap their present. The experimenter asked children to turn around in their seat (facing a hidden camera) so that he or she could wrap the present "so it will be a big surprise" and reminded the children not to peek. The experimenter then wrapped a small gift box noisily in a standardized manner (rifling through a paper bag, cutting wrapping paper with scissors, folding the paper around the box, and tearing off tape) for 60 sec. Peeking behavior was recorded.

Pinball (Reed et al., 1984).   A children's tabletop pinball machine was installed with a digital timer that recorded the length of time the plunger was held back half way or more. The experimenter demonstrated the pinball game for children and gave them a turn. After this warm-up, the experimenter explained that children were to wait until she said "Go!" before releasing the plunger. Six test trials followed with delay times of 10, 15, 25, 15, 20, and 10 sec, respectively. Scores were the number of correct (full wait) trials.

Motor Sequencing (Carlson & Moses, 2001; Welsh, Pennington, & Groisser, 1991).   The experimenter presented a child-size musical keyboard that had four differently colored keys. She demonstrated how to play the keyboard by pressing each key in order from left to right with her index finger, and then she invited the children to try it. Next, the experimenter instructed children to press the keys in sequence over and over again, as fast as they could, until she said "Stop!" She signaled children to start and then recorded the number of complete sequences completed in 10 sec.

Count and Label (Gordon & Olson, 1998).   Children were shown three objects (e.g., a key, a shoe, and a toy dog) and asked to label them. Then the experimenter suggested they count the objects. She demonstrated how to count the objects and label them each in turn (e.g., "one is a key, two is a shoe, three is a dog"). There were two test trials using different objects. Children were scored as incorrect if (a) they labeled the objects and then counted them or vice versa, or (b) (more commonly) if they said "one is a key, one is a shoe, one is a dog" or the equivalent.

Backward Digit Span (Davis & Pratt, 1996).   The   experimenter   introduced children to a puppet named Ernie and said that whatever she says, Ernie likes to say it backward. She demonstrated, saying "1, 2" and then made Ernie say

"2, 1." Children were invited to try (using the same example). The experimenter then suggested they do some more like that, explaining that whatever she says, the children should say it backward. She began with two digits and increased the number of digits until children erred on three consecutive trials. The highest level of success was recorded (two, three, four, or five digits). (A 1 was assigned when children failed at two digits.)

Standard Dimensional Change Card Sort (Standard DCCS; Frye, Zelazo, & Palfai, 1995; Zelazo et al., 2003).   Children were introduced to two recipe boxes that had rectangular slots cut in the top. Target cards (e.g., a red rabbit and a blue boat) were affixed to the front of the boxes. The experimenter presented a series of cards (red and blue rabbits and boats) and instructed children to place all the rabbits in the box with the red rabbit and to place all the boats in the box with the blue boat in the "shape game." After five consecutively correct trials, the experimenter announced that they would stop playing the shape game and now play the "color game." In this case, all the red things would go in the box with the red rabbit affixed and all the blue things would go in the box with the blue boat affixed. She announced the rule before each trial, presented a card and labeled it (e.g., "Here's a red boat"), and then handed the card to the children. We followed the method of Frye et al. (1995, Exp .2), in which there were five postswitch trials including two trials that were compatible with the old sorting rule and three trials that were incompatible with it (i.e., sorting by the old rule would now lead to an incorrect response). The total number of correct incompatible postswitch trials was recorded.

In the Stars DCCS used with 5- and 6-year-olds (analogous to the Borders DCCS described in Hongwanishkul et al., this issue), we added a third sorting segment in which the experimenter explained that if there is a star on a card, then children should sort according to color, but if there is *not* a star, then they should sort according to shape. There were 20 trials (4 star, 16 nonstar). Scores were the total number of correct star trials.

Less is More (Carlson et al., 2005).   Less is More is a reverse reward contingency task in which children were asked to select between a larger and smaller array of candy placed in shallow trays (e.g., five vs. two jelly beans). (All children indicated that they preferred the larger amount.) They were told that whichever tray they choose, those treats will go to a naughty puppet and they will get the treats in the other, nonselected, tray. Children therefore need to infer that they should point to the smaller amount to get the larger amount of treats. The candies accumulated in clear plastic cups (one for the child and one for the puppet) across trials. After a brief practice and verbal rule check, 16 test trials followed with a rule reminder halfway through but without explicit feedback. We recorded the number of correct (smaller) treat selections.

Simon Says (Strommen, 1973).   In this version of a popular game for schoolchildren, the experimenter and child stood facing each other, and the experimenter first asked children to do some "silly" things with her, such as "touch your feet." Then she explained that they should do an action only if she prefaced the command with "Simon says." They were to remain perfectly still otherwise. The experimenter issued commands in quick succession and performed all actions, regardless of whether it was a "Simon says" trial. This is an advanced anti-imitation task similar to Bear/Dragon but greater in difficulty. There were 10 trials (5 with and 5 without "Simon says"). The anti-imitation trials were scored in the same manner as Bear/Dragon.

Kansas Reflection-Impulsivity Scale for Preschoolers (KRISP; Carlson & Moses, 2001; Wright, 1971).   Children were shown a book oriented vertically and told to find the shape on the bottom page that exactly matched the target shape on the top page (e.g., to warm up, there was a spoon on top and a choice of a spoon, fork, and knife on the bottom). Items increased in difficulty as the task progressed, with more highly similar items to choose from, so that an impulsive response (quickly selecting a similar but not exact match) would be recorded as an error. For 3- and 4-year-olds there were 10 trials; for 5- to 6-year-olds, 5 additional trials were added. Accuracy was recorded.

Forbidden Toy (adapted from Lewis, Stanger, & Sullivan, 1989).   The experimenter introduced children to an attractive, 20 in. tall Magic Robot toy that speaks and makes sounds when touched on its hands, tummy, or head (Playskool's® Magic Screen Learning Pal). After briefly demonstrating the features of the toy, she explained that she had to leave the room for a few minutes but that the children should not touch the toy while she was gone, "because I really want us to play with this robot together when I get back." The children were left alone in the room (seated and directly facing the toy) for 5 min. (Children were praised if they did not touch the toy or, if they did, they were told it was okay because sometimes it is really hard to wait.)

Disappointing Gift (Saarni, 1984).   Children were given the Gift Delay task in which the experimenter wrapped a present behind their backs. Then they opened the highly anticipated gift, only to discover that it was a plain-looking wood chip. We recorded children's facial and vocal expressions following Saarni's (1984) coding scheme, in which children received 1 point for each positive expression (e.g., smiling eye contact with the experimenter), 0 points for transitional responses (e.g., abrupt loss of smile), and minus 1 point for each negative expression (e.g., nose wrinkling, negative vocalization). Total scores were recorded. Although most children have difficulty exaggerating a positive expression until about 9 years of age, we were interested in the extent to which they could at least neutralize their negative expressions on this task. (All children then received a more desirable gift.)

RESULTS

Preliminary Analyses

Scores were converted on each task to pass/fail for ease of comparison across measures having different scales. This method was preferred over conversion to z scores, which preserves individual differences relative to the mean but makes it difficult to compare absolute levels of performance on multiple tasks as a function of age. As well, performance on most tasks had a binary distribution, suggesting that a pass/fail analysis was appropriate. Passing was determined using the binomial theorem to derive scores where the probability of passing by chance was less than .05. For example, to be scored as passing, children needed to succeed on 10 of 12 trials on Reverse Categorization, 12 of 16 trials on Less is More, and 3 of 3 incompatible trials on the DCCS. Exceptions were tasks where failure was self-evident (e.g., peeking at a gift or touching a forbidden toy), and Whisper, where the number of scored trials varied according to whether children knew the character's name. We therefore considered passing as whispering for all trials scored. One task (Spatial Conflict) had a ceiling problem (with only one child failing) and so was excluded from further analysis. Table 3 provides the scoring criteria for each task included in the analyses with age.

We then examined whether there were differences in performance on a given task across studies (after controlling for age, because there were significant age differences between some studies). A logistic regression was conducted for each task administered in more than one study, with age as a covariate. Logistic regression is an appropriate analysis for binary (pass/fail) data. Tasks (and number of studies compared) included Grass/Snow (3), Bear/Dragon (6), Tower (3), Whisper (6), Gift Delay (wrap; 7), Backward Digit Span (2), Standard DCCS (2), Less is More (2), KRISP (2), and Simon Says (2). These analyses confirmed there were no systematic differences in performance according to study sampling or experimenter (all $ps > .10$). There were also no differences in the child refusal rate on a given task across studies. (Note that refusals were considered missing data and were excluded from analyses.) Although the tasks were presented in a fixed order within a study rather than counterbalanced (which is appropriate for studies of individual differences; see Carlson & Moses, 2001), we were able to compare means on tasks that were given in the first half of the session in some studies and given in the second half of the session in other studies. (One exception was Gift Delay [wrap], which was always done at the end of a session.) There were no significant differences, which suggests that child fatigue did not influence our assessment of task difficulty. Given these preliminary results, we were able to combine data across studies on these measures to get a more complete picture of developmental changes in performance and comparisons among tasks.

Age Trends in EF Performance

Table 3 shows developmental trends in performance for tasks administered to more than one age group. Logistic regression was used to analyze the effect of age for each task. Of the 17 tasks, 11 (65%) showed a significant age effect, 1 was marginally significant, and 5 were nonsignificant in the age groups tested. It is important to note that it remains possible that age effects might be significant if younger and/or older children were also tested, as was done in some of the original studies using these tasks (e.g., the Day/Night task; Gerstadt et al., 1994). Our focus was on development from 3 to 5 years. Also shown in Table 3, the average proportion of tasks passed increased significantly as a function of age. Post hoc analyses (Tukey's Honestly Significant Difference) indicated no significant difference from young 3 (36–41 months) to older 3 (42–47 months) but showed significant improvement from young and older 3 to young 4, and again from young 4 to older 4 and 5+ ($ps < .05$).

EF performance is often strongly related to individual differences in verbal ability (e.g., Carlson & Moses, 2001; Hughes, 1998). Thus it was possible that the observed age differences in EF were merely a proxy for increasing verbal skills across the preschool period. In the combined data set, however, age group remained significantly related to the proportion of EF tasks passed by each participant, even after covarying scores on the Peabody Picture Vocabulary Test (PPVT; Dunn & Dunn, 1981, 1997), which were obtained for the majority of children: effect of PPVT, $F(1, 427) = 25.42$, $p < .001$; effect of Age Group (after controlling for PPVT), $F(4, 427) = 9.71$, $p < .001$.

EF Task Difficulty

Having established the developmental trends in EF performance, we examined task difficulty within each age category in the second set of analyses. Logistic regression was used to test the interaction of person ability and task difficulty on performance outcomes. This is a probabilistic approach to scale construction that estimates item difficulty and within-subject ability levels with dichotomous data. The model can be summarized as

$$y_{ij} = \mu + a_i + b_j$$

The probability of success for a given child on a given task (y_{ij}) is equal to the overall rate of success (μ) plus child-specific rates of success (a_I), plus specific task

TABLE 3
Percentage Passing Executive Function Tasks According to Age

Task	Pass Criteria	Young 3	Older 3	Young 4	Older 4	5	Age Effect
Day/Night	12/16	50 (14)	47 (45)	48 (25)	68 (19)	—	ns
Grass/Snow	12/16	40 (86)	52 (75)	55 (64)	84 (37)	—	$\chi^2(3, N = 262) = 21.99$***
Bear/Dragon	4/5	51 (108)	76 (119)	88 (102)	94 (69)	100 (13)	$\chi^2(4, N = 411) = 65.23$***
Tower	8/10	24 (107)	42 (77)	67 (63)	66 (38)	—	$\chi^2(3, N = 285) = 38.56$***
Whisper	All whisper	62 (122)	63 (120)	74 (103)	90 (69)	92 (13)	$\chi^2(4, N = 427) = 26.85$***
Gift Delay (wrap)	No peek	42 (125)	48 (120)	53 (117)	60 (74)	74 (34)	$\chi^2(4, N = 470) = 14.29$**
Pinball	5/6	67 (15)	74 (46)	81 (26)	95 (19)	—	ns
Motor Sequencing	2	27 (15)	60 (45)	77 (26)	79 (19)	—	$\chi^2(3, N = 105) = 12.92$**
Count/Label	2/2	26 (31)		55 (22)	71 (21)	77 (13)	$\chi^2(4, N = 87) = 18.92$**
Backward Digit	3+	9 (47)	17 (41)	37 (35)	69 (13)		$\chi^2(4, N = 136) = 25.67$***
Standard DCCS	3/3	10 (29)	25 (79)	48 (65)	76 (38)	—	$\chi^2(3, N = 211) = 42.58$***
Less is More	12/16	24 (25)	34 (62)	61 (38)	68 (19)	—	$\chi^2(3, N = 144) = 15.75$**
Simon Says	4/5	—	—	25 (20)		46 (69)	$\chi^2(2, N = 89) = 5.75$†
Delay of Gratification (5 min)	Full wait	64 (14)	61 (31)	64 (39)	84 (19)	—	ns
KRISP	8/10	0 (15)	41 (46)	81 (26)	75 (20)	94 (49)	$\chi^2(4, N = 156) = 69.60$***
Forbidden Toy	No touch	—	—	47 (19)		67 (21)	ns
Disappointing Gift	No negative expression	—	—	32 (19)		43 (21)	ns
Average Proportion of Tasks Passed (SD)		.40 (.28)	.45 (.31)	.61 (.28)	.73 (.21)	.69 (.27)	$F(4, 564) = 28.63$***

Note. Total sample sizes for individual tasks are shown in parentheses. Numbers appearing between two age groups reflect the combined data, occurring when a cell contained fewer than 12 participants.

†$p < .10$. *$p < .05$. **$p < .01$. ***$p < .001$.

effects (b_j). At 24 months, both main effects were significant: Person, $\chi^2(117, N = 118) = 254.79$, and Task, $\chi^2(4, N = 5) = 166.03$, $ps = .000$. This analysis yields parameter estimates representing the probability of passing a given task (between-subject variability) while taking into account within-subject variability. The mean parameter estimates for tasks given to 24-month-olds are illustrated in Figure 1. Multilocation Search was least difficult, followed by Gift Delay (bow), Shape Stroop, Snack Delay, and Reverse Categorization (most difficult). Examination of the 95% confidence intervals indicated significant differences at each step in the scale, with the exception of Snack Delay and Shape Stroop, which did not differ (indicated by brackets). This model suggests that a child with a given ability level is likely to succeed on tasks with difficulty levels below that person's ability and likely to fail on tasks with difficulty levels greater than that person's ability.

The data for 3-, 4-, and 5- to 6-year-olds were obtained from multiple studies that included different combinations of EF tasks. Therefore we used the probabilities of passing each task at a given age in data analyses of these groups. They were derived from binary logistic regressions with age (in months) as a covariate. These probabilities were then entered into a repeated measures analysis of variance. The parameter estimates on 17 EF tasks for 288 three-year-olds are illustrated in Figure 2. The multivariate test was significant, $F(6, 282) = 3.46E^{+10}$, $p = .000$. Examination of the 95% confidence intervals indicated that each task in succession (from left to right in Figure 2) was significantly more difficult than the previous one, with the following exceptions: Bear/Dragon and Whisper did not differ; Gift Delay, Motor Sequencing, Grass/Snow, and Hand Game did not differ; and Tower and KRISP did not differ from one another.

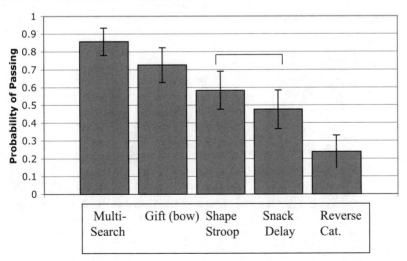

FIGURE 1   Task scale at 24 months ($N = 118$).

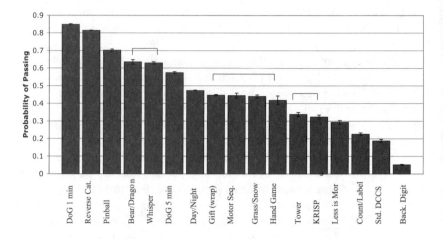

FIGURE 2   Task scale at 3 years ($N = 288$).

We next carried out the same procedure for the 4-year-olds ($N = 194$). The multivariate test was again significant, $F(6, 188) = 1.78E^{+10}$, $p = .000$. The parameter estimates and 95% confidence intervals for 18 EF tasks are shown in Figure 3. Each task in succession (from left to right) was significantly harder than the previous one, with the following exceptions: Motor Sequencing and Whisper did not differ; Tower, Grass/Snow, and KRISP did not differ; Standard DCCS and Less is More did not differ; Gift Delay, Day/Night, and Count and Label did not differ; and Simon Says and Disappointing Gift did not differ from one another in difficulty.

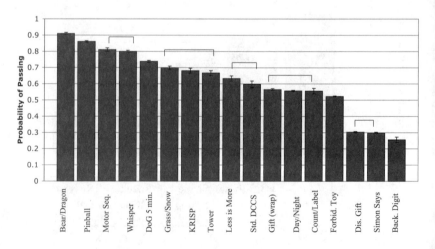

FIGURE 3   Task scale at 4 years ($N = 194$).

Last, the parameter estimates on 10 EF tasks for the 5- to 6-year-olds ($N = 83$) are shown in Figure 4. The multivariate test was significant, $F(6, 77) = 2.6E^{+10}, p = .000$. The 95% confidence intervals indicated that each task represented a significant increase in difficulty (left to right) with two exceptions: Whisper and Count and Label did not differ, and Disappointing Gift and Simon Says did not differ significantly from one another.

DISCUSSION

We analyzed the responses of 602 preschool children on batteries of EF tasks to provide a more comprehensive picture of development and task difficulty scales in each major age group tested (24 months, 3 years, 4 years, and 5 to 6 years). Among the tasks that were administered to more than one age group, the majority (65%) showed significant age-related improvement. The cases where age was not significant were likely due to a restricted age range and sample size (e.g., Forbidden Toy). Indeed, it is a limitation of this research that sample sizes varied; ideally, all tasks would be administered to all participants. Similarly, our analytic approach dictated the use of categorical variables for age group and pass/fail on the tasks, which might have resulted in a loss of sensitivity. Nevertheless, the overall finding replicates numerous studies of EF in preschool children showing age-related changes (e.g., Diamond & Taylor, 1996; Frye et al., 1995; Hughes, 1998). Aggregate EF scores also improved significantly from 3 to 5 years, even after we controlled for

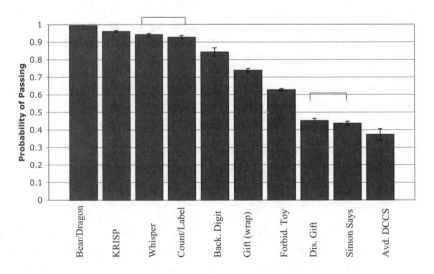

FIGURE 4   Task scale at 5 to 6 years ($N = 83$).

the relation between EF and verbal ability. Hence it is likely that maturational changes at both the biological (brain basis) and contextual (social experience) levels are governing EF development, over and above children's increasing comprehension of task rules and the verbal self-regulation needed to follow them.

These analyses also allowed us to establish a scale of task difficulty for each age group. We determined the probability of passing each EF task at a given age and ability level. This resulted in four scales (24 months, 3 years, 4 years, and 5–6 years) describing the relative difficulty level of each task while taking within-subject variability into account. A scale indicates that children who passed a given task were likely to pass the other tasks at that level, as well as all easier tasks (all tasks located to the left in the figure), and children who failed a given task were likely to fail the other tasks at that level as well as all harder tasks (all tasks located to the right in the figure). (See Andrich, 1985, and Wellman & Liu, 2004, for a similar approach using a Rasch model.) We hope that researchers can benefit from this information in selecting EF tasks according to age and desired level of difficulty. For example, in correlation studies involving EF, researchers would want to select tasks that are likely to capture the greatest variability of individual differences at a given age. If group discrimination is the goal (e.g., in investigations of atypical development), then one might select tasks that are normally mastered by the age group of interest.

Examination of the difficulty scales might also shed light on the different task demands inherent in these measures. For instance, it is possible to conceptualize the tasks as containing primarily inhibition demands (e.g., Gift Delay), primarily working memory demands (e.g., Count and Label), or a combination of both (e.g., Grass/Snow). Previous research suggested that these task demands are dissociable (e.g., Carlson et al., 2002; Diamond, Kirkham, & Amso, 2002; Espy & Bull, this issue; Hughes, 1998). It is also possible to label tasks according to whether they are relatively cool (nonaffective, arbitrary rules) or hot (affective, reward sensitive). The difficulty scales we produced showed no consistent pattern of certain hot/cool task features or inhibition and working memory demands being easier or passed earlier than others. Hot and cool tasks can both be seen at the easy and hard ends of the spectrum, as can tasks that call for inhibition and working memory. However, in all age groups, it was found that the very hardest tasks were those that are thought to involve a combination of inhibition and working memory: Reverse Categorization at age 2, DCCS and Backward Digit Span at age 3, Simon Says and Backward Digit Span at age 4, and the Advanced DCCS at age 5 to 6. (Note that forward digit span is more aptly considered a pure measure of working memory, whereas the backward span task has inhibition demands as well.) These findings suggest that the ways of fractionating EF do not clearly map onto age or difficulty levels. Instead, these divisions (hot/cool; inhibition/working memory) might be most meaningful at the level of *individual differences* regardless of age. As well, EF might be a relatively undifferentiated construct in young children but one that becomes more modular with age (Zelazo & Müller, 2002). Our findings on EF task interrelations (which were consistently strong) are presented elsewhere (Carlson et al., 2005; Carlson, Mandell, & Williams, 2004; Carlson & Moses, 2001; Carlson et al., 2002; Carlson, Moses, & Claxton, 2004).

This study helps to address some of Fletcher's (1996) earlier observations about the state of EF research in children. First, large data sets of this kind with typically developing children are important to establish what is "normal" at a given age and the expected rate of development. Second, we have described children's performance on a large (although by no means exhaustive) set of EF tasks developed for preschool children, with the aim of better operationalization of the construct. This information should facilitate further inquiry into EF development and deficits.

Our data also do not shed light on what factors aside from age may contribute to EF development. Relatively little is known about environmental influences on EF. Distal factors awaiting further study include social disadvantage, school and neighborhood effects, and cultural construals of the self. More proximal factors to investigate are child nutrition, parental discipline, sibling relations, language, and symbolic play.

This analysis of EF from our data collected across nine studies is a further step toward understanding and tracing the development of executive control skills in preschoolers. Eventually, with developmentally sensitive measurement tools in hand, investigators will be able to select EF tasks that are appropriate to the age range and goals of the research design (e.g., basic development, individual differences, or atypical development). There is also likely to be more overlap in task selection and hence a large corpus of data from which to establish age norms on standardized procedures. Rather than homogenizing EF research altogether, however, these efforts are likely to lead to further innovation and improvement of measures and, in turn, increased understanding of the complex role of EF in cognitive and social development. Beyond the borders of the academic research community, as evidence grows on the importance of EF in early childhood, clinicians and educators need valid diagnostic and assessment tools (e.g., to predict school readiness, Blair, 2002). This exchange of information will lead to exciting advances in our understanding of brain-behavior relations in development.

ACKNOWLEDGMENTS

This research was supported, in part, by Grant RO3–041473–02 from the National Institute of Child Health and Human Development; by a gift to the University of Washington Center for Mind, Brain, and Learning from the Apex Foundation, the charitable foundation of Bruce and Jolene McCaw; by a University of Washington Royalty Research Award; and by an American Psychological Association Dissertation Research Award.

I thank the participating families, child care centers, and several research assistants. Peter Hoff provided statistical consultation.

REFERENCES

Andrich, D. (1985). An elaboration of Guttman scaling with Rasch models for measurement. *Sociological Methodology, 15*, 33–80.

Barkley, R. A. (1997). Behavioral inhibition, sustained attention, and executive functions: Constructing a unifying theory of ADHD. *Psychological Bulletin, 121*, 65–94.

Beveridge, M., Jarrold, C., & Pettit, E. (2002). An experimental approach to executive fingerprinting in young children. *Infant and Child Development, 11*, 107–123.

Blair, C. (2002). School readiness: Integrating cognition and emotion in a neurobiological conceptualization of children's functioning at school entry. *American Psychologist, 57*, 111–127.

Bosacki, S., & Astington, J. W. (1999). Theory of mind in preadolescence: Relations between social understanding and social competence. *Social Development, 8*, 237–255.

Canfield, R. L., Kreher, D. A., Cornwell, C., & Henderson, C. R., Jr. (2003). Low-level lead exposure, executive functioning, and learning in early childhood. *Child Neuropsychology, 9*, 35–53.

Carlson, S. M., Davis, A. C., & Leach, J. G. (2005). Less is more: Executive function and symbolic representation in preschool children. *Psychological Science, 16*, 609–616.

Carlson, S. M., Mandell, D. J., & Williams, L. (2004). Executive function and theory of mind: Stability and prediction from age 2 to 3. *Developmental Psychology, 40*, 1105–1122.

Carlson, S. M., & Moses, L. J. (2001). Individual differences in inhibitory control and children's theory of mind. *Child Development, 72*, 1032–1053.

Carlson, S. M., Moses, L. J., & Breton, C. (2002). How specific is the relation between executive function and theory of mind? Contributions of inhibitory control and working memory. *Infant and Child Development,11*, 73–92.

Carlson, S. M., Moses, L. J., & Claxton, L. J. (2004). Individual difference in executive functioning and theory of mind: An investigation of inhibitory control and planning ability. *Journal of Experimental Child Psychology, 87*, 299–319.

Davis, H. L., & Pratt, C. (1996). The development of children's theory of mind: The working memory explanation. *Australian Journal of Psychology, 47*, 25–31.

Dempster, F. N. (1992). The rise and fall of the inhibitory mechanism: Toward a unified theory of cognitive development and aging. *Developmental Review, 12*, 45–75.

Denckla, M. B. (1996). Research on executive function in a neurodevelopmental context: Applications of clinical measures. *Developmental Neuropsychology, 12*, 5–16.

Dennis, M., Barnes, M. A., Donnelly, R. E., Wilkinson, M., & Humphreys, R. P. (1996). Appraising and managing knowledge: Metacognitive skills after childhood head injury. *Developmental Neuropsychology, 12*, 77–104.

Diamond, A., Kirkham, N., & Amso, D. (2002). Conditions under which young children can hold two rules in mind and inhibit a prepotent response. *Developmental Psychology, 38*, 352–362.

Diamond, A., Prevor, M. B., Callender, G., & Druin, D. P. (1997). Prefrontal cortex cognitive deficits in children treated early and continuously for PKU. *Monographs of the Society for Research in Child Development, 62*(4, Serial No. 252).

Diamond, A., & Taylor, C. (1996). Development of an aspect of executive control: Development of the abilities to remember what I said and to "Do as I say, not as I do". *Developmental Psychobiology, 29*, 315–334.

Dunn, L. M., & Dunn, L. M. (1981). *Peabody Picture Vocabulary Test–Revised: Form M*. Circle Pines, MN: American Guidance Service.

Dunn, L. M., & Dunn, L. M. (1997). *Peabody Picture Vocabulary Test–Third Edition.* Circle Pines, MN: American Guidance Service.

Engle, R. W. (2002). Working memory capacity as executive attention. *Current Directions in Psychological Science, 11,* 19–23.

Espy, K. A., & Bull, R. (2005/this issue). Inhibitory processes in young children and individual variation in short-term memory. *Developmental Neuropsychology, 28,* 669–688.

Espy, K. A., McDiarmid, M. M., Cwik, M. F., Stalets, M. M., Hamby, A., & Senn, T. E. (2004). The contribution of executive functions to emergent mathematics skills in preschool children. *Developmental Neuropsychology, 26,* 465–486.

Espy, K. A., Stalets, M. M., McDiarmid, M. M., Senn, T. E., Cwik, M. F., & Hamby, A. (2002). Executive functions in preschool children born preterm: Application of cognitive neuroscience paradigms. *Child Neuropsychology, 8,* 83–92.

Fletcher, J. M. (1996). Executive functions in children: Introduction to the special series. *Developmental Neuropsychology, 12,* 1–4.

Fletcher, J. M., Brookshire, B. L., Landry, S. H., Bohan, T. P., Davidson, K. C., Francis, D. J., et al. (1996). Attentional skills and executive functions in children with early hydrocephalus. *Developmental Neuropsychology, 12,* 53–76.

Frye, D., Zelazo, P. D., & Palfai, T. (1995). Theory of mind and rule-based reasoning. *Cognitive Development, 10,* 483–527.

Gerardi-Caulton, G. (2000). Sensitivity to spatial conflict and the development of self-regulation in children 24–36 months of age. *Developmental Science, 3,* 397–404.

Gerstadt, C. L., Hong, Y. J., & Diamond, A. (1994). The relationship between cognition and action: Performance of children 3.5–7 years old on a Stroop-like day-night test. *Cognition, 53,* 129–153.

Gordon, A. C. L., & Olson, D. R. (1998). The relation between acquisition of a theory of mind and the capacity to hold in mind. *Journal of Experimental Child Psychology, 68,* 70–83.

Hongwanishkul, D., Happaney, K. R., Lee, W. S. C., & Zelazo, P. D. (2005/in press). Assessment of hot and cool executive function in young children: Age-related changes and individual differences. *Developmental Neuropsychology, 28,* 617–644.

Hughes, C. (1998). Finding your marbles: Does preschoolers' strategic behavior predict later understanding of mind? *Developmental Psychology, 34,* 1326–1339.

Hughes, C., & Ensor, R. (2005/this issue). Executive function and theory of mind in 2 year olds: A family affair? *Developmental Neuropsychology, 28,* 645–668.

Isquith, P. K., Gioia, G. A., & Espy, K. A. (2004). Executive function in preschool children: Examination through everyday behavior. *Developmental Neuropsychology, 26,* 403–422.

Kerr, A., & Zelazo, P. D. (2004). Development of "hot" executive function: The Children's Gambling Task. *Brain and Cognition, 55,* 148–157.

Kochanska, G., Murray, K. T., & Harlan, E. T. (2000). Effortful control in early childhood: Continuity and change, antecedents, and implications for social development. *Developmental Psychology, 36,* 220–232.

Kochanska, G., Murray, K. T., Jacques, T. Y., Koenig, A. L., & Vandegeest, K. A. (1996). Inhibitory control in young children and its role in emerging internalization. *Child Development, 67,* 490–507.

Levin, H. S., Fletcher, J. M., Kufera, J. A., Harward, H., Lilly, M. A., Mendelsohn, D., et al. (1996). Dimensions of cognition measured by the Tower of London and other cognitive tasks in head-injured children and adolescents. *Developmental Neuropsychology, 12,* 17–34.

Lewis, M., Stanger, C., & Sullivan, M. W. (1989). Deception in 3-year-olds. *Developmental Psychology, 25,* 439–443.

Luria, A. R., Pribram, K. H., & Homskaya, E. D. (1964). An experimental analysis of the behavioral disturbance produced by a left frontal arachnoidal endothelioma (meningioma). *Neuropsychologia, 2,* 257–280.

Mischel, W., Shoda, Y., & Rodriguez, M. L. (1989). Delay of gratification in children. *Science, 244,* 933–938.

Miyake, A., Friedman, N. P., Emerson, M. J., Witzki, A. H., Howerter, A., & Wager, T. D. (2000). The unity and diversity of executive functions and their contributions to complex "frontal lobe" tasks: A latent variable analysis. *Cognitive Psychology, 41,* 49–100.

Ozonoff, S., Pennington, B. F., & Rogers, S. J. (1991). Executive function deficits in high-functioning autistic individuals: Relationship to theory of mind. *Journal of Child Psychology and Psychiatry, 32,* 1081–1095.

Reed, M., Pien, D. L., & Rothbart, M. K. (1984). Inhibitory self-control in preschool children. *Merrill Palmer Quarterly, 30,* 131–147.

Roberts, R. J., Jr., & Pennington, B. F. (1996). An interactive framework for examining prefrontal cognitive processes. *Developmental Neuropsychology, 12,* 105–126.

Saarni, C. (1984). An observational study of children's attempts to monitor their expressive behavior. *Child Development, 55,* 4804–1513.

Senn, T. E., Espy, K. A., & Kaufmann, P. M. (2004). Using path analysis to understand executive function organization in preschool children. *Developmental Neuropsychology, 26,* 445–464.

Strommen, E. A. (1973). Verbal self-regulation in a children's game: Impulsive errors on "Simon says." *Child Development, 44,* 849–853.

Taylor, H. G., Schatschneider, C., Petrill, S., Barry, C. T., & Owens, C. (1996). Executive dysfunction in children with early brain disease: Outcomes post Haemophilus Influenzae Meningitis. *Developmental Neuropsychology, 12,* 35–52.

Wellman, H. M., & Liu, D. (2004). Scaling of theory of mind tasks. *Child Development, 75,* 523–541.

Welsh, M. C., Pennington, B. F., & Groisser, D. B. (1991). A normative-developmental study of executive function: A window on prefrontal function in children. *Developmental Neuropsychology, 7,* 131–149.

Wright, J. C. (1971). *KRISP (Kansas Reflection-Impulsivity Scale for Preschoolers).* Lawrence: University of Kansas.

Zelazo, P. D., Carter, A., Reznick, J. S., & Frye, D. (1997). Early development of executive function: A problem-solving framework. *Review of General Psychology, 1,* 1–29.

Zelazo, P. D., Jacques, S., Burack, J. A., & Frye, D. (2002). The relation between theory of mind and rule use: Evidence from persons with autism-spectrum disorders. *Infant and Child Development, 11,* 171–195.

Zelazo, P. D., & Müller, U. (2002). Executive function in typical and atypical development. In U. Goswami (Ed.), *Handbook of childhood cognitive development* (pp. 445–469). Oxford, England: Blackwell.

Zelazo, P. D., Müller, U., Frye, D., & Marcovitch, S. (2003). The development of executive function in early childhood. *Monographs of the Society for Research in Child Development, 68*(3, Serial No. 274).

Zelazo, P. D., Reznick, J. S., & Spinazolla, J. (1998). Representational flexibility and response control in a multistep multilocation search task. *Developmental Psychology, 34,* 203–214.

DEVELOPMENTAL NEUROPSYCHOLOGY, 28(2), 617–644

Assessment of Hot and Cool Executive Function in Young Children: Age-Related Changes and Individual Differences

Donaya Hongwanishkul
Institute of Child Development
University of Minnesota

Keith R. Happaney
Department of Psychology
Lehman College
City University of New York

Wendy S. C. Lee and Philip David Zelazo
Department of Psychology
University of Toronto

Although executive function (EF) is often considered a domain-general cognitive function, a distinction has been made between the "cool" cognitive aspects of EF more associated with dorsolateral regions of prefrontal cortex and the "hot" affective aspects more associated with ventral and medial regions (Zelazo & Müller, 2002). Assessments of EF in children have focused almost exclusively on cool EF. In this study, EF was assessed in 3- to 5-year-old children using 2 putative measures of cool EF (Self-Ordered Pointing and Dimensional Change Card Sort) and 2 putative measures of hot EF (Children's Gambling Task and Delay of Gratification). Findings confirmed that performance on both types of task develops during the preschool period. However, the measures of hot and cool EF showed different patterns of relations with each other and with measures of general intellectual function and temperament. These differences provide preliminary evidence that hot and cool EF are indeed distinct, and they encourage further research on the development of hot EF.

Correspondence should be addressed to Philip David Zelazo, Department of Psychology, University of Toronto, Canada M5S 3G3. E-mail: zelazo@psych.utoronto.ca

Executive function (EF), which refers to the psychological processes involved in cognitive control, is usually considered a domain-general cognitive function (e.g., Denckla & Reiss, 1997; Zelazo, Carter, Reznick, & Frye, 1997). Although it is recognized that EF encompasses a variety of subfunctions (e.g., working memory, attentional flexibility) that work together in the service of goal-directed problem solving, it is generally assumed that these subfunctions, as well as the higher order function of EF, operate in a consistent fashion across content domains ranging from theory of mind (e.g., Frye, Zelazo, & Palfai, 1995; Hughes, 1998; Perner & Lang, 1999) to understanding symbols and word meaning (e.g., Bialystok & Martin, 2003; Deák , 2000; O'Sullivan, Mitchell, & Daehler, 2001) to reasoning about physical causality (e.g., Frye, Zelazo, Brooks, & Samuels, 1996).

In contrast to a domain general view of EF, however, recent research on the functions of ventral and medial regions of prefrontal cortex (VM–PFC) suggests that EF may operate differently in different contexts (e.g., Bechara, 2004; Clark, Cools, & Robbins, 2004; Damasio, 1994; Dias, Robbins, & Roberts, 1996; Hauser, 1999; Miller & Cohen, 2001; Rolls, 2004). In light of this research, Zelazo and Müller (2002) distinguished between two aspects of EF—the relatively "hot" affective aspects associated with VM–PFC and the more purely cognitive, "cool" aspects associated with dorsolateral prefrontal cortex (DL–PFC; cf. Metcalfe & Mischel, 1999). According to this heuristic framework, cool EF is more likely to be elicited by abstract, decontextualized problems (e.g., sorting by color, number, or shape in the Wisconsin Card Sorting Test [WCST]; Grant & Berg, 1948), whereas hot EF is more likely to be elicited by problems that involve the regulation of affect and motivation (i.e., the regulation of basic limbic system functions), as when one is required to reappraise the motivational significance of a stimulus (e.g., learning to choose advantageously in the Iowa Gambling Task; Bechara, Damasio, Damasio, & Anderson, 1994). Although it seems likely that measures of EF always require a combination of hot and cool EF (e.g., Manes et al., 2002) and, hence, that the difference between hot and cool EF is always a matter of degree, the hot–cool distinction encourages researchers to adopt a broader conception of EF that captures its more affective aspects.

Prefrontal cortex as a whole undergoes considerable growth during the course of childhood, as indicated by age-related changes in volumes of gray and white matter (Giedd et al., 1999; Gogtay et al., 2004; Matsuzawa et al., 2001; Pfefferbaum et al., 1994), and interhemispheric connectivity (P. M. Thompson et al., 2000), among other measures. Until recently, however, research on the functional implications of these structural changes has focused almost exclusively on DL–PFC and cool EF. This research indicates that cool EF improves considerably between 3 and 4 years of age (e.g., Espy, Kaufmann, Glisky, & McDiarmid, 2001; Hughes, 1998; Zelazo, Müller, Frye, & Marcovitch, 2003; see also Zelazo & Müller, 2002, for review). Much less is known about the development of hot EF, although there is some indication that VM–PFC develops earlier than DL–PFC (e.g., Gogtay et al., 2004; Orzhekhovskaya, 1981), and interest in hot EF is growing (e.g., Blair, 2002; Carlson, Davis, & Leach, in press; Kerr & Zelazo, 2004; Pérez-Edgar & Fox, in press; Prencipe & Zelazo, 2005; see Happaney, Zelazo, & Stuss, 2004, and the June 2004 special issue of *Brain and Cognition*). In particular, there has been growing interest in the development of affective decision making, or decision making about events that have emotionally significant consequences (i.e., meaningful rewards and/or losses).

The distinction between hot and cool EF requires further clarification, but it has the potential to shed light on the role of EF in clinical disorders with childhood onset. Although deficits in EF have been implicated in a wide variety of disorders, including autism (e.g., Hughes, Russell, & Robbins, 1994), phenylketonuria (e.g., Diamond, Prevor, Callender, & Druin, 1997), and various externalizing disorders (e.g., Barkley, 1997; Hughes, Dunn, & White, 1998; Pennington, 1997), it seems unlikely that the same aspects of EF are involved in each disorder (Pennington & Ozonoff, 1996). Indeed, Zelazo and Müller (2002) suggested that whereas autism may be primarily a disorder of hot EF with secondary impairments in cool EF (cf. Dawson, Meltzoff, Osterling, & Rinaldi, 1998), ADHD may be mainly a disorder of cool EF (although differences may exist among subtypes and as a function of comorbidity; e.g., see Dinn, Robbins, & Harris, 2001).

The study presented here was designed to examine the early development of cool and hot EF in a single study. It was also designed to examine whether (and if so, how) these two aspects of EF may be related to one another and to measures of general intellectual functioning and temperament. Performance on two putative measures of cool EF—Self-Ordered Pointing task (Petrides & Milner, 1982) and a version of the Dimensional Change Card Sort (DCCS; Zelazo et al., 2003)—was compared to performance on two putative measures of hot EF—the Children's Gambling Task (Kerr & Zelazo, 2004) and a Delay of Gratification task (Prencipe & Zelazo, 2005). The rationale for selecting these measures is reviewed next.

MEASURES OF COOL EF

EF has long been considered synonymous with DL–PFC function, and two classic cases of DL–PFC function are working memory and flexible rule use. Working memory involves the simultaneous manipulation and maintenance of a representation so that this representation can guide responding (e.g., Baddeley, 1986; Daneman & Merikle, 1996). Neuropsychological and neuroimaging studies have consistently demonstrated the involvement of DL–PFC in working memory, in both adults (e.g., Curtis, Zald, & Pardo, 2000; Jacobson, 1936; Kane & Engle, 2002; Petrides & Milner, 1982) and children (Tsujimoto, Yamamoto, Kawaguchi, Koizumi, & Sawaguchi, 2004).

A common measure of working memory in adult patients is the Self-Ordered Pointing task (Petrides & Milner, 1982), in which participants are presented with a visual array of items, with the position of these items randomly changing from trial to trial. Participants begin by pointing to one item and are instructed not to point to the same item twice. Thus, to perform well, participants must keep the previously selected items in mind and use this information to inform subsequent responses. Developmental research has shown that performance on measures of working memory similar to the Self-Ordered Pointing task increases during the preschool period (see Gathercole, 1998, for a review). For example, Diamond et al. (1997) used a task in which rewards were placed in several (three or six) clearly distinct boxes that were scrambled from trial to trial. These authors found that children's performance improved from 15 months to about 7 years of age (the oldest age tested). Similar improvement on a spatial self-ordered working memory task from the Cambridge Neuropsychological Testing Automated Battery has been found during the early and middle childhood period (Luciana & Nelson, 1998, 2002). Archibald and Kerns (1999) used a more standard version of this task, in which children were presented with drawings of objects arranged in a matrix. The same objects were presented on each trial but in different locations, and children were instructed to point to a different picture on each trial. However, these authors examined older children—children between the ages of 7 and 12 years. To our knowledge, a standard picture version of the Self-Ordered Pointing task has never been used with preschoolers.

Flexible rule use has frequently been assessed by the WCST (Grant & Berg, 1948), which is often regarded as "the prototypical EF task in neuropsychology" (Pennington & Ozonoff, 1996, p. 55). In this task, participants are presented with target cards that differ on various dimensions (shape, color, and number) and then shown test cards that match different target cards on different dimensions. Participants must discover the rule according to which each card must be sorted. After a certain number of consecutive correct responses, the correct dimension is switched, and participants must discover this new rule. Patients with DL–PFC lesions typically perseverate on the WCST, continuing to sort by the initial dimension (Milner, 1964). Recent research has confirmed the role of DL–PFC in performance on the WCST and other measures of task switching (e.g., Lombardi et al., 1999; Nagahama et al., 2001; Rogers, Andrews, Grasby, Brooks, & Robbins, 2000; Sohn, Ursu, Anderson, Stenger, & Carter, 2000; Wang, Kakigi, & Hoshiyama, 2001; see Demakis, 2003, for a review).

Research with children reveals that flexible rule use improves considerably between 3 and 5 years of age. One frequently used measure is the DCCS (Frye, Zelazo, & Palfai, 1995; Zelazo et al., 2003), in which children are asked to sort a series of colored shapes, first by one dimension (e.g., color) and then by the other (e.g., shape). Whereas 4-year-olds switch flexibly, 3-year-olds systematically perseverate on the preswitch rules during the postswitch phase, despite being able to describe the rules they fail to use (e.g., Bialystok, 1999; Carlson & Moses, 2001; Jacques, Zelazo, Kirkham, & Semcesen, 1999; Kirkham, Cruess, & Diamond,

2003; Munakata & Yerys, 2001; Perner, Stummer, & Lang, 1999; Zelazo, Frye, & Rapus, 1996). That is, like DL–PFC patients on the WCST, 3-year-olds display what Teuber (see Discussion section in Milner, 1964) called "a curious dissociation between knowing and doing" (p. 333). The DCCS resembles the WCST in that cards must be sorted first by one dimension and then by another. In contrast to the WCST, however, children are explicitly told the rules by which to sort cards; they do not need to infer them. In our study, children who passed the postswitch phase of the standard version were given a new, more difficult border version (see the Method section).

MEASURES OF HOT EF

Interest in hot aspects of EF has been bolstered by findings that patients with VM–PFC damage exhibit substantial impairments in their social and emotional decision-making abilities despite good performance on traditional (i.e., cool) measures of EF, such as working memory and flexible rule use (e.g., Anderson, Bechara, Damasio, Tranel, & Damasio, 1999; Bechara, Damasio, Tranel, & Anderson, 1998). To study the basis of these impairments in the laboratory, researchers have developed a number of measures, including measures of gambling (e.g., Bechara, 2004), risky decision making (e.g., Rogers, Everitt, et al., 1999; Rogers, Owen, et al., 1999), guessing with feedback (e.g., Elliot, Frith, & Dolan, 1997), and delay discounting (Monterosso, Ehrman, Napier, O'Brien, & Childress, 2001). Despite their differences, these measures all assess flexible decision making about events that have emotionally significant consequences (i.e., meaningful rewards and/or losses).

One of the most widely used measures of VM–PFC function is the Iowa Gambling Task (Bechara et al., 1994). In this task, participants are presented with four decks of cards that, when turned, reveal a combination of gains and losses (measured in play money). Participants are initially given a stake of $2,000 facsimile dollars and asked to win as much money as possible by choosing cards from any of the four decks (one card per trial). Consistently selecting from two of the decks (the advantageous decks) results in a net gain, whereas selecting from the other two (the disadvantageous decks) results in a net loss. Each card from the disadvantageous decks provides a higher reward than each card from the advantageous decks ($100 vs. $50), but the variable (and unpredictable) losses associated with cards from disadvantageous decks are much larger on average than the losses associated with the advantageous decks. Bechara and colleagues have demonstrated that, whereas healthy controls learn to avoid the disadvantageous decks, patients with damage to VM–PFC continue to choose from these disadvantageous decks (e.g., Bechara et al., 1994; Bechara, Tranel, & Damasio, 2000; Bechara, Tranel,

Damasio, & Damasio, 1996; but see Manes et al., 2002, for some qualifications regarding lesion focus and extent).

Kerr and Zelazo (2004) created the Children's Gambling Task (a simplified version of the Iowa Gambling Task), in which children had to choose between (a) cards that offered more rewards (candies) per trial but were disadvantageous across trials due to occasional large losses and (b) cards that offered fewer rewards per trial but were advantageous overall. On later trials, 4-year-olds made more advantageous choices than would be expected by chance, whereas 3-year-olds made fewer. Other adaptations of the Iowa Gambling Task have revealed age-related improvements in performance in somewhat older children (Crone & van der Molen, 2004; Garon & Moore, 2004). However, 4-year-olds in the study by Kerr and Zelazo were far from ceiling, and we expected that this task would be developmentally sensitive until at least 5 years of age.

Another measure of affective decision making is delay discounting (e.g., Green, Myerson, & Ostaszewski, 1999; Monterosso et al., 2001), a paradigm originally developed for use with nonhuman animals. In this task, individuals are asked to choose between smaller, immediate rewards and larger, delayed rewards (e.g., $9 immediately vs. $10 in 1 week). By varying the delay and the amount offered immediately, it is possible to calculate the rate at which a reward is discounted over time. Rats with lesions to orbitofrontal cortex, a part of VM–PFC, are more likely than controls to opt for small, immediate rewards (e.g., Mobini et al., 2002; Kheramin et al., 2003), and evidence suggests that similar regions of PFC play an important role in this type of decision making in human participants as well (e.g., Krawczyk, 2002; Rahman, Sahakian, Cardinal, Rogers, & Robbins, 2001; Rogers, Owen, et al., 1999). In addition, Monterosso et al. (2001) found that performance on the Iowa Gambling Task was significantly correlated with performance on the delay discounting task in a group of cocaine-dependent individuals, and these authors concluded that the two tasks tap similar affective decision-making processes.

Versions of this delay paradigm (referred to as Delay of Gratification) have been used extensively with children (Mischel, Shoda, & Rodriguez, 1989, for review). In one version (the choice version), children choose between an immediate reward of lower value and a delayed reward of higher value. Although early studies found few age differences within the preschool range (e.g., Schwarz, Schrager, & Lyons, 1983; Toner, Holstein, & Hetherington, 1977), C. Thompson, Barresi, and Moore (1997) used a modified choice paradigm and found a significant increase between 3 and 4 years of age in children's tendency to choose delayed rewards. Prencipe and Zelazo (2005) adapted the procedure used by C. Thompson et al. to include additional trials. These authors used nine trial types, created by crossing three types of reward (stickers, pennies, candies) and three types of choice (one now vs. two later, one now vs. four later, one now vs. six later), and found that 4-year-olds were more likely to choose delayed rewards than were 3-year-olds. In addition, whereas 3-year-olds were less likely to choose delayed rewards than would be expected based on chance responding, 4-year-olds were more likely to do so. These results were robust across all three types of reward.

THIS STUDY: OBJECTIVES AND HYPOTHESES

The study presented here was designed to investigate the development of both cool and hot EF in a single sample of children to assess whether these aspects of EF were related and whether they showed similar patterns of relations with measures of general intellectual functioning and temperament. Two putative measures of cool EF—a Self-Ordered Pointing task and a modified DCCS—were compared to two putative measures of hot EF—the Children's Gambling Task and Delay of Gratification. It was expected that the measures of cool EF would be more highly correlated with each other than with the measures of hot EF, and vice versa.

It should be kept in mind, however, that like VM–PFC and DL–PFC, hot and cool EF are presumed to be parts of an interactive functional system—in the normal case, they should work together, even in a single situation. Thus, it is probably impossible to design a task that is a pure measure of hot or cool EF (although it should be possible to design tasks that emphasize one or the other). For this reason, and because the same genetic and environmental influences may affect all aspects of PFC, it was expected that hot and cool measures would be related to one another to some extent.

It was also expected that hot and cool measures might show different patterns of correlations with measures of general intellectual functioning and temperament. More specifically, it was expected that performance on cool EF tasks would be highly related to general intellectual functioning, given both the relatively abstract nature of measures of general intellectual functioning and previous research using measures of cool EF (e.g., Ardila, Pineda, & Rosselli, 2000; Arffa, Lovell, Podell, & Goldberg, 1998; Duncan et al., 2000; Gray, Chabris, & Braver, 2003). In contrast, given the well-documented failure of standardized measures of intelligence to capture differences in emotional and social competence (e.g., Gardner, 1983; Goleman, 1995), performance on measures of hot EF tasks was expected to be only weakly related to general intellectual functioning, if at all. Finally, hot and cool EF were expected to be related to different dimensions of temperament, as assessed by the Children's Behavior Questionnaire (CBQ; Rothbart, Ahadi, & Hershey, 1994). Whereas children's emotional reactivity to negative situations (i.e., the factor of Negative Affectivity) was expected to be positively related to hot EF (just as adults' levels of self-reported negative affect are related to VM–PFC activity; Zald, Mattson, & Pardo, 2002), children's attentional self-regulation (i.e., the factor of Effortful Control) was expected to be positively related to cool EF (e.g., Rothbart et al., 1994; Ruff & Rothbart, 1996; Wolfe & Bell, 2003).

METHODS

Participants

One hundred six children between 3.0 and 5.9 years of age were recruited from a database of parents who had expressed interest in having their children participate in research. The study consisted of two separate sessions, which occurred approximately 2 weeks apart. Six of the initial 106 children did not return for the second session, and 2 refused to play during both sessions. The remaining 98 children were divided into three age groups, with the final sample consisting of 33 children at 3 years (16 girls, 17 boys; $M = 41.02$, $SD = 3.84$, range $= 35.9$–46.8 months), 32 at 4 years (16 girls, 16 boys; $M = 54.06$, $SD = 3.61$, range $= 48.0$–58.8 months), and 33 at 5 years (16 girls, 17 boys; $M = 66.13$, $SD = 3.00$, range $= 61.4$–71.3 months).

Design and Overview of the Procedure

Children were tested individually. At the beginning of each session, the experimenter played with children for 10 min to help them become comfortable with both the experimenter and experimental setting. In the first session, children received three standardized tests of general intellectual function, administered in a counterbalanced order. In addition, parents were asked to fill out the CBQ, which took about 30 min to complete. The first session took approximately 1 hr to complete.

In the second session, children received four measures of EF in a counterbalanced order: the Self-Ordered Pointing task, the DCCS, the Children's Gambling Task, and Delay of Gratification. This session took approximately 1 hr 15 min, with a break (approximately 10 min) provided after completion of the first two tasks.

Measures of Cool EF

Self-Ordered Pointing task. Children were shown sets of pictures presented on laminated sheets of paper (21.6 × 27.9 cm) in a three-ring binder (see Figure 1). The pictures across sets were distinct. To demonstrate the task, children were first shown a sheet containing two pictures and instructed to select one, after which the page was turned and a new sheet was shown that contained the same two pictures in different locations. Children were told that they must point to a picture they had not yet chosen. If children responded correctly to these instructions, the test phase began. If children did not respond correctly, they were given another demonstration trial. All children successfully completed this practice phase within two demonstration trials.

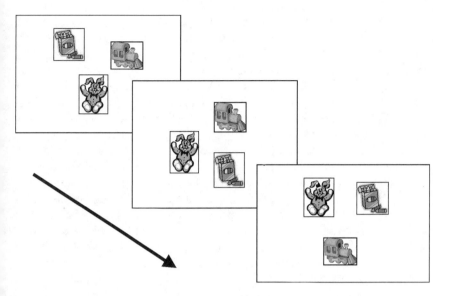

FIGURE 1   Sample picture set from the Self-Ordered Pointing task.

Test trials were presented in the same fashion as the demonstration trial(s). However, test trials started with 3 pictures, and the number of pictures per trial set was increased by 1 (up to a maximum of 10) until children erred on two consecutive trials. That is, if children erred on a particular trial set (e.g., if they chose the same picture twice), they received an additional trial set containing the same number of pictures. If children erred on this second trial set, the task was terminated. The dependent measure was the highest number of pictures in the last trial set on which children were correct.

DCCS.   All children received the standard version of the DCCS. The order in which dimensions were presented (e.g., color first) was counterbalanced across age and sex. Target cards (a blue rabbit and a red boat) were first affixed to sorting trays, where they remained (visible) throughout the task (both versions). Children were then told a pair of rules (i.e., shape rules or color rules) for separating test cards, which consisted of red rabbits and blue boats. Children who sorted by color during the preswitch phase were told, "If it's red put it here, but if it's blue put it there." The experimenter then sorted two test cards facedown into each tray to illustrate what children were supposed to do. After these demonstration trials, preswitch test trials commenced. On each of six preswitch trials, the experimenter stated the relevant rules, randomly selected a test card (with the constraint that the same type of card was not presented on more than two consecutive trials), labeled the card by the relevant dimension only, and asked children, "Where does this go?" Children were required to place the card facedown in one of the trays. No feedback was provided; after children sorted each card, the experimenter simply said, "Let's do another one," and then proceeded to the next trial.

When they had completed six trials, children were told to stop playing the first game and to switch to a new game. They were then given six postswitch trials, which were identical to the preswitch trials except that children were told the rules for sorting by the other dimension (e.g., shape: "If it's a boat put it here, but if it's a rabbit put it there."). As in previous research, children were considered to have passed a phase in the standard version when they correctly sorted five or more cards out of six in that phase ($p < .05$, on the basis of the binomial theorem).

To capture developmental changes across the entire age range of interest in this study, children who passed the postswitch phase of the standard version were given a new, more difficult border version (Figure 2). This version commenced immediately after completion of the postswitch phase of the standard version. To explain this version, children were first shown two test cards like those used in the standard version as well as two new test cards that had black

Target Cards:

Test Cards:

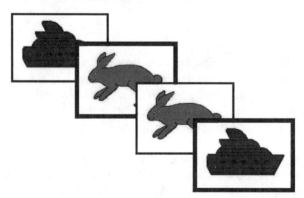

FIGURE 2   The border version. Children are told to sort test cards by one dimension (e.g., color) when there is a black border and by the other dimension (e.g., shape) when there is no border.

borders. Children were then told that the black borders indicated that they must play a particular game (e.g., "If there's a black border, you have to play the color game; if there is no black border, you have to play the shape game"). The dimension indicated by the black border was counterbalanced across participants. Test trials then commenced. On each of 12 trials, the experimenter stated the rules, randomly selected a test card (with the constraint that no more than two cards in a row were of the same type—with borders or without), labeled it according to the relevant dimension, and asked children, "Where does this go?" As was the case for the standard version, no feedback was provided. Children were considered to have passed this phase when they correctly sorted on 9 out of these 12 trials ($p < .05$, on the basis of the binomial theorem).

Measures of Hot EF

Children's Gambling Task.   On each of 40 trials, children chose from one of two decks of cards (each card being 18 × 29 cm), a striped deck and a dotted deck. When turned, cards displayed a number of happy and sad faces, corresponding to the number of rewards (candies) won and lost, respectively. Cards in one deck (striped) offered more rewards per trial but were disadvantageous across trials due to occasional large losses; cards in the other deck (dotted) offered fewer rewards per trial but were advantageous overall. More specifically, cards in the advantageous deck always offered one reward (i.e., they showed one happy face) together with losses of nothing or one candy (with a net average of five candies gained per 10 cards). Cards in the disadvantageous deck always offered two rewards together with losses of nothing, four, five, or six candies (with a net average of five candies lost per 10 cards). The order of cards in each deck was fixed and followed the win–loss contingencies used by Kerr and Zelazo (2004).

At the start of the task, children were instructed that they should try to win as many candies as possible and that they could select from whichever deck they wished. They were then given a stake of 10 candies with which to begin the task. During 8 initial demonstration trials, in which the experimenter sampled four cards from each deck, children were told (and shown) that the happy faces on the cards indicated the number of candies won, whereas sad faces indicated the number of candies lost. When a card was turned over, only the happy faces were visible initially, because the sad faces were covered with a sticky note. After the number of candies won was revealed to the child and the candies distributed, the sticky note was removed, and the number of candies lost was revealed (this was done to ensure that children attended to both wins and losses). The rewards were deposited into, and removed from, a graduated cylinder situated in front of the child, at an equal distance from each of the two decks. The task proper consisted of 40 test trials. Forty rather than 50 trials (Kerr & Zelazo, 2004) were used because the task was presented as part of a relatively lengthy battery of tasks. In keeping with evidence that data from the second half of the Iowa Gambling Task provide a more reliable index of performance (Monterosso et al., 2001), the dependent variable was the net score on these trials (i.e., the number of advantageous choices minus number of disadvantageous choices made in the last 20 trials). Thus, higher scores indicated better performance.

Delay of Gratification task.   The Delay of Gratification task administered in this study was taken from Prencipe and Zelazo (2005), who adapted the procedure used by C. Thompson et al. (1997). Nine test trial types, created by crossing three types of reward (stickers, pennies, candies) and three types of choice (one now vs. two later, one now vs. four later, one now vs. six later), were each depicted graphically on a separate card (14 × 11 cm). There were also two demonstration trials, one in which the option was one candy now versus one candy later and one option for one candy now versus eight candies later.

The two demonstration trials were presented first. On both trials, the experimenter read the decision aloud and made a choice herself. For each trial, the choice was explained verbally and visually by placing the two reward options in separate piles (i.e., immediate pile vs. delay pile). For the one candy now versus one candy later option, the experimenter chose the immediate reward. For the one candy now versus eight candies later option, she chose the delayed reward.

Nine test trials were then presented, involving all nine trial types presented in a random order. Test trials were presented in the same fashion as demonstration trials. However, on each trial, the experimenter asked, "What do you want to do?" The experimenter provided no feedback regarding the wisdom of children's choices, apart from administering the consequences (i.e., dispensing the rewards). When children chose the immediate option, they were allowed to eat the candy, stick their stickers on a special piece of paper, or put their pennies in a penny box. Delayed rewards were placed in an envelope and set aside. Scores were the number of times that children chose to delay.

General Intellectual Functioning

Verbal mental age.   Verbal mental age (VMA) was assessed via the Peabody Picture Vocabulary Test–Third Edition–Revised (PPVT–III–R; Dunn & Dunn, 1997), which was presented in the standard fashion. The PPVT–III–R took between 5 to 20 min to complete, depending on children's performance, with better performing children taking longer due to more words being presented. VMA was obtained by determining the raw score (subtracting the number of errors from the number of items administered) and matching this score to its age equivalent from the norms provided in the testing manual.

Performance mental age.   Performance mental age (PMA) was assessed via children's performance on the Bead Memory and Pattern Analysis subtests of the Stanford–Binet Intelligence Scale–Fourth Edition (Thorndike, Hagen, & Sattler, 1986). Scores for each subtest were obtained by subtracting the number of errors from the highest number of items administered, and standard age scores on each task were then derived from the norms in the scoring manual. PMA was estimated by averaging the two standard age scores. The two tasks combined took approximately 15 to 40 min, depending on children's performance.

CBQ.   The CBQ consists of 195 statements describing typical child behaviors. Parents rated these behaviors on a 7-point Likert scale, ranging from *extremely untrue of your child* to *extremely true of your child*. Items from the CBQ are grouped into 15 scales, which have been shown to load reliably on three distinct factors–Effortful Control, Surgency/Positive Affect, and Negative Affectivity (Rothbart et al., 1994). Following Rothbart et al., Effortful Control scores were derived from scales of Low-Intensity Pleasure, Inhibitory Control, Perceptual Sensitivity, and Attentional Focusing. Surgency scores were computed from scores on the scales of Impulsivity, Approach, High-Intensity Pleasure, Smiling/Laughter, Shyness (negatively scored), and Activity Level. Finally, Negative Affectivity scores were calculated from scores on the scales of Discomfort, Fear, Anger/Frustration, Soothability (negatively scored), and Sadness.

RESULTS

Preliminary analyses revealed no effect of task order and no interactions between task order and any of the variables of interest (i.e., age and sex). Thus, data were combined across task orders for purposes of subsequent analyses, which first examined age-related changes in performance on measures of EF, and then assessed relations among all measures.

Age-Related Changes on Measures of Cool EF

Self-Ordered Pointing.   One 3-year-old boy refused to complete the task, so analyses for this task were based on 97 children. An Age × Sex analysis of variance (ANOVA) on the highest number of items that children were able to remember yielded only a main effect for age, $F(2, 91) = 7.86, p < .001, \eta_p^2 = .15$. Tukey's honestly significant difference (HSD) tests indicated that 5-year-olds performed better than 3-year-olds ($p < .001$), as did 4-year-olds ($p = .02$; see Figure 3). Neither the effect of sex, $F(1, 91) = .018, ns, \eta_p^2 < .001$, nor the interaction between age and sex, $F(2, 91) = 2.77, ns, \eta_p^2 = .06$, were significant.

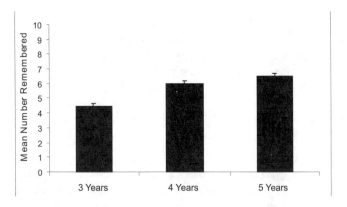

FIGURE 3   Mean (plus 1 standard error) number of items that children were able to remember in the Self-Ordered Pointing task, by age group.

DCCS.   One 4-year-old boy indicated that he was deliberately placing the cards in the wrong sorting trays, so his data were excluded and analyses for this task, as with Self-Ordered Pointing, were based on 97 children. Preliminary analyses revealed no effects of dimension order (color or shape first) in the standard version, or of the sorting dimension associated with the border in the border version, so data were collapsed across these variables. Children's performance on the DCCS task was classified into four categories reflecting their highest level of performance. Children who failed the preswitch phase on the standard version were given a score of 0. Those who failed the postswitch phase on the standard version were given a score of 1. Those who passed the postswitch phase of the standard version but failed the border version were given a score of 2. Those who passed the postswitch phase of the standard version as well as the border version were given a score of 3. Due to the categorical nature of these data, a nonparametric (chi-square) analysis was conducted. This analysis demonstrated a significant effect of age across the four categories, $\chi^2(6, N = 97) = 41.88, p < .001, \phi = .66$ (see Figure 4). Further analyses revealed that the following comparisons were significant: 5-year-olds versus 4-year-olds, $\chi^2(2, N = 64) = 12.77, p < .01, \phi = .47$; 4-year-olds versus 3-year-olds, $\chi^2(3, N = 64) = 10.68, p < .05, \phi = .41$; and 5-year-olds versus 3-year-olds, $\chi^2(3, N = 66) = 28.59, p < .001, \phi = .66$. Performance did not differ as a function of sex, $\chi^2(3, N = 97) = 3.11, ns, \phi = .18$. In all cases, older children outperformed younger ones.

Children's Gambling Task.   Five children (three 3-year-old boys, one 3-year-old girl, and one 4-year-old boy) stopped playing before the task was finished, and data from an additional child (a 5-year-old boy) were compromised because a fire alarm interrupted the procedure. Therefore, analyses for this task were

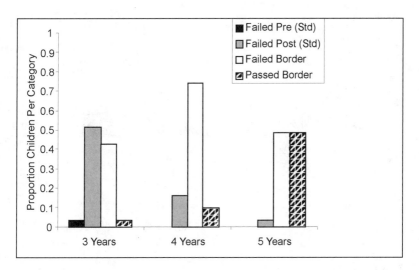

FIGURE 4   Classifications based on children's highest level of performance on the Dimensional Change Card Sort. Percentages of children at each age who were classified as (a) failing the preswitch phase of the standard version, (b) passing the preswitch phase of the standard version but failing the postswitch phase, (c) passing the standard version but failing the border version, and (d) passing both the standard and border versions.

based on 92 children. An Age × Sex ANOVA on children's net scores revealed a main effect of age, $F(2, 86) = 3.74, p < .05, \eta_p^2 = .08$; but no effect of sex, $F(1, 86) = .07, ns, \eta_p^2 = .001$; and no interaction between age and sex, $F(2, 86) = 2.40, p < .10, \eta_p^2 = .05$. Tukey's HSD test showed that 5-year-olds performed better than 3-year-olds ($p = .02$; see Figure 5). T tests indicated that 3-year-olds performed significantly worse than chance, $t(29) = -2.16, p = .04$, but that neither 4- nor 5-year-olds differed from chance, $t(30) = -.19, ns$, and $t(31) = 1.46, ns$, respectively.

Delay of Gratification task.   All children in the final sample ($N = 98$) completed this task. Preliminary analyses indicated no significant differences in performance across type of reward (pennies, stickers, candies) and type of choice (one vs. two, one vs. four, one vs. six), so data were collapsed across these variables for further analysis, and scores were calculated out of nine. An Age × Sex ANOVA on the number of delay choices revealed a main effect of age, $F(2, 92) = 11.11, p < .001, \eta_p^2 = .20$. Post-hoc Tukey's HSD tests indicated that 3-year-olds chose to delay less often than 4-year-olds ($p < .005$) and 5-year-olds ($p < .001$), although the latter two groups did not differ (see Figure 6). Neither the effect of sex, $F(1, 92) = 1.65, ns, \eta_p^2 = .02$, nor the interaction between age and sex, $F(2, 92) = .28, ns, \eta_p^2 = .006$, were significant. T tests indicated that both 4- and 5-year-olds performed significantly above chance, $t(31) = 2.69, p = .01$, and $t(32) = 4.90, p < .001$, respec-

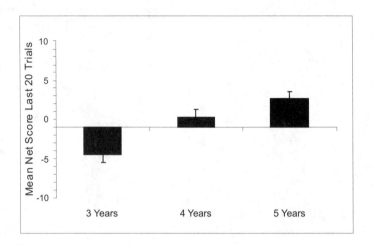

FIGURE 5   Mean (plus 1 standard error) number advantageous minus disadvantageous choices (i.e., net score) on the last 20 trials of the Children's Gambling Task, by age group.

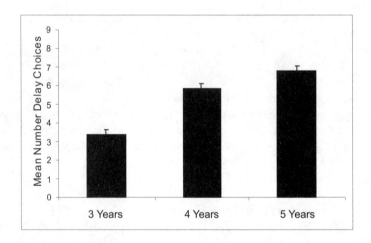

FIGURE 6   Mean (plus 1 standard error) number of times children chose to delay (out of nine) on the modified Delay of Gratification task, by age group.

tively. There was a trend toward 3-year olds performing worse than chance, $t(32) = -1.85, p = .07$.

VMA and PMA. An Age × Sex multivariate analysis of variance (MANOVA) was conducted on estimates of VMA and PMA. Significant effects of age were obtained for both VMA, $F(2, 92) = 40.78, p < .001, \eta_p^2 = .47$, and

PMA, $F(2, 92) = 47.98$, $p < .001$, $\eta_p^2 = .51$ (see Table 1). Tukey's HSD tests revealed differences between each of the three age groups ($p < .005$ for all comparisons). Neither the effect of sex, $F(1, 92) = .15$, ns, $\eta_p^2 = .002$, for VMA and $F(1, 92) = .09$, ns, $\eta_p^2 = .001$, for PMA nor the Age $\times$ Sex interaction, $F(2, 92) = 1.17$, ns, $\eta_p^2 = .025$, for VMA, and $F(2, 92) = .08$, ns, $\eta_p^2 = .002$, for PMA were significant.

CBQ.   Parents of six children (one boy from each age group, one 4-year-old girl, and two 5-year-old girls) failed to complete the CBQ, leaving data from 92 children for analysis. Parent ratings on the CBQ were used to derive scores for the three temperament factors of Effortful Control, Surgency, and Negative Affectivity. An Age $\times$ Sex MANOVA on all three scores indicated effects of age, $F(2, 86) = .59$, $p = .001$, $\eta_p^2 = .14$, and sex, $F(1, 86) = 19.64$, $p < .001$, $\eta_p^2 = .15$, that were limited to Effortful Control (see Table 1). There was no interaction between these variables. More specifically, girls scored higher than boys, and a Tukey's HSD test showed that 5-year-olds scored higher than 3-year-olds on this measure ($p = .001$). No other effects were detected.

TABLE 1
Verbal Mental Age (VMA), Performance Mental Age (PMA), and Children's
Behavior Questionnaire (CBQ) Factors (Effortful Control, Surgency, and
Negative Affectivity)

Variable	M	SD	Range
VMA (months)			
3 years	48.90	19.11	21.6–86.4
4 years	65.88	12.84	49.2–88.8
5 years	82.44	12.39	44.4–105.6
PMA (months)			
3 years	44.76	7.32	36.0–60.0
4 years	55.63	14.10	45.6–84.0
5 years	74.02	13.69	51.6–98.4
CBQ–Effortful Control			
3 years	19.05	2.57	14.97–24.62
4 years	19.89	2.22	14.70–23.43
5 years	21.01	1.84	17.22–25.43
CBQ–Surgency			
3 years	22.58	3.65	12.92–28.54
4 years	20.52	3.81	13.31–26.90
5 years	21.22	2.91	14.85–26.62
CBQ–Negative Affectivity			
3 years	10.96	2.76	6.69–18.31
4 years	12.10	3.83	5.14–20.24
5 years	12.49	2.94	6.31–18.08

Relations Among Measures

Pearson correlations were conducted to assess whether performance on the measures of hot and cool EF were related to each other and to individual differences in general intellectual functioning and temperament. Due to missing data (see previous sections), correlations were based on total sample sizes ranging from 86 to 98.

Relations among measures of EF.   As shown in Table 2, there was a highly significant positive relation between performance on the two measures of cool EF—the DCCS and Self-Ordered Pointing task. This relation remained significant even when chronological age (CA) in months was partialled out and even when both CA and mental age (MA; i.e., both VMA and PMA) were partialled out. Simple correlations failed to reveal a relation between the two measures of hot EF, but after partialling, a significant negative relation emerged. The only other relation to remain significant after partialling out CA (and CA and MA) was a positive relation between performance on the Self-Ordered Pointing task and performance on the Children's Gambling Task.

Relations between EF and measures of general intellectual function and temperament.   As can be seen in Table 3, performance on both of the two measures of cool EF was highly positively related to both VMA and PMA. Relations with VMA remained significant even when CA was partialled out, as did the relation between the DCCS and PMA. No other relations with VMA or PMA were significant after partialling out CA.

Temperament factors (as assessed by parent ratings on the CBQ) were also related to the measures of cool EF, whereas no correlation was found with measures of hot EF (see Table 3). Among the three factors, significant relations were found for both Effortful Control and Surgency. Effortful Control (which is related to age; see previously) was significantly positively related to both Self-Ordered Pointing and the DCCS, although both relations become nonsignificant after controlling for

TABLE 2
Simple and Partial Correlations Among Measures of Executive Function

Variable	DCCS	CGT	DoG
SOP	.50*** (.34**) [.28**]	.33** (.25*) [.29**]	−.01 (−.19) [−.17]
DCCS		.07 (−.15) [−.09]	.21* (−.07) [.00]
CGT			−.07 (−.22*) [−.24*]

Note.   Chronological-age-partialled correlations appear in parentheses. Chronological-age- and mental-age-partialled correlations appear in brackets. SOP = Self-Ordered Pointing; DCCS = Dimensional Change Card Sort; CGT = Children's Gambling Task; DoG = Delay of Gratification.
*p < .05. **p < .01. ***p < .001.

TABLE 3
Simple (and Chronological-Age-Partialled) Correlations Among Measures
of Executive Function, Measures of General Intellectual Functioning, and
Measures of Temperament

Variable	SOP	DCCS	CGT	DoG
VMA	.41*** (.28***)	.70*** (.44***)	.20 (–.04)	.18 (–.15)
PMA	.37** (.15)	.69*** (.46***)	.08 (–.20)	.23* (–.10)
Effortful Control	.27** (.17)	.21* (–.01)	.14 (.05)	.12 (–.01)
Surgency	–.25* (–.23*)	–.07 (–.01)	–.01 (.01)	–.08 (–.05)
Negative Affect	.10 (.04)	.14 (.05)	.09 (.06)	.06 (–.01)

Note. SOP = Self-Ordered Pointing; DCCS = Dimensional Change Card Sort; CGT = Children's Gambling Task; DoG = Delay of Gratification; VMA = verbal mental age; PMA = performance mental age.
*p < .05. **p < .01. ***p < .001.

CA. Surgency was significantly negatively related to performance on the Self-Ordered Pointing task, and this relation remained significant after controlling for CA.

DISCUSSION

Assessments of EF in children have relied almost exclusively on the cool, cognitive aspects of EF associated with DL–PFC. Much less is known about the hot, affective aspects associated with VM–PFC, but interest in the topic is growing. Our study investigated the development of both hot and cool EF in the same sample of children to assess whether these aspects of EF were related and whether they showed similar patterns of relations with measures of general intellectual functioning and temperament.

Age-related improvements in performance were found for all four measures of EF, consistent with the notion that both hot and cool aspects of EF develop rapidly during the preschool years (e.g., Zelazo & Müller, 2002)—a period during which PFC as a whole undergoes considerable growth (e.g., see Diamond, 2002; Fuster, 2002, for reviews). In particular, reliable age-related improvements were seen on the Self-Ordered Pointing task, the DCCS, the Children's Gambling Task, and the Delay of Gratification task. This version of the Self-Ordered Pointing task had never been used with preschoolers, and the DCCS included a new, more difficult border version that proved sensitive to developmental changes between 4 and 5 years of age.

Despite the finding that all four measures were developmentally sensitive within this age range, different patterns of relations were found among measures of EF. The two measures of cool EF were significantly positively related to one another, even after controlling for CA and MA. This finding suggests that performance on these tasks relies on common processes and indicates that although cool EF was related to MA, it is not synonymous with general intelligence as measured by standardized tests. Surprisingly, the two hot EF tasks (the Children's Gambling Task and the Delay of Gratification task) correlated with one another in a negative direction, suggesting that they may differ in important ways and that the construct of hot EF may need to be further refined. This finding with preschool-age children differs from previous findings with cocaine-dependent adults, showing that the Iowa Gambling Task is positively related to delay discounting (e.g., Monteresso et al., 2001).

There are several fundamental differences between the two measures of hot EF that may account for the lack of a positive relation between them. In contrast to the Children's Gambling Task, which requires learning to avoid disadvantageous decks across a series of 40 trials, the Delay of Gratification task involves a smaller series of nine independent choices. Thus, although both tasks require consideration of affectively significant future consequences (relative pros and cons associated with each of two options), only the Children's Gambling Task requires children to track the wins and losses associated with each deck across trials. Tracking wins and losses may require working memory, consistent with the finding that the Children's Gambling Task was related to the Self-Ordered Pointing task in this study and with recent evidence from adults suggesting that working memory may play a role in the Iowa Gambling Task. For example, Manes et al. (2002) found that patients with DL–PFC damage performed worse than a control group on the Iowa Gambling Task. More direct evidence of the role of working memory on the Iowa Gambling Task comes from Hinson, Jameson, and Whitney (2002), who found that performance declined when participants' working memory was taxed (via dual task conditions). It is possible, therefore, that the Children's Gambling Task and the Iowa Gambling Task entail *both* the flexible appraisal of emotional stimuli (a VM–PFC function) *and* working memory (a DL–PFC function) to track the feedback provided by previous selections and, hence, that neither task provides a "pure" measure of hot EF.

It is also important to note, however, that other studies have failed to find a relation between working memory and performance on the Iowa Gambling Task or variants of this task (see Crone & van der Molen, 2004; Hooper, Luciana, Conklin, & Yarger, 2004; Wilder, Weinberger, & Goldberg, 1998). Resolving this issue will be important in understanding the processes underlying affective decision making. For example, Schoenbaum and Setlow (2001) suggested that orbitofrontal cortex (OFC; a subregion of VM–PFC) may support its own working memory function. That is, although DL–PFC-mediated working memory may involve the storage and manipulation of objects and places (absent affective content), OFC-mediated working memory may involve the storage and manipulation of the incentive value of objects. However, much of Schoenbaum and Setlow's evidence was based on relatively simple tasks with nonhuman animals, and it is still unclear whether OFC plays a role in working memory in human beings. Further work is required to refine the construct of working memory and explore its relation to different aspects of EF at different points in development.

Another difference between Delay of Gratification and the Children's Gambling Task is the extent to which one can be certain that prudent choices will yield subsequent rewards. That is, whereas choice contingencies are clear in the Delay of Gratification task (e.g., one now vs. two later), the Children's Gambling Task, like the Iowa Gambling Task, was designed to make the contingencies associated with each choice uncertain. According to Bechara (2004), VM–PFC is most likely to be implicated in decisions under uncertainty. Once again, further investigation is required to explore the possibility that hot EF, although perhaps distinct from cool EF, may itself be a heterogeneous construct.

The measures of hot and cool EF also showed different patterns of relations with general intellectual functioning. Strong positive (age-partialled) relations were found between VMA and the two measures of cool EF and between PMA and performance on the DCCS. These findings suggest that there may be substantial overlap between the construct of cool EF and the construct of intelligence (as conceptualized in standardized tests; e.g., Duncan et al., 2000), and they are consistent with previous research using the DCCS (e.g., Bialystok, 1999) and tests of working memory (e.g., Carlson, Moses, & Breton, 2002). It is noted that the Bead Memory subscale used to assess PMA is a measure of short-term memory (involving passive storage of content) rather than working memory (involving both storage and manipulation of content), which may partly explain why PMA was not more highly related to the Self-Ordered Pointing task than to the DCCS.

The finding that measures of hot EF were not related to general intellectual functioning is consistent with the suggestion that hot EF may be related to a different form of intelligence than that assessed in this study. More specifically, in contrast to standard measures of general intellectual function, hot EF, with its more emotional nature, may be more related to emotional intelligence (e.g., Goleman, 1995; Salovey & Mayer, 1990), emotional and social intelligence (Bar-On, 2000), or personal intelligence (Gardner, 1983). Consistent with this possibility, Rosso, Young, Femia, and Yurgelun-Todd (2004) found that a measure of emotional intelligence was unrelated to abstract reasoning (matrix reasoning) in 9- to 18-year-olds. It is of interest that these authors found significant age differences on matrix reasoning but not emotional intelligence, which they interpret in terms of "differential developmental trajectories across various cognitive and emotional domains of frontal lobe functioning" (Rosso et al., 2004, p. 355). Indeed, whereas DL–PFC may be more closely linked to standard measures of intelligence (Duncan et al., 2000), VM–PFC and related structures may play a greater role in emotional intelligence. This suggestion is supported by a recent study showing that performance on the Iowa Gambling Task was positively related to scores on a measure of emotional and social intelligence but not to scores on the Wechsler Adult Intelligence Scale (Bar-On, Tranel, Denburg, & Bechara, 2003). From this perspective, one may or may not expect some aspects of temperament to be related to performance on hot EF tasks; the relation between temperament and emotional intelligence in childhood is unclear.

In fact, although cool EF was related to temperament, hot EF was not. First, a negative relation between Surgency and Self-Ordered Pointing (even after controlling for age) was found and may reflect the fact that Surgency has an impulsive component (Davis, Bruce, & Gunnar, 2002). For example, in this working memory task, it was necessary to avoid selecting the same picture twice despite the fact that having responded to a particular picture once may have primed responding to that picture again in the future (repetition priming).

The two measures of cool EF were positively related to Effortful Control before controlling for age, although the relations became nonsignificant after controlling for age. The relations were expected based on previous research and theory (e.g., Rothbart et al., 1994; Ruff & Rothbart, 1996; Wolfe & Bell, 2003), and given that there was a significant effect of age on Effortful Control, it is perhaps not surprising that these relations were attenuated when age was controlled. Parent ratings of Effortful Control may well be based in large part on parents' observations of children's developing cool EF.

In contrast, neither measure of hot EF was related to Effortful Control or any other temperament factor. Effortful Control is conceptually and empirically related to EF, but previous research has focused mainly on cool EF, and the developmental correlates of hot EF remain largely unknown. Although some previous work has considered delay of gratification in relation to Effortful Control (e.g., Davis et al., 2002; Kochanska, Murray, & Harlan, 2000), these studies used delay versions of delay of gratification that differ in important respects from the choice version used in our study (i.e., in delay versions, one measures how long children wait before engaging in a desired activity). Overall, the finding that hot EF was unrelated to temperament is consistent with the suggestion that hot and cool EF reflect distinct aspects of EF.

CONCLUSION

Although researchers traditionally have treated EF as a domain-general cognitive function and have focused almost exclusively on cool, cognitive aspects of EF, the findings from this study support a distinction between hot and cool aspects of EF, and they underscore the need for more comprehensive assessments of EF that include measures of hot EF. The findings also suggest that whereas cool EF seems to be a reasonably coherent functional construct, hot EF is not. Much less is known about hot EF than cool EF, and further research is clearly warranted. This research will fill an important gap in our understanding of EF and its development, and it has the potential to shed light on the complex interactions between emotion and cognition. In addition, it may have practical implications for children with disorders such as autism and conduct disorder, where social and emotional deficits are prominent.

ACKNOWLEDGMENT

This research was supported by grants from the Natural Sciences and Engineering Research Council and the Canada Research Chairs Program to Philip David Zelazo.

REFERENCES

Anderson, S. W., Bechara, A., Damasio, H., Tranel, D., & Damasio, A. R. (1999). Impairment of social and moral behavior related to early damage in human prefrontal cortex. *Nature Neuroscience, 2*, 1032–1037.

Archibald, S. J., & Kerns, K. A. (1999). Identification and description of new tests of executive functioning in children. *Child Neuropsychology, 5*, 115–129.

Ardila, A., Pineda, D., & Rosselli, M. (2000). Correlation between intelligence test scores and executive function measures. *Archives of Clinical Neuropsychology, 15*, 31–36.

Arffa, S., Lovell, M., Podell, K., & Goldberg, E. (1998). Wisconsin Card Sorting Test performance in above average and superior school children: Relationship to intelligence and age. *Archives of Clinical Neuropsychology, 13*, 713–720.

Baddeley, A. (1986). *Working memory.* New York: Clarendon Press/Oxford University Press.

Barkley, R. A. (1997). Behavioral inhibition, sustained attention, and executive functions: Constructing a unifying theory of ADHD. *Psychological Bulletin, 121*, 65–94.

Bar-On, R. (2000). Emotional and social intelligence: Insights from the Emotional Quotient Inventory. In R. Bar-On & J. D. A. Parker (Eds.), *The handbook of emotional intelligence: Theory, development, assessment, and application at home, school, and in the workplace* (pp. 363–388). San Francisco: Jossey-Bass.

Bar-On, R., Tranel, D., Denburg, N. L., & Bechara, A. (2003). Exploring the neurological substrate of emotional and social intelligence. *Brain, 126*, 1790–1800.

Bechara, A. (2004). The role of emotion in decision-making: Evidence from neurological patients with orbitofrontal damage. *Brain and Cognition, 55*, 30–40.

Bechara, A., Damasio, A., Damasio, H., & Anderson, S. (1994). Insensitivity to future consequences following damage to human prefrontal cortex. *Cognition, 50*, 7–15.

Bechara, A., Damasio, H., Tranel, D., & Anderson, S. W. (1998). Dissociation of working memory from decision-making within the human prefrontal cortex. *The Journal of Neuroscience, 18*, 428–437.

Bechara, A., Tranel, D., & Damasio, H. (2000). Characterization of the decision-making deficit of patients with ventromedial prefrontal cortex lesions. *Brain, 123*, 2189–2202.

Bechara, A., Tranel, D., Damasio, H., & Damasio, A. R. (1996). Failure to respond autonomically to anticipated future outcomes following damage to prefrontal cortex. *Cerebral Cortex, 6*, 215–225.

Bialystok, E. (1999). Cognitive complexity and attentional control in the bilingual mind. *Child Development, 70*, 636 644.

Bialystok, E., & Martin, M. (2003). Notation to symbol: Development in children's understanding of print. *Journal of Experimental Child Psychology, 86*, 223–243.

Blair, C. (2002). School readiness: Integrating cognition and emotion in a neurobiological conceptualization of children's functioning at school entry. *American Psychologist, 57*, 111–127.

Carlson, S. M., Davis, A. C., & Leach, J. G. (in press). Less is more: Executive function and symbolic representation in preschool children. *Psychological Science.*

Carlson, S. M., & Moses, L. J. (2001). Individual differences in inhibitory control and theory of mind. *Child Development, 72*, 1032–1053.

Carlson, S. M., Moses, l. J., & Breton, C. (2002). How specific is the relation between executive function and theory of mind? Contributions of inhibitory control and working memory. *Infant and Child Development, 11*, 73–92.

Clark, L., Cools, R., & Robbins, T. W. (2004). The neuropsychology of ventral prefrontal cortex: Decision-making and reversal learning. *Brain and Cognition, 55*, 41–53.

Crone, E. A., & van der Molen, M. W. (2004). Developmental changes in real life decision-making: Performance on a gambling task previously shown to depend on the ventromedial prefrontal cortex. *Developmental Neuropsychology, 25*, 251–279.

Curtis, C. E., Zald, D. H., & Pardo, J. V. (2000). Organization of working memory within the human prefrontal cortex: A PET study of self-ordered object working memory. *Neuropsychologia, 38*, 1503–1510.

Damasio, A. R. (1994). *Descartes' error: Emotion, rationality, and the human brain.* New York: Putnam.

Daneman, M., & Merikle, P. M. (1996). Working memory and language comprehension: A meta-analysis. *Psychonomic Bulletin and Review, 3*, 422–433.

Davis, E. P., Bruce, J., & Gunnar, M. R. (2002). The anterior attention network: Associations with temperament and neuroendocrine activity in 6-year-old children. *Developmental Psychobiology, 40*, 43–56.

Dawson, G., Meltzoff, A. N., Osterling, J., & Rinaldi, J. (1998). Neuropsychological correlates of early symptoms of autism. *Child Development, 69*, 1276–1285.

Deák , G. O. (2000). The growth of flexible problem solving: Preschool children use changing verbal cues to infer multiple word meanings. *Journal of Cognition and Development, 1*, 157–191.

Demakis, G. J. (2003). A meta-analytic review of the sensitivity of the Wisconsin Card Sorting Test to frontal and lateralized frontal brain damage. *Neuropsychology, 17*, 255–264.

Denckla, M. B., & Reiss, A. L. (1997). Prefrontal-subcortical circuits in developmental disorders. In N. A. Krasnegor, G. R. Lyon, & P. S. Goldman-Rakic (Eds.), *Development of the prefrontal cortex: Evolution, neurobiology, and behavior* (pp. 283–293). Baltimore: Brookes.

Diamond, A. (2002). Normal development of prefrontal cortex from birth to young adulthood: Cognitive functions, anatomy, and biochemistry. In D. T. Stuss & R. T. Knight (Eds.), *Principles of frontal lobe function* (pp. 466–503). London: Oxford University Press.

Diamond, A., Prevor, M., Callender, G., & Druin, D. P. (1997). Prefrontal cortex cognitive deficits in children treated early and continuously for PKU. *Monographs of the Society for Research in Child Development, 62*(4, Whole No. 252).

Dias, R., Robbins, T. W., & Roberts, A. (1996, March 7). Dissociation in prefrontal cortex of affective and attentional shifts. *Nature, 380*, 69–72.

Dinn, W. M., Robbins, N. C., & Harris, C. L. (2001). Adult attention-deficit/hyperactive disorder: Neuropsychological correlates and clinical representation. *Brain and Cognition, 46*, 114–121.

Duncan, J., Seitz, R. J., Kolodny, J., Bor, D., Herzog, H., Ahmed, A., et al. (2000, July 21). A neural basis for general intelligence. *Science, 289*, 457–460.

Dunn, L. M., & Dunn, L. M. (1997). *Peabody Picture Vocabulary Test* (3rd ed., Rev.). Circle Pines, MN: American Guidance Service.

Elliott, R., Frith, C. D., & Dolan, R. J. (1997). Differential neural response to positive and negative feedback in planning and guessing tasks. *Neuropsychologia, 35*, 1395–1404.

Epsy, K. A., Kaufman, P. M., Glisky, M. L., & McDiarmid, M. (2001). New procedures to assess executive functions in preschool children. *Clinical Neuropsychologist, 15*, 46–58.

Frye, D., Zelazo, P. D., Brooks, P. J., & Samuels, M. C. (1996). Inference and action in early causal reasoning. *Developmental Psychology, 32*, 120–131.

Frye, D., Zelazo, P. D., & Palfai, T. (1995). Theory of mind and rule-based reasoning. *Cognitive Development, 10*, 483–527.

Fuster, J. M. (2002). Frontal lobe and cognitive development. *Journal of Neurocytology, 31*, 373–385.

Gardner, H. (1983). *Frames of mind: The theory of multiple intelligences.* New York: Basic Books.

Garon, N., & Moore, C. (2004). Complex decision-making in early childhood. *Brain and Cognition, 55*, 158–170.

Gathercole, S. E. (1998). The development of memory. *Journal of Child Psychology, Psychiatry, and Allied Disciplines, 39*, 3–27.

Giedd, J. N., Blumenthal, J., Jeffries, N. O., Castellanos, F. X., Liu, H., Zijdendos, A., et al. (1999). Brain development during childhood and adolescence: A longitudinal MRI study. *Nature Neuroscience, 2*, 861–863.

Gogtay, N., Giedd, J. N., Lusk, L., Hayashi, K. M., Greenstein, D., Vaituzis, A. C., et al. (2004, May 25). Dynamic mapping of human cortical development during childhood through early adulthood. *Procedings of the National Academy of Science, USA*, 101, 8174–8179.

Goleman, D. (1995). *Emotional intelligence.* New York: Bantam.

Grant, D. A., & Berg, E. (1948). A behavioral analysis of degree of reinforcement and ease of shifting to new responses to Weigl-type card-sorting problem. *Journal of Experimental Psychology, 38*, 404–411.

Gray, J. R., Chabris, C. F., & Braver, T. S. (2003). Neural mechanisms of general fluid intelligence. *Nature Neuroscience, 6,* 207–208.

Green, L., Myerson, J., & Ostaszewski, P. (1999). Discounting of delayed rewards across the lifespan: age differences in individual discounting functions. *Behavioural Processes, 46*, 89–96.

Happaney, K. R., Zelazo, P. D., & Stuss, D. T. (2004). Development of orbitofrontal function: Current themes and future directions. *Brain and Cognition, 55*, 1–10.

Hauser, M. D. (1999). Perseveration, inhibition and the prefrontal cortex: A new look. *Current Opinion in Neurobiology, 9*, 214–222.

Hinson, J. M., Jameson, T. L., & Whitney, P. (2002). Somatic markers, working memory, and decision-making. *Cognitive, Affective, & Behavioral Neuroscience, 2*, 341–353.

Hooper, C. J., Luciana, M., Conklin, H. M., & Yarger, R. S. (2004). Adolescents' performance on the Iowa Gambling Task: Implications for the development of decision-making and ventromedial prefrontal cortex. *Developmental Psychology, 40*, 1148–1158.

Hughes, C. (1998). Executive function in preschoolers: Links with theory of mind and verbal ability. *British Journal of Developmental Psychology, 16,* 233–253.

Hughes, C., Dunn, J., & White, A. (1998). Trick or treat?: Uneven understanding of mind and emotion and executive dysfunction in "Hard-to-manage" preschoolers. *Journal of Child Psychology and Psychiatry, 39*, 981–994.

Hughes, C., Russell, J., & Robbins, T. W. (1994). Evidence for executive dysfunction in autism. *Neuropsychologia, 32*, 477–492.

Jacobson, C. F. (1936). Studies of cerebral functions in primates: I. The functions of the frontal association areas in monkeys. *Comparative Psychology Monographs, 13,* 1–30.

Jacques, S., Zelazo, P. D., Kirkham, N. Z., & Semcesen, T. K. (1999). Rule selection versus rule execution in preschoolers: An error-detection approach. *Developmental Psychology, 35*, 770–780.

Kane, M. J., & Engle, R. W. (2002). The role of prefrontal cortex in working-memory capacity, executive attention, and general fluid intelligence: An individual-differences perspective. *Psychonomic Bulletin & Review, 9*, 637–671.

Kerr, A., & Zelazo, P. D. (2004). Development of "hot" executive function: The Children's Gambling Task. *Brain and Cognition, 55,* 148–157.

Kheramin, S., Brody, S., Ho, M.-Y., Velazquez-Martinez, D. N., Bradshaw, C. M., Szabadi, E., et al. (2003). Role of the orbitofrontal cortex in choice between delayed and uncertain reinforcers: A quantitative analysis. *Behavioural Processes, 64*, 239–250.

Kirkham, N. Z., Cruess, L., & Diamond, A. (2003). Helping children apply their knowledge to their behavior on a dimension-switching task. *Developmental Science, 6*, 449–476.

Kochanska, G., Murray, K. T., & Harlan, E. T. (2000). Effortful control in early childhood: Continuity and change, antecedents, and implications for social development. *Developmental Psychology, 36*, 220–232.

Krawczyk, D. C. (2002). Contributions of the prefrontal cortex to the neural basis of human decision making. *Neuroscience and Biobehavioral Reviews, 26*, 631–664.

Lombardi, W. J., Andreason, P. J., Sirocco, K. Y., Rio, D. E., Gross, R. E., Umhau, J. C., et al. (1999). Wisconsin Card Sorting Test performance following head injury: Dorsolateral fronto-striatal circuit activity predicts perseveration. *Journal of Clinical & Experimental Neuropsychology, 21*, 2–16.

Luciana, M., & Nelson, C. A. (1998). The functional emergence of prefrontally-guided working memory systems in four- to eight- year old children. *Neuropsychologia, 36*, 273–293.

Luciana, M., & Nelson, C. A. (2002). Assessment of neuropsychological function through use of the Cambridge Neuropsychological Testing Automated Battery: Performance in 4- to 12- year old children. *Developmental Neuropsychology, 22*, 595–624.

Manes, F., Sahakian, B., Clark, L., Rogers, R., Antoun, N., Aitken, M., et al. (2002). Decision-making processes following damage to prefrontal cortex. *Brain, 125*, 624–639.

Matsuzawa, J., Matsui, M., Konishi, T., Noguchi, K., Gur, R. C., Bilker, W., et al. (2001). Age-related changes in brain grey and white matter in healthy infants and children. *Cerebral Cortex, 11*, 335–342.

Metcalfe, J., & Mischel, W. (1999). A hot/cool-system analysis of delay of gratification: Dynamics of willpower. *Psychological Review, 106*, 3–19.

Miller, E. K., & Cohen, J. D. (2001). An integrative theory of prefrontal cortex function. *Annual Review of Neuroscience, 24*, 167–202.

Milner, B. (1964). Some effects of frontal lobectomy in man. In J. M. Warren & K Akert (Eds.), *The frontal granular cortex and behavior* (pp. 313–334). New York: McGraw-Hill.

Mischel, W., Shoda, Y., & Rodriguez, M. L. (1989, May 26). Delay of gratification in children. *Science, 244*, 933–938.

Mobini, S., Body, S., Ho, M.-Y., Bradshaw, C. M., Szabadi, E., Deakin, J. F. W., et al. (2002). Effects of lesions of the orbitofrontal cortex on sensitivity to delayed and probabilistic reinforcement. *Psychopharmacology, 160*, 290–298.

Monterosso, J., Ehrman, R., Napier, K. L., O'Brien, C. P., & Childress, A. R. (2001). Three decision-making tasks in cocaine-dependent patients: Do they measure the same construct? *Addiction, 96*, 1825–1837.

Munakata, Y., & Yerys, B. E. (2001). All together now: When dissociations between knowledge and action disappear. *Psychological Science, 12*, 335–337.

Nagahama, Y., Okada, T., Katsumi, Y., Hayashi, T., Yamauchi, H., Oyanagi, C., et al. (2001). Dissociable mechanisms of attentional control within the human prefrontal cortex. *Cerebral Cortex, 11*, 85–92.

Orzhekhovskaya, N. S. (1981). Fronto-striatal relationships in primate ontogeny. *Neuroscience & Behavioral Physiology, 11*, 379–385.

O'Sullivan, L. P., Mitchell, L. L., & Daehler, M. W. (2001). Representation and perseveration: Influences on young children's representational insight. *Journal of Cognition and Development, 2*, 339–365.

Pennington, B. F. (1997). Dimensions of executive functions in normal and abnormal development. In N. A. Krasnegor, G. R. Lyon, & P. S. Goldman-Rakic (Eds.), *Development of the prefrontal cortex: Evolution, neurobiology, and behavior* (pp. 265–281). Baltimore: Brookes.

Pennington, B. F., & Ozonoff, S. (1996). Executive functions and developmental psychopathology. *Journal of Child Psychology & Psychiatry & Allied Disciplines, 37*, 51–87.

Pérez-Edgar, K., & Fox, N. A. (in press). A behavioral and electrophysiological study of children's selective attention under neutral and affective conditions. *Journal of Cognition and Development.*

Perner, J., & Lang, B. (1999). Development of theory of mind and cognitive control. *Trends in Cognitive Science, 3*, 337–344.

Perner, J., Stummer, S., & Lang, B. (1999). Executive functions and theory of mind: Cognitive complexity or functional dependence? In P. D. Zelazo, J. W. Astington, & D. R. Olson (Eds.), *Developing theories of intention: Social understanding and self-control* (pp. 133–152). Mahwah, NJ: Lawrence Erlbaum Associates, Inc.

Petrides, M., & Milner, B. (1982). Deficits on subject-ordered tasks after frontal- and temporal-lobe lesions in man. *Neuropsychologia, 20*, 249–262.

Pfefferbaum, A., Mathalon, D. H., Sullivan, E. V., Rawles J. M., Zipursky, R. B., & Lim, K. O. (1994). A quantitative magnetic resonance imaging study of changes in brain morphology from infancy to late adulthood. *Archives of Neurology, 51*, 874–887.

Prencipe, A., & Zelazo, P. D. (2005). Development of affective decision-making for self and other: Evidence for the integration of first- and third-person perspectives. *Psychological Science, 16*, 501–505.

Rahman, S., Sahakian, B. J., Cardinal, R. N., Rogers, R. D., & Robbins, T. W. (2001). Decision making and neuropsychiatry. *Trends in Cognitive Sciences, 5*, 271–277.

Rogers, R. D., Andrews, T. C., Grasby, P. M., Brooks, D. J., & Robbins, T. W. (2000). Contrasting cortical and subcortical activations produced by attentional-set shifting and reversal learning in humans. *Journal of Cognitive Neuroscience, 12*, 142–162.

Rogers, R. D., Everitt, B. J., Baldacchino, A., Blackshaw, A. J., Swainson, R., Wynne, K., et al. (1999). Dissociable deficits in the decision-making cognition of chronic amphetamine abusers, opiate abusers, patients with focal damage to prefrontal cortex, and tryptophan-depleted normal volunteers: Evidence for monoaminergic mechanisms. *Neuropsychopharmacology, 20*, 322–339.

Rogers, R. D., Owen, A. M., Middleton, H. C., Williams, E. J., Pickard, J. D., Sahakian, B. J., et al. (1999). Choosing from small, likely rewards and large, unlikely rewards activated inferior and orbital prefrontal cortex. *The Journal of Neuroscience, 20*, 9029–9038.

Rolls, E. T. (2004). The functions of the orbitofrontal cortex. *Brain and Cognition, 55*, 11–29.

Rosso, I. M., Young, A. D., Femia, L. A., & Yurgelun-Todd, D. A. (2004). Cognitive and emotional components of frontal lobe functioning in childhood and adolescence. In R. E. Dahl & L. P. Spear (Eds.), *Adolescent brain development: Vulnerabilities and opportunities* (pp. 355–362). New York: New York Academy of Sciences.

Rothbart, M. K., Ahadi, S. A., & Hershey, K. L. (1994). Temperament and social behavior in childhood. *Merrill Palmer Quarterly, 40*, 21–39.

Ruff, H. A., & Rothbart, M. K. (1996). *Attention in early development: themes and variations*. London: Oxford University Press.

Salovey, P., & Mayer, J. D. (1990). Emotional intelligence. *Imagination, Cognition, and Personality, 9*, 185–211.

Schoenbaum, G., & Setlow, B. (2001). Integrating orbitofrontal cortex into prefrontal theory: Common processing themes across species and subdivisions. *Learning and Memory, 8*, 134–147.

Schwarz, J. C., Schrager, J. B., & Lyons, A. E. (1983). Delay of gratification by preschoolers: Evidence for the validity of the choice paradigm. *Child Development, 54*, 620–625.

Sohn, M. H., Ursu, S., Anderson, J. R., Stenger, V. A., & Carter, C. S. (2000). The role of prefrontal cortex and posterior parietal cortex in task switching. *Proceedings of the National Academy of Sciences, USA, 97*, 13448–13453.

Thompson, C., Barresi, J., & Moore, C. (1997). The development of future-oriented prudence and altruism in preschoolers. *Cognitive Development, 12*, 199–212.

Thompson, P. M., Giedd, J. N., Woods, R. P., MacDonald, D., Evans, A. C., & Toga, A. W. (2000, March 9). Growth patterns in the developing brain detected by using continuum mechanical tensor maps. *Nature, 404*, 190–193.

Thorndike, R. L., Hagen, E. P., & Sattler, J. M. (1986). *Stanford-Binet Intelligence Scale, Fourth edition* [Technical manual]. Chicago: Riverside.

Toner, I. J., Holstein, R. B., & Hetherington, E. M. (1977). Reflection-impulsivity and self-control in preschool children. *Child Development, 48*, 239–245.

Tsujimoto, S., Yamamoto, T., Kawaguchi, H., Koizumi, H., & Sawaguchi, T. (2004). Prefrontal cortical activation associated with working memory in adults and preschool children: an event-related optical topography study. *Cerebral Cortex, 14*, 703–712.

Wang, L., Kakigi, R., & Hoshiyama, M. (2001). Neural activities during Wisconsin Card Sorting Test–MEG observation. *Cognitive Brain Research, 12*, 19–31.

Wilder, K. E., Weinberger, D. R., & Goldberg, T. E. (1998). Operant conditioning and the orbitofrontal cortex in schizophrenic patients: Unexpected evidence for intact functioning. *Schizophrenia Research, 30*, 169–174.

Wolfe, C. D., & Bell, M. A. (2003). Working memory and inhibitory control in early childhood: Contributions from physiology, temperament, and language. *Developmental Psychobiology, 44*, 68–83.

Zald, D. H., Mattson, D. L., & Pardo, J. V. (2002). Brain activity in ventromedial prefrontal cortex correlates with individual differences in negative affect. *Proceedings of the National Academy of Sciences, USA, 99*, 2450–2454.

Zelazo, P. D., Carter, A., Reznick, J. S., & Frye, D. (1997). Early development of executive function: A problem-solving framework. *Review of General Psychology, 1*, 198–226.

Zelazo, P. D., Frye, D. & Rapus, T. (1996). An age-related dissociation between knowing rules and using them. *Cognitive Development, 11*, 37–63.

Zelazo, P. D., & Müller, U. (2002). Executive function in typical and atypical development. In U. Goswami (Ed.), *Handbook of childhood cognitive development* (pp. 445–469). Oxford: Blackwell.

Zelazo, P. D., Müller, U., Frye, D., & Marcovitch, S. (2003). The development of executive function in early childhood. *Monographs of the Society for Research in Child Development, 68*(3, Serial No. 274).

DEVELOPMENTAL NEUROPSYCHOLOGY, 28(2), 645–668

Executive Function and Theory of Mind in 2 Year Olds: A Family Affair?

Claire Hughes and Rosie Ensor
Centre for Family Research
University of Cambridge, England

Although numerous studies of preschoolers report robust associations between performance on tests of executive function (EF) and theory of mind (ToM), a lack of developmentally appropriate tasks so far has limited research on these cognitive skills in younger children. Here, we present new batteries of EF and ToM tasks that were administered to 140 two-year-olds from predominantly disadvantaged families, with analyses based on 129 children. Our results showed a strong association between EF and ToM, which remained significant when effects of verbal ability were controlled. Individual differences in EF and ToM were also examined in relation to both distal family factors (social disadvantage, number of siblings) and proximal family factors (quality of child's relationships with parents and siblings). Social disadvantage predicted significant variance in both EF and ToM but did not contribute to the association between these domains. Associations between positive parent–child relationships and both EF and ToM were nonsignificant when verbal ability was controlled. In contrast, positive *sibling* relationships predicted significant variance in ToM, even controlling for age, verbal ability, EF, social disadvantage, and parent–child relationships.

Two hot topics for research on young children's cognitive development are early executive functions (EF) and the emergence of a theory of mind (ToM). The term *executive function* refers to the higher order cognitive processes (e.g., inhibitory control, working memory, attentional flexibility) that underpin goal-directed behavior. Premack and Woodruff (1978) coined the term *theory of mind* to refer to the attribution of mental states (e.g., beliefs, feelings, desires) in explaining and predicting behavior. Although at first glance these constructs appear to be quite distinct, numerous studies provide converging evidence for a robust association.

Correspondence should be addressed to Claire Hughes, Centre for Family Research, University of Cambridge, Free School Lane, Cambridge, England CB2 3RF. E-mail: ch288@cam.ac.uk

For example, research with typically developing children highlights the synchrony of developmental milestones in EF and ToM: Across the preschool years, children show marked improvements in both EF (Diamond, 1988; Gerstadt, Hong, & Diamond, 1994; Zelazo, Frye, & Rapus, 1996) and ToM (Wellman, Cross, & Watson, 2001). Studies of typically developing children also show consistently strong correlations between individual differences in EF and ToM, even with effects of age and IQ controlled (Carlson & Moses, 2001; Carlson, Moses, & Breton, 2002; Frye, Zelazo, & Palfai, 1995; Hughes, 1998a, 1998b; Perner & Lang, 1999). In addition, research with clinical groups has shown widespread, pronounced impairments in both EF and ToM for individuals with autism (Ozonoff, Pennington, & Rogers, 1991), schizophrenia (Corcoran, Mercer, & Frith, 1995), and frontal lobe pathologies (Channon & Crawford, 2000).

Despite the consensus that developments and deficits in EF and ToM typically appear hand in hand, there is much less agreement as to how these associations should be explained. At least three different kinds of account have been offered. The first of these is the neuroanatomical proximity account, in which EF and ToM are seen as independent functions that happen to depend on neighboring neural substrates (Bach, Happe, Fleminger, & Powell, 2000; Ozonoff et al., 1991; Saxe, Carey, & Kanwisher, 2004). Much of the evidence for this view comes from studies of adult clinical groups that demonstrate dissociations in performance: impaired EF coupled with intact ToM (Lough, Gregory, & Hodges, 2001) or intact EF coupled with impaired ToM (Fine, Lumsden, & Blair, 2001). Setting aside both the difficulties in defining intact and impaired performance and the problems associated with the generally small sample sizes involved, findings from adult samples are difficult to extrapolate to children. Indeed, Karmiloff-Smith (1992; Karmiloff-Smith, Scerif, & Ansari, 2003) has argued that neuropsychological development is characterized by progressive modularization, so that systems that appear quite independent by adulthood may well be closely entwined in early development.

The second type is the expression account, which hinges on the common task demands of both EF and ToM tasks. Advocates of this view note that both types of tasks place significant verbal demands on the child; in addition, many ToM tasks require the child to hold a complex narrative in working memory (Davis & Pratt, 1995; Gordon & Olson, 1998) and to inhibit prepotent responses based on the child's own knowledge of the situation (Carlson, Moses, & Hix, 1998; Leslie & Polizzi, 1998; Russell, Mauthner, Sharpe, & Tidswell, 1991). Closely related to these expression accounts is the view that EF and ToM tasks place common demands on embedded if–if–then reasoning, such that developmental improvements in both EF and ToM can be explained in terms of an age-related increase in cognitive complexity and control (Zelazo & Frye, 1997; Zelazo, Jacques, Burack, & Frye, 2002).

The third type is the emergence account, which posits a genuinely functional relationship between EF and ToM. For example, Perner and colleagues (Perner &

Lang, 1999; Perner, Lang, & Kloo, 2002) have argued that meta-representational ToM skills provide a foundation for self-monitoring and inhibitory control. Conversely, others (Hughes & Russell, 1993; Russell, Jarrold, & Potel, 1994) have proposed that prerepresentational capacities for goal-directed action support conceptual developments in the understanding of intentions and desires. Note that these two viewpoints are not mutually exclusive, as different directions of influence may come to the fore at different developmental periods (Tager-Flusberg, 2001). This kind of developmental shift probably also characterizes the relationship between ToM and language: Early ToM supports language acquisition (L. Bloom & Tinker, 2001; P. Bloom, 2002), but later semantic and/or syntactic aspects of language development may well facilitate the development of a more advanced, representational ToM (J. de Villiers, 2000).

Just as the false-belief paradigm clearly requires significant non-ToM skills, traditional EF tasks are typically complex and multicomponential. As a result, associations between EF and ToM performance in preschoolers can be difficult to interpret. Identifying an association between younger children's performance on simpler tests of EF and ToM is an important test of the strength and stability of the association between these constructs. To date however, the scarcity of developmentally appropriate tasks tapping higher order cognitive functions (such as EF) in the 2-year-olds has hampered research in this field. However, recent research has seen a rapid growth in the number of suitable tasks available (Archibald & Kerns, 1999; Carlson et al., 2002; Frye, 1999; Griffith, Pennington, Wehner, & Rogers, 1999; Hughes, 1998a; Hughes & Graham, 2002; McEvoy, Rogers, & Pennington, 1993). Our study adds to this expansion of research tools by presenting a set of EF tasks that has been successfully administered to a sample of 140 two-year-olds. Our first aim in this study was to examine whether fledgling EF and ToM skills were associated in children as young as 2 years of age, and if so, whether this association remained significant when individual differences in verbal ability were controlled.

To our knowledge, only one other study has presented a battery of EF and ToM tasks to 2-year-olds (Carlson et al., 2002); these authors found no significant association at age 2 (although the predicted relationship was found 1 year later, when the children were 3). In contrast with the middle-class sample recruited in Carlson et al.'s study, our study included a large proportion of children from disadvantaged families; our hope was that the diversity of our sample would lead to striking individual differences in task performance and so would provide the study with greater power to detect associations between EF and ToM.

At this point, two methodological issues are of note. First, although there is growing support for componential or 'fractionated' models of EF, both in adults (Shallice & Burgess, 1991) and in children (Hughes, 1998a; Welsh, Pennington, & Groisser, 1991), cognitive assessments of 2-year-olds need to be as brief as possible, and so only a limited number of tasks for each EF component can be given. We therefore elected to construct a single aggregate measure of EF, as this was likely to provide a more stable and unbiased estimator of individual differences in performance (Rushton, Brainerd, & Pressley, 1983). Second, in many studies that report robust associations between EF and ToM, the two test batteries are administered in the same session by the same researcher. Day-to-day and diurnal variations in motivation and alertness, as well as in children's interest in and rapport with the researcher, will therefore have a common influence on performance on the two sets of tasks, potentially inflating the association between EF and ToM. To avoid this problem, a more conservative approach was taken in our study, in that different researchers administered the two sets of tasks on different days and in different settings.

Our other main aim was to examine whether EF and ToM show common or distinct links with distal versus proximal family factors. With respect to distal factors, individual differences in ToM are known to show clear associations with family socioeconomic background (Cutting & Dunn, 1999; Hughes et al., in press) and the presence of siblings (Perner, Ruffman, & Leekam, 1994; Ruffman, Perner, Naito, Parkin, & Clements, 1998). In contrast, it is not known whether these family factors also predict individual differences in EF. This is surprising, as common links with family factors (e.g., social disadvantage) may contribute to the association between EF and ToM.

With regard to proximal family factors, individual differences in ToM have been found to relate to the quality of both mother–child interactions (Hughes, Deater-Deckard, & Cutting, 1999; Meins et al., 2002) and sibling interactions (Dunn, 2000). Note that number of siblings and quality of sibling interactions have yet to be directly compared as predictors of ToM: Addressing this gap in the literature was a secondary aim of this study. Although parent–child interactions have been identified as supporting general cognitive development (Rogoff, 1990), specific features of child–child interactions (e.g., teasing, jokes, squabbles, pretend play) appear closely entwined with ToM in particular (Dunn, 1996, 2000). We therefore hypothesized that individual differences in early EF and ToM skills would show overlapping *and* independent associations with family factors. Specifically, we hypothesized that EF and ToM would show overlapping associations with distal family factors (e.g., social disadvantage) but independent associations with proximal factors with, for example, a strong and specific association between ToM and sibling relationships.

In sum, the first aim of this study was to establish whether individual differences in EF and ToM are associated in 2-year-olds, even when effects of verbal ability are controlled. The second aim of the study was to explore individual differences in EF and ToM in relation to both distal and proximal family factors and to examine the extent to which the relationship between EF and ToM can be attributed to common associations with family factors.

METHOD

Recruitment and Participants

Recruitment was carried out through face-to-face contact with 420 mothers accessed via 25 schools and 30 mother/toddler groups in low-income neighborhoods. Eligibility for the study was established via follow-up phone interviews and postal screening questionnaires. Families were eligible if the target child was between 24 and 36 months of age at the first visit and spoke English as a first language. Beyond these core inclusion criteria, an enriched sampling design was used to maximize the number of participants exposed to high levels of social disadvantage or maternal depression/stress. Following the methods used by Moffitt and the E-Risk Study Team (2002), seven markers of social disadvantage were recorded (see Table 1). Of 420 families contacted, 192 were invited to take part, and informed consent was obtained from 140 (73%) families. The target children in these families included 85 male and 55 female 2-year-olds (*M* age = 2.37 years, *SD* = 4 months).

Procedures

Home visits. Two researchers visited each family for 2 hr at a time convenient to the families (but also scheduled so that the final 30 min would coincide with preparation of the family's mealtime). One researcher interviewed the mother, collecting information about family background and relationships. During

TABLE 1
Number of Families (Out of 140) Showing Each Marker of Social
Disadvantage

Specific Marker	No. of Families
Head of household has no educational qualifications	39
Head of household unemployed	24
Family income < £10,000	29
Family living in publicly funded housing	62
Family receiving noncontributory benefits	46
Family has no access to a car	35
Family living in a very poor neighbourhood	13
Total markers of social disadvantage	
0	46
1–3	63
≥ 4	31

this time, the second researcher filmed the children playing for 20 min and then gave the target child the ToM tasks (distractor tasks and toys were provided for the older children during the testing, which lasted approximately 30 min). Next, the mother was then filmed for 10 min playing with the target child (and any other children present) and for a 5-min tidy-up task. Finally, 30 min of unstructured family interaction were filmed. Researcher home-visit questionnaire (Moffitt & the E-Risk Study Team, 2002) ratings of parenting style were based on this final 30 min and were made by both researchers immediately after the visit. Families were paid £20 per visit in appreciation for their time.

Lab visits.   Just over 1 month after the home visit ($M = 39$ days, $SD = 32$ days), pairs of mother/2-year-old dyads visited the lab for another 2-hr session. During this time, each mother/2-year-old dyad was filmed playing together for 25 min (10 min free play, 5 min tidy-up, and 10 min structured play) using the following props: a baby doll, bath, cot, pajamas, and feeding accessories; an Early Learning Centre Happy Track set with a post office, figures, and animals; six jigsaw puzzles ranging in difficulty from simple inset to 25-piece interconnected; a LEGO® Duplo set of Bob the Builder and Scoop; and a Mrs. Potato Head set. This play session was filmed and the videotapes later coded using the Parent–Child Interaction System (Deater-Deckard, Pylas, & Petrill, 1997). Next, while the 2-year-olds completed EF tasks (25 min) and verbal ability assessments (15 min), mothers completed the 25-item Strengths and Difficulties Questionnaire (Goodman, 1997). At the end of each visit, researchers completed the Bayley rating scale (Bayley, 1993) of 2-year-olds' behaviors. Refunds for taxi rides and parking and a video of the full visit were provided for all families.

Tasks

Executive function.   Each child was given five EF tasks in a set order established in a pilot study of 50 2- and 3-year-olds. The tasks are described in the order in which they were presented. The props for the Spin the Pots task (a multilocation search task) included a set of eight visually distinct pots (e.g., candy tins, jewelry boxes, decorated wooden boxes) that were arranged on a lazy susan tray, a supply of attractive stickers, and a silk scarf. The experimenter said, "We're going to play a game that's lots of fun, and you can win lots of stickers. Would you like that? Let's open each of these pots. Now we'll put a sticker in six of them, like this [a sticker was put in all but a gray jewelry pot and wooden flower pot]. We haven't got enough stickers for all the pots, so these two pots are empty. Now I'll cover it up like this [places silk scarf over tray]. Now, we're going to spin the tray, and I want you to choose a pot. Can you do that? Show me which pot you want to open." As soon as the child chose a pot, the remaining pots were covered with the scarf ready for the next search trial. Children were congratulated and encouraged after each trial, and the chosen pot was recorded on the score sheet. The task ends when all six stickers have been found, with a maximum of 16 trials. Performance scores were calculated as 16 minus the total number of errors made.

For the Trucks task, the experimenter showed the child a "treasure chest" filled with raisins (or stickers for children who didn't like raisins) and said, "Now we're going to play a guessing game, and you can win lots of raisins! Here are some yellow cards; each has two pictures of trucks—one truck is the right one that will give you a treat, and one is not. You have to guess which truck will give you a treat." The pictures are shown in Figure 1; on the reverse face of each card was a red or blue dot, used to help the experimenter record correct and incorrect choices. The child's choice on the first trial was always counted as correct; the researcher then noted whether this corresponded to the red or the blue rule. The second pair of trucks was shown on the next trial. Children were praised if they happened to choose the truck that also corresponded to the red or blue rule; if not, they were encouraged to choose the other truck next time. Success on subsequent trials depended on choos-

FIGURE 1   The picture cards for the Trucks task.

ing the same truck. Thus, rather than discriminating on the basis of truck size, color, or position, children were required to recognize individual trucks. The cards were presented in a pseudo-random order, and each time the child picked the correct truck the experimenter gave the child a treat and said, "Well done! Try to remember that one! Now let's have another go." If the child picked the incorrect truck, the experimenter said, "Oh, that wasn't the truck with the treat. Never mind, let's try with another card."

On each trial, the experimenter noted whether the child had chosen the correct or the incorrect picture and whether this picture had been on the left-hand side or on the right-hand side. After eight trials, the experimenter noted the child's performance. Children who had chosen the correct truck for at least four of the last five trials were invited to play the reversal phase of this task, in which the same pictures were mounted on green cards and success depended on choosing the previously unreinforced pictures. Instructions for this phase of the task were as follows: "Now we're going to play with these green cards, and this time you need to choose the other trucks to win the treats. Let's see how many you can win now." Children received eight postreversal trials. Performance on this task was rated by the total number of rules passed. Children who failed the first rule received a score of 0; children who passed the first rule only received a score of 1, and children who passed both rules received a score of 2.

The props for the Baby Stroop task were a baby cup and spoon and a regular cup and spoon. Children were randomly assigned to either Group A (cup trials followed by spoon trials) or Group B (spoon trials followed by cup trials). On each trial, the experimenter showed the child a big "mommy" spoon and cup and a little "baby" spoon and cup, and the experimenter checked that the child understood which was which by asking them to point to the mommy spoon and cup and then to the baby spoon and cup. The experimenter repeated these instructions until the child clearly understood. Next, the experimenter said, "Now we are going to play a topsy-turvy game— we're going to swap the two spoons/cups around. So now Mommy is going to use the baby spoon/cup, and baby can use the big spoon/cup." Then the experimenter hid both spoons/cups behind her back and brought one forward, saying "In this topsy-turvy game, is this a baby spoon/cup or a mommy spoon/cup? You tell me." The experimenter gave feedback for each trial, which was presented in the following, pseudo-random order: mommy/baby/mommy/baby/baby/mommy. Performance was rated by the number of correct trials across all cup and spoon trials.

Next, children completed the Beads task from the Stanford–Binet Intelligence Scales (Thorndike, Hagen, & Sattler, 1986). First, the child was shown a photograph depicting an array of 12 beads (red, blue, and white beads in four shapes: sphere, cone, cylinder, and disc). On each trial, the child was asked to point to the bead (or pair of beads) that exactly matched the bead(s) shown by the experimenter (for 2 sec for single beads and 3 sec for bead pairs). Feedback was given for each of

4 warm-up trials. Next, children were given 5 single-bead trials followed by 5 two-bead trials. Children who passed at least 3 two-bead trials then completed a third (16-trial) section of the task, in which for each trial they were asked to look closely for 5 sec at a picture of beads arranged on a stick. The picture was then removed, and children were asked to build a matching tower of beads. Performance was rated by the total number of correct trials across all three sections.

The Detour-Reaching task was presented at the end of the session, as even tired children were interested by the metal "box"; this had a Perspex window at the front, with a centrally placed hole through which children were invited to reach for a marble positioned on a platform in the middle of the box (see Hughes & Russell, 1993, for full details of the apparatus). After two failures (a photo-electric circuit was wired so that reaching through the window caused the marble to drop through a trapdoor in the platform) the child was shown that a yellow light was lit and told "When the yellow light is on, you need to turn this knob on the side to get the marble" (the knob was attached to a lever paddle that knocked the marble down a chute to a catch tray at the front). This knob route was demonstrated twice, and then the child was asked to retrieve the marble using the knob. Feedback (praise/reminder of the rule) was given on each trial. After three consecutively correct trials (achieved by all but 5 children), a lock was thrown so that the knob route was blocked. Locking this route also caused a green light to come on instead of the yellow light. The child was then told "Look, there's a green light on, and now the knob doesn't work anymore. When the green light is on, you need to flick this switch here [pointing to switch on right-hand side of box] and then reach in with your hand for the marble." To ensure that the children were motivated to execute the more difficult means–end action sequence required by the switch route, the marble was replaced with a larger ball that flashed when the child bounced it on the floor. Again, feedback (praise/reminder of the rule) was given on each trial. Performance on this task was rated by the number of trials needed to achieve the criterial run of 3 correct trials on the switch route (with a maximum of 12 trials allowed).

For most of the EF tasks, the distribution of scores was non-normal. In line with the scoring procedures adopted in previous studies (Hughes et al., 2000), we therefore adopted a simple pass/fail approach, using the binomial theorem to derive criteria for success for which the probability of passing by chance was less than .05 and selecting thresholds that were approximately equivalent to a median split. This corresponded to a score of at least 10 of 12 for the Stroop task and 12 of 16 for the Pots task, passing at least one pair of rules for the Trucks task, passing at least five trials on the Beads task, and achieving 3 consecutively correct trials on the Detour-Reaching box.

ToM.   Each child completed three ToM tasks. The first was a penny-hiding game that has been used in previous studies of preschoolers (Hughes, Dunn, & White, 1998) and children with autism (Baron-Cohen, 1992). The experimenter hid a coin behind her back and, bringing both hands forward with the coin concealed in one hand, asked the child to guess which hand held the coin. This was repeated three times, after which the experimenter announced that it was now the child's turn to hide the coin. For each of the following three test trials, the experimenter gave 1 point for each of the following: hiding both hands behind back, bringing both hands forward, keeping hand closed, and keeping coin hidden. (Note that this is a considerably more lenient scoring system than that used with preschoolers, for whom all four criteria had to be met to receive credit on a trial.)

The second ToM task (Charman & Baron Cohen, 1997; Fein, 1975) involved elicited pretend play. First, the child was shown four objects: two realistic (toy horse and plastic grass) and two less realistic (Duplo models of a horse and hay). In the baseline condition, the child was shown the realistic objects only. In the single substitution condition, the child was shown the prototypical horse and the junk hay. In the double substitution condition, the child was shown the junk horse and the junk hay. Three trials were coded for each condition: display, modeling, and suggestion. In the display trials, the child was asked simply, "Show me how you can play with these" and given 10 sec to respond. In the modeling trials, the experimenter pretended to feed the horse, saying 'yum yum' and clicking his or her tongue before allowing 10 sec for the child to respond. In the suggestion trials, the experimenter said, "Let's pretend he's still hungry. You give him something to drink," and then waited 10 sec for the child to respond. For each trial, 1 point was awarded for any pretend play actions (e.g., making the horse walk, feeding the horse).

The third ToM task was a deceptive-identity task (also used by Hughes, 1998b) that involved a pop-up picture book (Moerbeek, 1994). The first five pages of this book showed an eye peeping through a hole in the page. On the final page, what had initially appeared to be an eye was revealed to be a spot on a snake's tail. After turning back to the penultimate page, the child was asked the test question "Before we turned the page, what did you think this would be, an eye or a spot?" and the reality question "What is it really, an eye or a spot?" Next, the researcher showed the child a puppet and said, "Look, this is Charlie. Charlie has never seen this book before. If we show him this picture, what will he think it is, an eye or a spot?" and then asked the second reality control question "What is it really, an eye or a spot?". The order of the alternatives was counterbalanced across children, who were credited with success on the memory-for-own-false-belief and predicting-other's-false-belief questions only if they also passed the corresponding reality control question.

Note that the range of scores on each ToM task varied widely (0–2 points for the most difficult deceptive identity task, 0–9 for the elicited pretense task, and 0–12 for the penny-hiding game). Scores from each task were therefore weighted so that each task had an (equivalent) range of 0 to 12 points.

Verbal ability.   Children's expressive and receptive language skills were assessed using the Naming and Comprehension subtests of the British Abilities

Scales (BAS; Elliott, Murray, & Pearson, 1983). The Naming subtest is based on a small picture book of simple objects (e.g, fish, cup, watch). The Comprehension subtest includes a large picture card of a teddy bear, a box of eight small items (toy car, toy horse, toy watch, toy soldier, miniature cat, miniature dog, button, pencil), and an inset puzzle with nine elements (two boys, big and small versions of a house and a tree, car, van, bridge). Standard scoring procedures for the BAS were applied and gave a possible range of 0 to 20 points for vocabulary and 0 to 27 for comprehension. Primarily because of lack of verbal comprehension and ability, 5 children (3.5%) failed to complete the Comprehension subtest and 10 children (7%) failed to complete the Naming subtest, so they were scored as failing. The BAS Verbal Comprehension and Naming subtests were strongly correlated with each other ($r[140] = 0.77$, $p < .001$), and were summed to provide an overall measure of children's language skills (total possible range = 0–47). Cronbach's alpha for this combined measure was 0.83, indicating good internal consistency. Overall language scores (receptive plus expressive) showed a mean value of 21.20 ($SD = 9.25$, range = 2–39).

Interview and Observational Measures

Positive parenting.   The researchers' home visit rating scale included 18 three-point items that related to positive parenting (e.g., responsiveness, humoring sour mood, or conflict). The two researchers' ratings were averaged to create an aggregate scale that had good internal consistency (Cronbach's $\alpha = .90$, range = 0–54). Video-based ratings of positive parenting in the lab visit were made using three 7-point ratings from the PARCHISY (Deater-Deckard et al., 1997):

1. Positive control: Use of explanation, praise, and open-ended questioning.
2. Responsiveness: Responsiveness to and expansion on child's comments, questions, and behaviors.
3. Talk: Amount of speaking.

These three behaviors were rated during every other 30-sec segments and then averaged for each setting (free play/tidy up/structured play). Two coders independently rated 20% of all videotapes. Inter-rater agreement for each scale was good or excellent. Spearman's rho was .92 for positive control, .74 for responsiveness, and .78 for verbalization.

Sibling relationship.   Mothers completed the Sibling Relationship Interview (Dunn, Stocker, & Plomin, 1990; Stocker, Dunn, & Plomin, 1989). Mothers were asked about the quality of the sibling relationship and about the child's behavior toward their sibling. Analyses of positive sibling behaviors are based on 13 questions concerning affection, comforting and concern, helping and teaching, time spent together, playing together, and pretend play. Answers were rated on a 6-point scale ranging from 0 (*almost never*) to 5 (*regularly*) and were averaged.

RESULTS

In this section we first present preliminary descriptive results and justify the construction of our aggregate scores for EF and ToM. Next we consider the results in relation to the three hypotheses addressed by this study. The first prediction was that individual differences in 2-year-olds' performances on EF and ToM tasks would be significantly correlated, even with effects of verbal ability controlled. The second prediction was that EF and ToM would show common associations with distal family factors (e.g., social disadvantage). The third prediction was that EF and ToM would show distinct associations with proximal family factors: In particular, sibling relationships were predicted to show clearer associations with ToM than with EF.

Descriptive Statistics and Data Reduction

EF tasks.   The numbers of children (out of 140) who failed to complete individual EF tasks were 1 for the Spin the Pots task, 2 for the Trucks task, 5 for the Detour Reaching box, 13 for the Baby Stroop, and 22 for the Beads task. In total, 111 children (79.3%) completed all five EF tasks, 132 (94.3%) completed at least four tasks, and 139 (99.3%) completed at least three tasks. Data from the single child who failed to complete three EF tasks were excluded.

Pass/fail phi-contingency coefficients for success on individual EF tasks are shown in Table 2. For each task, success was significantly related to success on at least two other tasks, so to simplify analyses a single aggregate was created (total EF tasks passed). Cronbach's alpha for this aggregate scale was .61, indicating

TABLE 2
Phi Contingencies for Success or Failure on Each Executive Function Task

Variable	Stroop	Trucks	Spin the Pots	DRB	Beads
Stroop	—				
Trucks	.27**	—			
Pots	.39**	.08	—		
DRB	.18*	.29**	.08	—	
Beads	.20*	.25**	.20*	.09	—

Note.   DRB = Detour Reaching Box.
*$p < .05$. **$p < .01$.

modest but acceptable internal consistency. The mean total number of EF tasks passed was 2.30 (SD = 1.59, range = 0–5).

ToM tasks.   The numbers of children (out of 139) who failed to complete individual ToM tasks were 2 for the Pretend Play task, 23 for the Penny-hiding game, and 43 for the Deceptive Identity task. In total, 85 children completed all three ToM tasks, and 129 children completed at least two tasks. All of these children had also completed at least three EF tasks; our analyses are based on this sample of 129 children. To avoid additional loss of data, uncompleted tasks (which was rare and usually the Beads task) were scored according to the performance (e.g., number of trials correct) on the completed section.

Children's scores on the Deceptive Identity task were significantly correlated with scores from both the Penny-hiding game, $r(129)$ = .31, p < .01, and the Pretense task, $r(129)$ = .21, p < .05, and so a single aggregate, with a possible range of 0 to 36 points, was created. Cronbach's alpha for this aggregate scale was 0.61, indicating modest but acceptable internal consistency. The mean overall ToM score was 13.25 (SD = 8.15, range = 0–32).

Social disadvantage.   Scale reliability analysis showed that Cronbach's alpha for the aggregate measure of social disadvantage was 0.76, indicating good internal consistency. The mean social disadvantage score was 1.77 (SD = 1.84, range = 0–7). Because these scores showed a strong positive skew (z = 4.10, p < .001) families were categorized as showing low, middle, or high levels of social disadvantage (see Table 1).

Positive parenting.   Researchers' home visit ratings for positive parenting showed a mean value of 47.28 (SD = 6, range = 26–54) and a strong negative skew (z = 2.47). To address this, three equal groups were constructed according to whether the home visit ratings for positive parenting were low (n = 47), medium (n = 46), or high (n = 47).

Video-based ratings of maternal positive control, responsiveness, and talk in the lab visit were strongly correlated across the free-play, tidy-up, and structured-play settings (average r = .36, range = .18–.71, p < .05, for all) and so were first summed to create three 0 to 18 point scales. These scales were significantly correlated with each other (r = .33–.53, p < .01, for all) and so were averaged to create a lab visit rating of positive parenting. This scale had good internal consistency (Cronbach's α = .84), and a normal distribution.

Because the home visit and lab visit ratings of positive parenting were significantly correlated, $r(129)$ = .27, the two scales (converted to T scores to equalize variance) were averaged to form an overall composite index of positive parenting. This composite score had very high internal consistency (Cronbach's α = .89) and an approximately normal distribution (M = 49.99, SD = 7.93, range = 28.61–69.52).

Sibling relationship.   Cronbach's alpha for the aggregate measure of positive sibling behaviors was 0.74, indicating good internal consistency. The mean positive sibling behavior score was 34.17 (SD = 6.98, range = 7–49).

No significant gender differences were found for five of the six measures previously described. The exception was the EF task aggregate, for which girls outperformed boys, $t(1,128) = 2.29, p < .05$. The results, however, were similar when performed separately for girls and boys, and so to simplify the analyses the data are reported for the whole sample in the following sections.

Links Between ToM, EF, and Verbal Ability

Table 3 presents full and age and verbal ability (VA) partialled correlations between all measures in the study. Individual differences in VA were strongly correlated with individual differences in both ToM, $r(129) = .53, p < .001$, and EF, $r(129) = .59, p < .001$. It is thus not surprising that a strong correlation was also found between EF and ToM, $r(129) = .50, p < .001$. However, when individual differences in

TABLE 3
Correlations Between EF and ToM and Distal and Proximal Family Factors

Variable	Age	VA	EF	ToM	Social Dis	Pos Parenting	No. of Sibs	Pos Sib Reln
Age	—							
VA	.46**	—						
EF	.32**	.59**	—					
ToM	.28**	.53**	.50**	—				
Social dis	.03	−.18*	−.22*	−.15	—			
Pos parenting	.08	.39**	.27**	.26**	−.27**	—		
No. of sibs	.08	.06	.14	.13	−.05	−.01	—	
Pos sib reln	.12	.18*	.07	.22*	.00	.05	−.06	—
EF			—					
ToM			.29**	—				
Social dis			−.15	.02	—			
Pos parenting			.16	.05	−.21*	—		
No. of sibs			.00	−.05	.11	−.06	—	
Pos sib reln			−.01	.18*	.03	−.01	−.01	—

Note.   Full correlations (above) and with age and verbal ability partialled (below). EF = executive function; ToM = theory of mind; VA = verbal ability; dis = disadvantage; pos = positive; sib = sibling; reln = relationship.
    $*p < .05. **p < .01.$

VA were controlled, the correlation between EF and ToM was attenuated but remained significant, $r(129) = .29, p < .01$.

A hierarchical regression analysis with EF as the dependent variable showed
that age, VA, and ToM predicted 40% of variance in EF ($R^2 = .40, F = 26.81, p < .001$), and ToM uniquely explained 5% of variance in EF ($\Delta R^2 = .05, F_{change} = 10.49, p < .01$). Likewise, age, VA, and EF predicted 34% of variance in ToM ($R^2 = .34, F = 21.15, p < .001$), and EF uniquely explained 6% of variance in ToM ($\Delta R^2 = .06, F_{change} = 10.49, p < .001$).

Relations Between EF and ToM and Distal Family Factors

Squaring the correlation coefficients shown in Table 3 shows that social disadvantage explained 13% of variance in ToM and 8% of variance in EF. To examine
these relations in more detail, separate regression analyses were conducted with
social disadvantage, age, and verbal ability as predictors of EF and ToM. (Note that
the number of siblings was not included in these analyses, as the correlation coefficients were nonsignificant; see Table 3). Together, these predictors explained 37%
of the variance in EF ($R^2 = .37, F = 23.93, p < .001$) and 29% of the variance in
ToM ($R^2 = .29, F = 16.49, p < .001$). Next, hierarchical regression analyses were
used to assess whether age, verbal ability or social disadvantage explained *unique*
variance in either ToM or EF. Significant unique predictive effects of verbal ability
were found for both ToM ($\Delta R^2 = .19, F_{change} = 32.29, p < .0001$) and EF ($\Delta R^2 = .21, F_{change} = 41.92, p < .0001$). Effects of age on EF and ToM overlapped entirely with
effects of verbal ability. However, social disadvantage predicted marginally signif-
icant unique variance in EF ($\Delta R^2 = .02, F_{change} = 2.94, p < .10$).

Given the significant association between social disadvantage and EF performance, a further partial correlation was computed to assess whether the relationship between EF and ToM was attenuated when individual differences in social
disadvantage were taken into account. Compared with the full correlation, $r(129) = .50, p < .001$, this partial correlation was little changed, $r(129) = .44, p < .001$. Thus,
social disadvantage did not contribute to the association between EF and ToM.

Relations Between EF and ToM and Proximal Family Factors

Hierarchical regression analyses showed that positive parent–child and sibling relations jointly explained 8% of variance in ToM ($R^2 = .08, F = 4.72, p < .01$) and
8% of variance in EF ($R^2 = .08, F = 4.51, p < .01$). These predictive associations
were attenuated when effects of age, verbal ability, and social disadvantage were
controlled at the first step but remained significant for ToM. Specifically, when
these two proximal family factors were entered separately at Step 2 and Step 3 of
the model, only positive sibling relations explained unique variance in ToM ($\Delta R^2 = $

.03, $F_{change} = 3.45$, $p < .05$; see Table 4). Note that this result was unchanged when EF was also included as a Step 1 predictor. In addition, when VA was covaried, positive sibling relations were significantly more strongly correlated with ToM than with EF ($z = 1.83$, $p < .05$, one-tailed). Together these findings indicate a highly specific association between individual differences in positive sibling relations and in ToM.

DISCUSSION

Three sets of findings emerged from this study of 2-year-olds. First, there was a strong association between individual differences in EF and ToM that remained significant when effects of age and verbal ability were controlled. Second, social disadvantage predicted significant variance in both EF and ToM but did not contribute to the association between these measures; when verbal ability was included as a predictor, social disadvantage predicted marginal unique variance in EF only. Third, although the number of siblings was unrelated to ToM, the quality of sibling relationships predicted significant variance in ToM, even when age, verbal ability, EF, social disadvantage, and parent–child relationship quality were all controlled. Themes that will emerge in our discussion of these findings include functional relationships between EF and ToM, the prominence of language-related differences in 2-year-olds, and distinctive features of the sibling relationship.

TABLE 4
Summary of Hierarchical Regression Analyses: Positive Sibling
Relationships Explained Unique Variance in ToM

		ToM		
Step	Variable	B	SE B	β
1	Age	.88	1.34	0.06
	Verbal ability	.21	0.04	4.68**
	Social disadvantage	.17	0.57	0.03
2	Age	.96	1.35	0.07
	Verbal ability	.20	0.05	4.25**
	Social disadvantage	.24	0.58	0.04
	Positive parenting	.03	0.05	0.06
3	Age	.73	1.34	0.05
	Verbal ability	.19	0.05	0.43**
	Social disadvantage	.21	0.58	0.03
	Positive parenting	.03	0.05	0.06
	Positive sibling relationship	.11	0.06	0.16*

Note. $R^2 = .24**$ for Step 1; $\Delta R^2 = .00$ for Step 2; $\Delta R^2 = .03*$ for Step 3. ToM = theory of mind.
*$p < .05$. **$p < .01$.

A Robust Association Between ToM And EF in 2-Year-Olds

In contrast to the large and rapidly growing number of studies of infants and of pre-schoolers, there is a dearth of research with 2-year-olds—indeed, this period has been referred to as the "dark ages" of cognitive development (Meltzoff, Gopnik, & Repacholi, 1999). In part, the paucity of research reflects the very real challenges of working with this age group: Unlike infants, 2-year-olds do not stay still, and unlike preschoolers, they have only limited verbal skills. Moreover, 2-year-olds show strong day-to-day and diurnal variations in motivation and alertness; factors such as interest in and rapport with the researcher may also influence task performance. Given these considerations, two points are worth making. First, the two sets of tasks in the current study were clearly developmentally appropriate, because only 11 of the 140 two-year-olds failed to complete more than half of both EF and ToM task sets. Second, given that the two sets of tasks were completed on different days, in different settings, and with different researchers, the strength of the correlation between EF and ToM ($r = .50$) is rather striking.

It is also worth noting that our findings are consistent with the progressive modularization account of development proposed by Karmiloff-Smith (1992). Specifically, whereas studies of 3- and 4-year-olds consistently report a significant but moderate correlation between ToM and verbal ability (P. de Villiers, in press; Astington & Jenkins, 1999; Farrar & Maag, 2002; Happé, 1995; Hughes, 1998a), this correlation was considerably stronger in this sample of 2-year-olds ($r = .60$). Common associations with verbal ability clearly contributed to the association between EF and ToM, because controlling for verbal ability did attenuate the correlation between these two measures. This finding can be taken as providing some support for expression accounts of the relation between EF and ToM. (Note also that the 11 children who failed to complete the tasks all showed very poor verbal skills, so that although the tasks were designed to minimize verbal demands, a verbal "threshold" for understanding the tasks appeared all the same.)

Emergence accounts of the relation between EF and ToM also received some support, as the correlation between these measures remained significant ($r = .29, p < .05$), even when effects of age and verbal ability were controlled. Longitudinal data are needed to examine the direction of this association; these will be provided by the 1-year follow-up assessments of the children currently in progress. Of interest, whereas studies of preschoolers have shown small but significant gender differences in ToM (Charman, Ruffman, & Clements, 2002), there was no gender difference in ToM scores in this sample of 2-year-olds, although girls did outperform boys on the EF tasks. Hughes (1998b) did suggest that the influence of EF on ToM may be socially mediated, as children with poor EF skills are less likely to engage in the kind of sustained connected conversations that fuel and foster improvements in ToM. An age-3 gender difference in ToM related to this age-2 gender difference in EF would support this account.

Social Disadvantage, EF, and ToM

Research into cognitive development is based overwhelmingly on homogeneous middle-class samples. Although obviously convenient, this restricted range of socioeconomic backgrounds clearly limits both the generalizability of findings and the validity of cognitive models of disorders such as attention deficit hyperactivity disorder and conduct disorder, as these appear particularly frequently in children from disadvantaged families (Pineda et al., 1999).

The handful of studies that have examined individual differences in ToM in relation to socioeconomic background (Cutting & Dunn, 1999; Shatz, Diesendruck, Martinez Beck, & Akar, 2003) have shown clear relations, with social background for example accounting for around 12% of the variance in ToM scores (Cutting & Dunn, 1999). To our knowledge, no study has yet examined the relationship between social background and early EF. In our study, social disadvantage explained similar proportions of variance in EF and ToM (13% and 8%, respectively), but the correlation between EF and ToM was unchanged when individual differences in social disadvantage were partialled out. When verbal ability was also entered as a predictor, social disadvantage remained a marginally significant predictor of EF but not ToM. Hughes et al. (2005) conducted a large-scale study (involving 1,116 pairs of 5-year-old twins; half from teen-parent families) and found that over half the phenotypic correlation between ToM and verbal ability was explained by shared environmental influences, of which family socioeconomic status was a significant component. And in a cross-cultural study, Shatz et al. (2003) compared preschoolers who were native speakers of languages that either include explicit terms to refer to false belief (e.g., Turkish and Puerto Rican Spanish) or lack these explicit terms (e.g., Brazilian Portuguese and English). Their findings demonstrated a local effect of lexical explicitness but a more general and robust effect of socioeconomic status on ToM.

Our findings are less strong but also point to a significant overlap in the relations between social disadvantage and ToM versus verbal ability. In this respect, the findings from the previously cited studies differ from those reported by Cutting and Dunn (1999), who found that family background (indexed by maternal education) was a significant predictor of preschoolers' ToM scores, even with verbal ability controlled. These contrasting findings may reflect differences in the samples involved, as both the large-scale twin study conducted by Hughes et al. (in press) and our study included a substantial proportion of teen-parent families, who show particularly high levels of social disadvantage (Moffitt & E-Risk Study Team, 2002). Thus the links between family factors and ToM may depend on the kinds of families (and/or the level of social disadvantage), with common influences on verbal ability and ToM for the least advantaged families and more specific influences for more advantaged families.

Note also that although the *quantity* of language input is often brought up as a key predictor of vocabulary development (Hoff, Laursen, & Tardif, 2002;

Hoff-Ginsberg, 1998; Walker, Greenwood, Hart, & Carta, 1994), the *quality* of language input (e.g., talk about feelings, causal talk) is the best predictor of ToM performance (Brown, Donelan-McCall, & Dunn, 1996; Brown & Dunn, 1991, 1992; Dunn, Brown, & Beardsall, 1991). It is not yet known, however, whether individual differences in these forms of family talk mediate the relation between SES and ToM.

Quality of Sibling Relationships as a Specific Predictor of ToM

A secondary aim of the study was to compare number of siblings and quality of sibling relationships as predictors of ToM. Here, our results were clear-cut. No relationship was found between the number of siblings and ToM. Other researchers working with more diverse samples have also not found any significant relationship between the number of siblings and ToM (e.g., Cutting & Dunn, 1999). Such nonsignificant findings suggest that it may be the *quality* (rather than the simple presence) of the sibling relationship that matters. Indeed, in our study the quality of sibling relationships predicted significant variance in ToM, even when age, verbal ability, EF, social disadvantage, and parent–child relationship quality were all controlled. This strong positive association between the quality of sibling relations and ToM performance in 2-year-olds is open to two contrasting (but not mutually exclusive) interpretations. Interactions between siblings may provide a fertile context for young children's increasing awareness of others for several reasons, including the emotional intensity and overt nature of conflict and the greater symmetry of interests in ToM-related activities such as pretend play, humor, and competition. Two-year-olds who get along well with their siblings are likely to spend more time with them and therefore have more opportunities to develop their ToM skills. Equally, 2-year-olds with more advanced ToM skills are likely to make better playmates for their older siblings (most of the siblings in this study were older) and so enjoy more frequent and more positive interactions with their siblings. Again, longitudinal data are needed to compare these two accounts. However, our findings highlight that the association between ToM and the quality of children's relationships with their siblings is essentially independent from verbal ability, whereas the association between ToM and the quality of children's relationships with their caregivers overlaps closely with the association with verbal ability. This contrasts with previous findings of specific predictive relations between mother–infant interactions and later ToM (Fonagy, Redfern, & Charman, 1997; Meins et al., 2002). This contrast may reflect either the diversity of our sample or the particular importance of individual differences in 2-year-olds, a period that marks the transition from nonverbal to verbal forms of communication. Once again, longitudinal data will help to resolve this issue.

CONCLUSIONS AND CAVEATS

Although our findings from 2-year-olds do not speak to the distinction between expression and emergence accounts of the ToM–EF relation, they are not consistent with the view that the ToM–EF relation reflects common family influences. For example, social disadvantage predicted significant variance in both EF and ToM but did not affect the relationship between these measures. Indeed, links between social disadvantage and both EF and ToM were somewhat indirect in that they overlapped entirely with the association between social disadvantage and verbal ability. Likewise, the quality of sibling relationships was significantly more closely correlated with individual differences in ToM than in EF, suggesting specific rather than common family influences.

As noted earlier, 2-year-oldhood has been described as the dark ages of cognitive development. The study presented here demonstrates the feasibility of assessing EF and ToM in toddlers and casts some light on individual differences in each domain in this age group; in doing so, it extends the span of our knowledge about associations between these domains. Nevertheless, the study does have a number of limitations that will need to be addressed in future research. First, our findings are based on cross-sectional correlations; adding longitudinal data will strengthen the conclusions considerably. Second, to maximize the reliability of our findings (without extending the length of the testing sessions), aggregate ratings of performance in EF and ToM were adopted, and yet there is some indication from studies of preschoolers that the links between EF and ToM may be rather specific (Carlson et al., 2002; Hughes, 1998a). When a greater consensus emerges from the literature on preschoolers, a more focused selection of tasks for toddlers may give studies greater sensitivity. Third, although our findings regarding the association between ToM and the quality of sibling relationships are strong, we should mention that maternal interview responses were the only source of information available for rating sibling relationships. The sample participants in this study were all filmed playing with their siblings; these sessions are currently being transcribed and we hope will provide a more detailed view of the mechanisms linking ToM with sibling interactions. Our study therefore represents only a first step toward elucidating the interplay between family relationships and children's early cognitive development.

REFERENCES

Archibald, S., & Kerns, K. (1999). Identification and description of new tests of executive functioning in children. *Child Neuropsychology, 5*, 115–129.

Astington, J., & Jenkins, J. (1999). A longitudinal study of the relation between language and theory-of-mind development. *Developmental Psychology, 35*, 1311–1320.

Bach, L., Happe, F., Fleminger, S., & Powell, J. (2000). Theory of Mind: Independence of executive function and the role of the frontal cortex in acquired brain injury. *Cognitive Neuropsychiatry, 5*, 175–192.

Baron-Cohen, S. (1992). Out of sight or out of mind? Another look at deception in autism. *Journal of Child Psychology and Psychiatry, 33*, 1141–1155.

Bayley, N. (1993). *Bayley Scales of Infant Development* (2nd ed.). San Antonio, TX: The Psychological Corporation.

Beck, A., Ward, C. H., Mendelson, M., Mock, J., & Erbaugh, J. (1961). An inventory for measuring depression. *Archives of General Psychiatry, 4*, 561–571.

Bloom, L., & Tinker, E. (2001). *The intentionality model and language acquisition* (Vol. 66). Boston: Blackwell.

Bloom, P. (2002). Mindreading, communication and the learning of names for things. *Mind and Language, 17*, 37–54.

Brown, J. R., Donelan-McCall, N., & Dunn, J. (1996). Why talk about mental states? The significance of children's conversations with friends, siblings, and mothers. *Child Development, 67*, 836–849.

Brown, J. R., & Dunn, J. (1991). "You can cry, mum": The social and developmental implications of talk about internal states. *British Journal of Developmental Psychology, 9*, 237–256.

Brown, J. R., & Dunn, J. (1992). Talk with your mother or your sibling? Developmental changes in early family conversations about feelings. *Child Development, 63*, 336–349.

Carlson, S., & Moses, L. (2001). Individual differences in inhibitory control and children's theory of mind. *Child Development, 72*, 1032–1053.

Carlson, S., Moses, L., & Breton, C. (2002). How specific is the relation between executive function and theory of mind? Contributions of inhibitory control and working memory. *Infant and Child Development, Special Issue on Executive Functions and Development, 11*, 73–92.

Carlson, S., Moses, L., & Hix, H. (1998). The role of inhibitory processes in young children's difficulties with deception and false belief. *Child Development, 69*, 672–691.

Channon, S., & Crawford, S. (2000). The effects of anterior lesions on a story comprehension test: Left anterior impairment on a theory-of-mind type task. *Neuropsychologia, 38*, 1006–1017.

Charman, A., & Baron Cohen, S. (1997). Brief report: Prompted pretend play in autism. *Journal of Autism and Developmental Disorders, 27*, 325–332.

Charman, T., Ruffman, T., & Clements, W. (2002). Is there a gender difference in false belief development? *Social Development, 11*, 1–10.

Cole, K., & Mitchell, P. (1998). Family background in relation to deceptive ability and understanding of the mind. *Social Development, 7*, 181–197.

Corcoran, R., Mercer, G., & Frith, C. D. (1995). Schizophrenia, symptomatology and social influence: Investigating "theory of mind" in people with schizophrenia. *Schizophrenia Research, 17*, 5–13.

Cutting, A., & Dunn, J. (1999). Theory of mind, emotion understanding, language, and family background: Individual differences and interrelations. *Child Development, 70*, 853–865.

Davis, H. L., & Pratt, C. (1995). The development of children's theory of mind: The working memory explanation. *Australian Journal of Psychology, 47*, 25–31.

Deater-Deckard, K., Pylas, M. V., & Petrill, S. A. (1997). *Parent–child interactive system (PARCHISY)*. London.

de Villiers, J. (2000). Language and theory of mind: What are the developmental relationships. In S. Baron-Cohen, H. Tager-Flusberg, & D. Cohen (Eds.), *Understanding other minds: Perspectives from developmental cognitive neuroscience* (pp. 83–123). Oxford, England: Oxford University Press.

de Villiers, P. (2005). Language as a causal factor in developing a representational theory of mind: What deaf children tell us. In J. W. Astington & J. Baird (Eds.), *Why language matters for theory of mind* (pp. 186–219). New York: Oxford University Press.

Diamond, A. (1988). Abilities and neural mechanisms underlying A not B performance. *Child Development, 59*, 523–527.

Dunn, J. (1996). The Emanuel Miller Memorial Lecture 1995: Children's relationships: Bridging the divide between cognitive and social development. *Journal of Child Psychology and Psychiatry, 37*, 507–518.

Dunn, J. (2000). State of the art: Siblings. *The Psychologist, 13*, 244–248.

Dunn, J., Brown, J., & Beardsall, L. (1991). Family talk about feeling states and children's later understanding of others' emotions. *Developmental Psychology, 27*, 448–455.

Dunn, J., Stocker, C., & Plomin, R. (1990). Assessing the relationship between young siblings: A research note. *Journal of Child Psychology and Psychiatry, 31*, 983–991.

Elliott, C., Murray, D., & Pearson, L. (1983). *British Abilities Scales*. Windsor, England: NFER–Nelson.

Farrar, M. J., & Maag, L. (2002). Early language development and the emergence of a theory of mind. *First Language, 22*, 197–213.

Fein, G. (1975). A transformational analysis of pretending. *Developmental Psychology, 11*, 291–296.

Fine, C., Lumsden, J., & Blair, R. (2001). Dissociations between 'theory of mind' and executive functions in a patient with early left amygdala damage. *Brain, 124*, 287–298.

Fonagy, P., Redfern, S., & Charman, T. (1997). The relationship between belief-desire reasoning and a projective measure of attachment security (SAT). *British Journal of Developmental Psychology, 15*, 51–61.

Frye, D. (1999). Development of intention: The relation of executive function to theory of mind. In P. Zelazo, J. Astington, & D. Olson (Eds.), *Developing theories of intention: Social understanding and self control* (pp. 119–132). Mahwah, NJ: Lawrence Erlbaum Associates, Inc.

Frye, D., Zelazo, P. D., & Palfai, T. (1995). Theory of mind and rule-based reasoning. *Cognitive Development, 10*, 483–527.

Gerstadt, C., Hong, Y., & Diamond, A. (1994). The relationship between cognition and action: performance of children 3½ – 7 years old on a stroop-like day-night test. *Cognition, 53*, 129–153.

Goodman, R. (1997). The Strengths and Difficulties Questionnaire: A research note. *Journal of Child Psychology and Psychiatry, 38*, 581–586.

Gordon, A. C. L., & Olson, D. R. (1998). The relation between acquisition of a theory of mind and the capacity to hold in mind. *Journal of Experimental Child Psychology, 68*, 70–83.

Griffith, E., Pennington, B., Wehner, E., & Rogers, S. (1999). Executive functions in young children with autism. *Child Development, 70*, 817–832.

Happé, F. (1995). The role of age and verbal ability in the theory of mind task performance of subjects with autism. *Child Development, 66*, 843–855.

Hoff, E., Laursen, B., & Tardif, T. (2002). Socioeconomic status and parenting. In M. Bornstein (Ed.), *Handbook of parenting* (2nd ed.). Mahwah, NJ: Lawrence Erlbaum Associates, Inc.

Hoff-Ginsberg, E. (1998). The relation of birth order and socioeconomic status to children's language experience and language development. *Applied Psycholinguistics, 19*, 603–629.

Hughes, C. (1998a). Executive function in preschoolers: Links with theory of mind and verbal ability. *British Journal of Developmental Psychology, 16*, 233–253.

Hughes, C. (1998b). Finding your marbles: Does preschoolers' strategic behaviour predict later understanding of mind? *Developmental Psychology, 34*, 1326–1339.

Hughes, C., Deater-Deckard, K., & Cutting, A. L. (1999). "Speak roughly to your little boy?" Sex differences in the relations between parenting and preschoolers' understanding of mind. *Social Development, 8*, 143–160.

Hughes, C., Dunn, J., & White, A. (1998). Trick or treat?: Uneven understanding of mind and emotion and executive function among "hard to manage" preschoolers. *Journal of Child Psychology and Psychiatry, 39*, 981–994.

Hughes, C., & Graham, A. (2002). Measuring executive functions in childhood: Problems & solutions? *Child and Adolescent Mental Health, 7*, 131–142.

Hughes, C., Jaffee, S., Happé, F., Taylor, A., Wilkins, K., Jackson, J., et al. (2005). Origins of individual differences in theory of mind: Findings from an environmentally informative study of five-year-old twins. *Child Development, 356–370.*

Hughes, C., & Russell, J. (1993). Autistic children's difficulty with mental disengagement from an object: Its implications for theories of autism. *Developmental Psychology, 29,* 498–510.

Hughes, C., White, A., Sharpen, J., & Dunn, J. (2000). Antisocial, angry and unsympathetic: 'Hard to manage' preschoolers' peer problems, and possible social and cognitive influences. *Journal of Child Psychology and Psychiatry, 41,* 169–179.

Karmiloff-Smith, A. (1992). *Beyond modularity: A developmental perspective on cognitive science.* Cambridge, MA: MIT Press.

Karmiloff-Smith, A., Scerif, G., & Ansari, D. (2003). Double dissociations in developmental disorders? Theoretically misconceived, empirically dubious. *Cortex, 39,* 161–163.

Leslie, A., & Polizzi, P. (1998). Inhibitory processing in the false-belief task: Two conjectures. *Developmental Science, 1,* 247–254.

Lough, S., Gregory, C., & Hodges, J. (2001). Dissociation of social cognition and executive function in frontal variant frontotemporal dementia. *Neurocase, 7,* 123–130.

McEvoy, R., Rogers, S. J., & Pennington, B. F. (1993). Executive function and social communication deficits in young autistic children. *Journal of Child Psychology and Psychiatry, 34,* 563–578.

Meins, E., Fernyhough, C., Wainwright, R., Gupta, M. D., Fradley, E., & Tuckey, M. (2002). Maternal mind-mindedness and attachment security as predictors of theory of mind understanding. *Child Development, 73,* 1715–1726.

Meltzoff, A., Gopnik, A., & Repacholi, B. (1999). Toddlers' understanding of intentions, desires and emotions: Explorations of the dark ages. In P. Zelazo, J. Astington, & D. Olson (Eds.), *Developing theories of intention: Social understanding and self-control* (pp. 17–41). Mahwah, NJ: Lawrence Erlbaum Associates, Inc.

Moerbeek, K. (1994). *Can't sleep.* London: Western Publishing.

Moffitt, T. E., & the E-Risk Study Team. (2002). Contemporary teen-aged mothers in Britain. *Journal of Child Psychology and Psychiatry, 43,* 727–742.

Ozonoff, S., Pennington, B. F., & Rogers, S. J. (1991). Executive function deficits in high functioning autistic children: Relationship to theory of mind. *Journal of Child Psychology and Psychiatry, 32,* 1081–1105.

Perner, J., & Lang, B. (1999). Development of theory of mind and executive control. *Trends in Cognitive Sciences, 3,* 337–344.

Perner, J., Lang, B., & Kloo, D. (2002). Theory of mind and self-control: More than a common problem of inhibition. *Child Development, 73,* 752–767.

Perner, J., Ruffman, T., & Leekam, S. R. (1994). Theory of mind is contagious: You catch it from your sibs. *Child Development, 65,* 1228–1238.

Pineda, D., Ardila, A., Rosselli, M., Arias, B., Henao, G., Gomez, L., et al. (1999). Prevalence of attention-deficit/hyperactivity disorder symptoms in 4- to 17-year-old children in the general population. *Journal of Abnormal Child Psychology, 27,* 455–462.

Premack, D., & Woodruff, G. (1978). Does the chimpanzee have a theory of mind? *Behaviour & Brain Sciences, 4,* 515–526.

Rogoff, B. (1990). *Apprenticeship in thinking.* Oxford, UK: Oxford University Press.

Ruffman, T., Perner, J., Naito, M., Parkin, L., & Clements, W. (1998). Older but not younger siblings facilitate false belief understanding. *Developmental Psychology, 34,* 161–174.

Rushton, J. P., Brainerd, C. J., & Pressley, M. (1983). Behavioral development and construct validity: The principle of aggregation. *Psychological Bulletin, 94,* 18–38.

Russell, J., Jarrold, C., & Potel, D. (1994). What makes strategic deception difficult for children—the deception or the strategy? *British Journal of Developmental Psychology, 12,* 301–314.

Russell, J., Mauthner, N., Sharpe, S., & Tidswell, T. (1991). The "windows task" as a measure of strategic deception in preschoolers and autistic subjects. *British Journal of Developmental Psychology, 9*, 331–349.

Saxe, R., Carey, S., & Kanwisher, N. (2004). Understanding other minds: Linking developmental psychology and functional neuroimaging. *Annual Review of Psychology, 55*, 87–124.

Shallice, T., & Burgess, P. (1991). Higher cognitive impairments and frontal lobe lesions in man. In H. Levin, H. Eisenberg, & A. Benton (Eds.), *Frontal lobe function and dysfunction* (pp. 125–138). Oxford, England: Oxford University Press.

Shatz, M., Diesendruck, G., Martinez Beck, I., & Akar, D. (2003). The influence of language and socioeconomic status on children's understanding of false belief. *Developmental Psychology, 39*, 717–729.

Stocker, C., Dunn, J., & Plomin, R. (1989). Sibling relationships: Links with child temperament, maternal behavior, and family structure. *Child Development, 60*(3), 715–727.

Tager-Flusberg, H. (2001). A re-examination of the Theory of Mind hypothesis of autism. In J. Burack, T. Charman, N. Yirmiya, & P. Zelazo (Eds.), *The development of autism: Perspectives from theory and research* (pp. 173–194). Mahwah, NJ: Lawrence Erlbaum Associates, Inc.

Thorndike, R. L., Hagen, E. P., & Sattler, J. M. (1986). *Stanford–Binet Intelligence Scale* (4th ed.). Chicago, IL: Riverside.

Walker, D., Greenwood, C., Hart, B., & Carta, J. (1994). Prediction of school outcomes based on early language production and socioeconomic factors. *Child Development, 65*, 606–621.

Wellman, H., Cross, D., & Watson, J. (2001). Meta-analysis of theory of mind development: The truth about false belief. *Child Development, 72*, 655–684.

Welsh, M. C., Pennington, B. F., & Groisser, D. B. (1991). A normative-developmental study of executive function: A window on prefrontal function in children. *Developmental Neuropsychology, 7*, 131–149.

Zelazo, P., & Frye, D. (1997). Cognitive complexity and control: A theory of the development of deliberate reasoning and intentional action. In M. Stamenov (Ed.), *Language structure, discourse, and the access to consciousness* (pp. 113–153). Amsterdam: Benjamins.

Zelazo, P. D., Frye, D., & Rapus, T. (1996). An age-related dissociation between knowing rules and using them. *Cognitive Development, 11*, 37–63.

Zelazo, P., Jacques, S., Burack, J., & Frye, D. (2002). The relation between theory of mind and rule use: Evidence from persons with autism-spectrum disorders. *Infant and Child Development, 11*, 171–196.

DEVELOPMENTAL NEUROPSYCHOLOGY, 28(2), 669–688
Copyright © 2005, Lawrence Erlbaum Associates, Inc.

Inhibitory Processes in Young Children and Individual Variation in Short-Term Memory

Kimberly Andrews Espy
Office of Research & Department of Psychology
University of Nebraska–Lincoln

Rebecca Bull
School of Psychology
University of Aberdeen, Scotland

A precise definition of executive control remains elusive, related in part to the variations among executive tasks in the nature of the task demands, which complicate the identification of test-specific versus construct-specific performance. In this study, tasks were chosen that varied in the nature of the stimulus (verbal, nonverbal), response (naming, somatic motor), conflict type (proactive interference, distraction), and inhibitory process (attention control, response suppression) required. Then performance differences were examined in 184 young children (age range = 3 years 6 months to 6 years 1 month), comparing those with high (5 or more digits) and low (3 or fewer digits) spans to determine the dependence on short-term memory. Results indicated that there was communality in inhibitory task demands across instruments, although the specific pattern of task intercorrelations varied in children with high and low spans. Furthermore, only performance on attention control tasks—that is, that require cognitive engagement/disengagement among an internally represented rule or response set that was previously active versus those currently active—differed between children of high and low spans. In contrast, there were differences neither between children with high and low spans on response suppression tasks nor on tasks when considered by type of stimulus, response, or conflict. Individual differences in well-regulated thought may rest in variations in the ability to maintain information in

Correspondence should be addressed to Kimberly Andrews Espy, Office of Research, University of Nebraska–Lincoln, 303 Canfield Administration Bldg., Lincoln, NE 68588–0433. E-mail: kespy2@siumed.edu

an active, quickly retrievable state that subserve controlling attention in a goal-rele-vant fashion.

Executive control plays a critical role in normative cognitive processes, such as memory, attention, and conciousness/theory of mind (e.g., Baddeley & Hitch, 1994; Desimone & Duncan, 1995; Posner & Petersen, 1990; Hughes, 1998b; Perner, Lang, & Kloo, 2002) and is related to important academic and behav-ioral/social outcomes (e.g., Bull, Johnston, & Roy, 1999; Bull & Scerif, 2001; Espy et al., 2004; Gathercole & Pickering, 2000; Hughes, White, Sharpen, & Dunn, 2000; Isquith, Gioia, & Espy, 2004; Ready, Stierman, & Paulsen, 2001). Not surprisingly, executive control is fundamental to etiology of, or at least a signifi-cant contributor to, diverse clinical disorders (e.g., Anderson, Anderson, Grimwood, & Nolan, 2004; Espy, Kaufmann, & Glisky, 1999; Espy et al., 2002; Ewing-Cobbs, Prasad, Landry, Kramer, & DeLeon, 2004; Pennington & Ozonoff, 1996). Although there are many models of executive control, largely derived from neuropsychological performance of adults, one underutilized method to under-stand the nature of executive control is to examine such skills early in ontogeny, when abilities are developing rapidly. There is substantial evidence across diverse tasks that the preschool period is a phase of rapid acquisition of executive compe-tencies that are supported by substantial maturation in prefrontal structures and functional systems (e.g., Huttenlocher & Dabholkar, 1997; Kinney, Brody, Kloman, & Gilles, 1988; Thatcher, 1997). In fact, Diamond and Kirkham (2005) recently noted that adults show the same stimulus-response biased performance on a simple card sorting task that most 4-year-old children "pass," suggesting sub-stantial continuity of executive control from early development to maturity.

Although the precise nature of executive control in adults, or children, is far from resolved, what differs among the various accounts is whether executive control is (a) viewed as a unitary process or composed of "fractionated," interdependent subprocesses; (b) the relative weights or uniqueness that these executive constructs are ascribed; (c) differentially localized within the brain, and/or (d) the manner or pattern of development during childhood. Executive control has been studied in typi-cally developing preschool children with several paradigms, including rule-gov-erned, attribute-based sorting tasks (Espy, Kaufmann, & Glisky, 1999; Hughes, 1998a) such as the Dimensional Change Card Sort task (DCCS; see Zelazo, Frye, & Rapus, 1996); tasks with manual selection or verbal naming of stimuli that conflict or interfere on the basis of natural associations (e.g., Carlson & Moses, 2001; Dia-mond, Briand, Fossella, & Gehlbach, 2004; Diamond, Kirkham, & Amso, 2002; Gerstadt, Hong, & Diamond, 1994; Prevor & Diamond, 2005; Wright, Waterman, Prescott, & Murdoch-Eaton, 2003); and manual search tasks with working memory maintenance demands (e.g., Espy, Kaufmann, Glisky, & McDiarmid, 2001; Dia-mond, Prevor, Callender, & Druin, 1997; Hughes, 1998a) and/or with inhibiting prepotent or prohibited somatic motor responses (e.g., Carlson & Moses, 2001; Diamond & Taylor, 1996; Espy, Kaufmann, McDiarmid, & Glisky, 1999; Kochanska, Murray, Jacques, Koenig, & Vandegeest, 1996; Korkman, Kirk, & Kemp, 1998; Reed, Pien, & Rothbart, 1984).

To provide a unified account across the diverse tasks used to measure executive control, Diamond recently argued that "attentional inertia" underlies the classic dysexecutive behavior that young children display, such as, persisting to search at a previously rewarded location that no longer contains the reward, sorting a new card to the previously active category despite explicit recall of the current sorting "rule," and impulsively performing a prohibited act (Kirkham, Cruess, & Diamond, 2003). Similar to the concept of task-set inertia discussed in the adult cognitive literature (Allport, Styles, & Hsieh, 1994; Allport & Wylie, 2000), Diamond and colleagues argued that the young child's attention gets pulled away from the response set at hand by conflicting stimulus properties, thereby disrupting performance and leading to the classic dissociation between knowledge and action. In this view, inhibition resolves the conflict among stimulus properties, response mappings, and current context demands, essentially permitting the child to activate one rule or response in one context, then cognitively disengage when the context changes and, in turn, engage another newly salient but competing response or set. Strong support for this type of conceptualization is provided in the adult cognitive literature, where evidence of backward inhibition (e.g., Mayr & Keele, 2000) and negative priming (e.g., Tipper & Cranston, 1985) are some likely mechanisms that might underlie such "inertia."

Unfortunately, in the developmental and pediatric literatures in particular, the term *inhibition* has been used to describe both the suppression of a prepotent (and typically somatic, motor response) and the control of attention—that is, cognitive engagement/disengagement among internally represented rules or response sets that are previously active versus those currently active (Harnishfeger, 1995; Nigg, 2000). In suppression tasks, the child must suppress somatic motor responses—for example, remaining still while the examiner tries to distract the child. In attention control tasks, the child must inhibit an internally represented rule or response set that had been previously active and now must be disengaged and controlled due to proactive interference, which interferes with the child's ability to engage and implement a new response or rule. Friedman and Miyake (2004) found evidence for such a distinction using structural equation modeling, where normative adult task performance was characterized by (a) inhibiting a prepotent response or resisting interference from irrelevant distraction versus (b) controlling attention to resist proactive interference from a previously active rule or response set. Although the attentional inertia conceptualization applies to the attention control view in a straightforward fashion, it is less clear how such attentional inertia might function in the suppression of a somatic motor response or whether, in fact, these two inhibitory processes are distinguishable (Bishop, Aamodt-Leaper, Creswell, McGurk,

& Skuse, 2001; Nigg, 2000; Wilson & Kipp, 1998), particularly in young children. Of note are the factor analytic findings of Carlson and Moses (2001), who identified two factors that best described the performance of 107 three- and four-year-olds on 10 inhibitory tasks, which they labeled *conflict* and *delay*. Inspection of the pattern matrix revealed that the conflict factor is composed of tasks that demand control of attention as described here, and the delay tasks were largely those that required response suppression (or moderation), consistent with this inhibitory framework.

Further complicating this issue is the fact that the nature of the conflict varies among executive tasks. In motor response suppression tasks, the conflict typically is derived through a prohibited action or resistance to obtaining reward. In other executive tasks like "Day-Night" (Gerstadt et al., 1994), Luria's tapping task (Diamond & Taylor, 1996), Dots (Diamond et al., 2004), and Color-Object Stroop (Prevor & Diamond, 2005), the conflict between the response and the stimulus conditions are derived from the child's experience in the natural environment. That is, there is a "natural" stimulus-response mapping, for example, between the picture of a sun in a sky and the word *day* that is entrenched from the child's participation in his or her everyday sensory, motor, and linguistic environment. Finally, in the DCCS, there is conflict between the stimuli properties and the required response, but the conflict between the two dimensions is arbitrary (e.g., color is not inherently related to shape). Inhibiting or controlling responding in light of conflict appears to be critical in engaging prefrontal systems (e.g., Casey et al., 2000; Durston et al., 2002), as some postulate that this conflict between stimulus-response mappings and new reward contingencies is the fundamental nature of executive control (e.g., Miller, 2000; O'Reilly, Noelle, Braver, & Cohen, 2002). In fact, even in very young children, conflict is critical to executive task performance, as 3-year-olds can sort the conflicting cards successfully when the second dimension is not present (Brooks, Hanauer, Padowska, & Rosman, 2003) or is irrelevant to sorting (Perner & Lang, 2002; Rennie, Bull, & Diamond, 2004), or when the response is not canonically related (Diamond et al., 2002). It remains unclear whether all types of conflict invoke executive control, or perhaps whether the nature of conflict required differs with age or cognitive proficiency.

Finally, most of the executive tasks developed to date are nonverbal in stimulus content and/or response. Dempster (1993) proposed that interference control in the motoric, linguistic, and perceptual domains may not be a unitary process. Indeed, Prevor and Diamond (2005) recently developed the Color-Object Stroop task that utilized a naming response of verbal material. They noted a significantly larger effect of conflict when the response was a naming response in comparison to a manual selection response. However, this distinction likely is complicated, as verbal material introduces another level of complexity with respect to semantic relations and phonological similarity, for example, which may or may not account for the conflict effects noted on a given task (Bull & Brown, 2004). The advantages of more verbally laden executive tasks is the potentially stronger relations to out-comes of interest that both more heavily demand verbal skills and utilize a verbal presentation format, such as emergent reading and mathematics achievement (e.g., Bull & Scerif, 2001; Espy et al., 2004; Gathercole & Pickering, 2000).

The purpose here was to better characterize the nature of executive control by examining inhibition task demands—the nature of the stimulus, response, conflict, and inhibitory process—as a function of individual differences in working mem-ory. For example, Diamond (1988) postulated that inhibition and working memory are inextricably linked, where if an individual is not able to maintain information over time and/or inhibit prepotent responses, he or she will continue to inflexibly choose the incorrect response. Similarly, Roberts and Pennington (1996) theorized that inhibition and working memory are in a competitive balance, so that as the de-mands for one increase, the other necessarily decreases. Both of these models are difficult to test empirically, particularly in young children. Engle and colleagues used an individual differences approach in adults to investigate this issue by com-paring performance in adults with high versus low working-memory spans on sev-eral attention/executive tasks, including Proactive Interference (Kane & Engle, 2000), Stroop (Kane & Engle, 2003), Prosaccade (Kane, Bleckley, Conway, & Engle, 2001), and Visual Attention (Bleckley, Durso, Crutchfield, Engle, & Khanna, 2003). Results consistently revealed that task performance was reduced only in high-span individuals (and not those with low spans) when the proactive intereference, distraction, or conflict load was increased relative to baseline task demands. Engle (2002) cogently concluded that the fundamental, domain-free ex-ecutive ability rests in individual differences in the ability to "control attention to maintain information in an active, quickly retrievable state … . It is about using at-tention to maintain or suppress information" (p. 20). Therefore, a similar individ-ual difference approach might be useful in young children to better understand the specific task conditions under which executive control is engaged.

Using this approach, individual differences in young children's memory span were hypothesized to reflect variation in the fundamental process of attention con-trol. Short-term memory span likely is utilized in attention control to maintain the currently active stimulus-response mapping among previously active mappings that now provide proactive interference and to retrieve the correct response to achieve flexible, well-regulated thought or behavior. Therefore, children with high spans should perform better than those with low spans on inhibitory tasks that de-mand attention control relative to those that instead require response suppression. For similar reasons, individual variation in memory span instead might subserve demands to resist interference from proactive information, more broadly, as pro-posed by Wilson and Kipp (1998). In this case, task performance will differ in chil-dren with high versus low spans across tasks where the conflict is derived through proactive interference rather than through distraction. Given the domain-specific views articulated by Dempster (1993) and the shared verbal nature of span and verbal executive tasks, task performance might differ as a function of stimulus type demands. However, in Baddeley's (1996) model of working memory, both verbal and nonverbal information is maintained through separate work spaces (the phonological loop and visual spatial sketch pad, respectively) and available for central executive processing; therefore, verbal and nonverbal stimulus-type task performance might not differ in children with high versus low spans. Similarly, response type can be considered an "output" mechanism, and therefore performance among tasks that differed in the type of response demands were not hypothesized to differ in children with high versus low spans.

METHOD

Participants

The sample was composed of 184 typically developing children who ranged in age from 3 years 6 months to 6 years 1 month (M_{age} = 4.84 years, SD_{age} = 0.50 years). There were 103 girls (56%) and 81 boys. Similar to the demographics of the local area, 85% (n = 156) of the sample were Caucasian, 19 children were African American, 7 were Asian, and 2 were of mixed race. Mean maternal education level of the sample was 14.2 years (SD = 2.3). By parental report, none of these children were diagnosed with any neurological, psychiatric, or developmental disorders.

Preschool children were divided into three groups according to their maximal string length recalled on a forward digit span subtest that was administered during the test session. There were 72 children with a digit span of 3 or fewer, 70 children with a span of 4, and 42 with a span of 5 or more. The sex distribution across digit span groups was comparable, $\chi^2(2, N = 184) = 1.83, p > .39$, however age was not. Not surprisingly, there were more younger children with a maximal digit span of 3 or fewer and more older children with a maximal span of 5 or more, $F(2, 181) = 9.19, p < .01$. Therefore, the effect of age was controlled in all analyses.

Materials

To parse children by span length, a standardized forward digit span task was administered; then after an initial practice session, a standard sequence of digits was presented orally, starting from a span length of two. Each child was instructed to recall the digit strings in the order of presentation, with a maximum of two trials at each string length, and the maximum digit span length was recorded. The relation between inhibitory processing and short-term memory was investigated by focusing on a verbal executive task, the Shape School (Espy, 1997; Espy, Bull, & Martin, 2005). Using a storybook format that is familiar and appealing to young children, conflict between the arbitrary relation between the stimulus properties and the response is progressively built up through the story theme. Then, other comparison tasks were chosen that varied in stimulus content (verbal vs. nonverbal), response type (somatic motor vs. naming), inhibitory demands (attention control vs. response suppression), and type of conflict (proactive interference vs. distraction) to form a matrix of comparative task demands, as depicted in Table 1. Consistent with the approach used by Friedman and Miyake (2004), the comparison tasks were selected purposefully among those that are commercially available or that have an extensive literature base in order to increase generalizability and applicability in the clinical context. Of course, the disadvantage of this approach is that the degree of task demand control is inherently reduced. Nonetheless, applicability to extant literature was central in task selection, particularly as an initial approach.

Shape School.   The Shape School, developed by Espy (1997), is designed to assess different aspects of executive control in young children by using colorful, affectively engaging stimuli presented in an age-appropriate, storybook format. The story begins by setting up the premise, showing stimulus figures (colored squares and circles with cartoon faces, arms, and legs) playing on a playground and then going on to different school activities throughout the story. In each condition, the child must "call"/name the figure for it to proceed to the relevant school activity by the relevant rule. Briefly (see Espy, 1997; Espy et al., 2005, for a more thorough description), in the first control condition to establish the stimulus-response mapping, the child is introduced to one classroom of figures whose names are their color, where the child then had to call/name the color of each figure arrayed in three lines of five across the page. In Condition B, children were told that not all of the story figures had finished their work, where Happy ($n = 9$) and Sad/Frustrated ($n = 6$) expressions were added to the stimulus figures' faces to depict this contingency. These facial expressions served as cues to which stimuli the

TABLE 1
Task Demands by Inhibitory Measures

Task	Stimulus Type	Response Type	Inhibitory Process	Conflict Type
Shape School–C	Verbal	Naming	Attention control	Proactive interference
Shape School–B	Verbal	Naming	Response suppression	Proactive interference
NEPSY Statue	Nonverbal	Somatic motor	Response suppression	Distraction
Delayed Search	Nonverbal	Somatic motor	Response suppression	Proactive interference
NEPSY Visual Attention	Verbal	Somatic motor	Attention control	Distraction

child was to name and which to suppress naming. In Condition C, a classroom was added where the stimulus figures wore hats; for figures with hats ($n = 8$), the names were the stimulus figure shapes, and for hatless figures ($n = 7$), the names remained the color. For each condition, there was a brief practice page on which children had to demonstrate success to ensure adequate rule knowledge prior to application in the test conditions. The experimenter recorded the response time and number of stimuli correctly identified (according to the pertinent rule) in each condition from when the child began naming the first figure to when he or she finished naming the last figure in the array. For the purposes here, an efficiency score was calculated for each condition by dividing the number of stimuli correctly named by the latency to complete each condition. Analysis of task demands of these two conditions reveals that both Conditions B and C utilize identical verbal stimuli and naming responses. For both conditions, the first stimulus-response mapping (name color) provides proactive interference for the implementation of the second (B = suppress color name; C = name shape), in light of a relatively constant working-memory load of maintaining two rules in mind where overt cues signal the correct stimulus-response mapping. The two conditions differ with respect to the type of inhibitory process demanded, with Condition B requiring response suppression and Condition C, attention control, as shown in Table 1.

Statue.   Statue is a NEPSY subtest (Korkman et al.,1998), where the child is asked to stand still in a set position as a "statue" pretending to hold a flag (i.e., with eyes closed, no body movements or vocalizations) over 75 sec. At set intervals to distract and induce the child to break the statue posture, the examiner coughs, knocks on the table, drops a pencil, or says "Ho Hum!". For each 5-sec epoch, the child is awarded 2 points if no inappropriate responding is noted (i.e., keeps eyes shut without movement or vocalization), 1 point for one inappropriate response, and 0 points if the child fails to inhibit more than one response, with a maximum score of 30. Like Shape School Condition B, this task demands suppression of response; however, it requires a somatic motor rather than naming response. Furthermore, conflict is provided through distraction, and the stimulus type is nonverbal.

Delayed Search task.   In this venerable task adapted from the neuroscience literature (e.g., Diamond, 1988), the child watched while a reward was hidden under a cup at one of two locations. After a 10-sec delay, the child retrieved the reward. This procedure was repeated for 10 trials, and the percentage of correct retrievals was scored. Here, the stimulus type is nonverbal, and the response type was somatic motor in nature. To inhibit reaching to the previously rewarded location, the child had to suppress a somatic motor response. The conflict is provided by the proactive interference from the previously searched and/or rewarded location.

Visual Attention.   In this NEPSY subtest (Korkman et al., 1998), the child was instructed to select only the items that match the target stimuli on the page containing both targets and distractors. Only the random cat array was used, as it is common to both older and younger children. The number of targets (maximum 20 cats) correctly identified and completion time (maximum 180 sec) were scored. Like the two Shape School tasks, the stimulus type is verbal; however, a somatic motor response is required to be suppressed. Like Statue, the conflict is engendered through irrelevant distractors arrayed on the page. Given the role of attention control in visual search processes (e.g., Bleckley et al., 2003; Han & Kim, 2004), this task was considered to be an attention control task, consistent with the task demands to search and select of relevant targets amidst consideration of irrelevant stimuli.

Procedure

Preschool children were administered the inhibitory tasks in a single 90- to 120-min session by a trained child clinical graduate student blind to the experimental hypotheses. Assessments were conducted individually in a quiet room, with the parent or guardian present in the back of the room, completing study forms, to minimize any separation issues in the youngest of children. To foster cooperation and interest, short breaks were used, and families received monetary and small trinket compensation for study participation.

RESULTS

First, Pearson correlations were conducted to determine the interrelatedness of the different inhibitory tasks. In the overall sample (in the bottom left quadrant in the first panel in Table 2), all but one correlation was significant. The magnitudes of the correlations were moderate. There was a relatively small difference in the pattern of correlations when partial correlations were examined with age controlled (in the top right quadrant of the same panel). Cronbach's alpha for the five outcome measures was .63, lending further support to a general communality in task demands. Furthermore, separate intertask Pearson correlations were calculated for children with low and high spans. Informal examination of the pattern of the strength of correlations across the three digit span groups revealed that performance on Shape School Condition B and Statue were unrelated in children with different span lengths. The association between performance on Statue and Shape School Condition C differed in magnitude across digit span groups, such that there was a moderate relation in children with a digit span of 3 or fewer and correlation close to zero in children with a digit span of 5 or more. The pattern also was similar for the relation between Visual Attention and Statue performance, again where

TABLE 2
Intertask Correlations for the Overall Sample and by Digit Span Group

Task	SS		Statue[b]	DS[c]	VA[d]
	C[a]	B[a]			
SS–C	—	.47****	.17*	.28***	.22**
SS–B	.53****	—	.02	.13	.23**
Statue	.18*	.05	—	.29***	.17*
DS	.30***	.16*	.30***	—	.16*
VA	.32****	.34****	.18*	.18*	—
SS–C	—	.46****	.26*	.35**	.26
SS–B	.60****	—	.09	.12	.29*
Statue	.00	.01	—	.40**	.33*
DS	.25	.10	.37*	—	.20
VA	.40*	.25	.00	.14	—

Note. First panel are the first-order correlations for the entire sample (bottom left) and partial correlations with age controlled (top right); second panel are the correlations for children with a digit span of ≤ 3 (bottom left), and top right of the second panel are the correlations for children with a digit span of ≥ 5. SS = Shape School; DS = Delayed Search; VA = NEPSY Visual Attention.
[a]$n = 184$. [b]$n = 159$. [c]$n = 146$. [d]$n = 143$.
*$p < .05$. **$p < .01$. ***$p < .001$. ****$p < .0001$.

moderate relations were observed in children with spans of 3 or fewer, and no relation was evident in children with spans 5 or more. The opposite pattern was observed for the association between Visual Attention and Shape School Condition C, where the magnitude of the association was higher in those with longer spans than in those children with span lengths of 3 or fewer digits.

The joint effect of short-term memory span capacity and task demand was examined using repeated measures multivariate analyses of variance (MANOVAs), comparing performance across the tasks collapsed by the four task demands (shown in Table 1) in children with high (maximal digit span length of 5 or more) and low (maximal span of 3 or fewer) digit recall spans, using Engle's individual difference approach. For example, the z scores from Shape School Condition C and Visual Attention performance were averaged to index Attention Control task performance, as were the z scores from Shape School Condition B, Statue, and Delayed Search to index Response Suppression. Then, these respective averaged z scores were treated as a within-subjects condition and compared between children with high and low spans. Separate MANOVAs were conducted for each task demand, with the pertinent variables transformed into averaged z scores to reduce individual variable scale effects. When there was missing data on an individual task (9 children with one task only [2 Statue, 1 Delayed Search, 6 Visual Attention], 11 children with two tasks [9 Delayed Search and Visual Attention; 2 Statue and Visual Attention]; and 21 children with three tasks [Statue, Delayed Search, and Visual Attention]), the averaged z score was based on the remaining task data. There were no differences in age between children with and without missing data for any task, $ps > .23$. Because there was an expected age difference between children of the varying span lengths (e.g., Cowan, 1995, 1999), all analyses were conducted controlling for age. Overall sample task performance, and that of the differing digit span lengths, is shown in Table 3.

Consistent with prediction, performance collapsed across inhibitory process demands (Attention Control vs. Response Suppression) differed in children with high and low span lengths, $F(1, 111) = 5.58, p < .02$. The average z score for performance on tasks that required attentional control (controlling for age) for children with a low span length was $-.21$, whereas for children with a high span length, average z score on attentional control tasks was .25. Follow-up analyses revealed that performance differed on attentional control tasks in children of high and low spans, $F(1, 111) = 8.53, p < .01$. Univariate analyses on each task revealed that task performance between children of high and low spans differed to a greater extent on Shape School Condition C, $F(1, 89) = 7.80, p < .001$, than on Visual Attention, $F(1, 89) = 0.84, p > .36$. As hypothesized, response suppression task performance did not differ between children of high and low spans, $F(1, 111) = 0.25, p > .61$, where the average z scores in the digit span groups were comparable ($M \leq 3$ digit span $z = -0.07$; $M \geq 5$ digit span $z = 0.01$).

Of interest, performance on tasks collapsed by conflict demand (i.e., comparing those that utilized proactive interference vs. those with distraction) did not differ in children with high and low spans, $F(1, 111) = 0.71, p > .40$. Because the overall Task × Digit Span Group effect was not significant, further group differences were not explored. Consistent with prediction, children of high and low spans per-

TABLE 3
Overall Sample Task Performance and Performance in Child of Varying
Digit Spans

Task	Overall Sample[a]		Digit Span ≤ 3[b]		Digit Span 4[c]		Digit Span ≥ 5[d]	
	M	SD	M	SD	M	SD	M	SD
Shape School								
Condition C	0.19	0.17	0.14	0.13	0.20	0.20	0.26	0.16
Condition B	0.63	0.31	0.57	0.28	0.65	0.33	0.73	0.33
Statue	22.59	7.19	21.64	6.95	23.53	7.10	22.53	7.65
Delayed Search	0.87	0.12	0.86	0.13	0.88	0.11	0.86	0.12
Visual Attention	0.23	0.09	0.21	0.08	0.23	0.09	0.25	0.09

Note. Shape School Condition efficiency = naming accuracy/completion time; Statue = subtest total raw score; Delayed Search = % of correct searches/total trials; Visual Attention efficiency = stamping accuracy/completion time.

formed equivalently on tasks that varied as a function of stimulus type (verbal vs. nonverbal), $F(1, 111) = 3.04, p > .08$. Contrary to prediction, performance on tasks that differed in response type (naming vs. somatic motor) differed marginally among children of high and low spans, $F(1, 111) = 3.70, p > .05$. The digit span effect was restricted to the naming response type only, $F(1, 111) = 6.93, p < .01$, in contrast to that for somatic motor response, $F(1, 111) = 0.28, p > .60$. Univariate analyses on each task revealed that task performance between children of high and low spans differed to a greater extent on Shape School Condition C, $F(1, 111) = 11.83, p < .001$, than on Shape School Conditon B, $F(1, 111) = 1.60, p > .20$

DISCUSSION

These findings suggest that these inhibitory processes, namely attention control and response suppression, indeed differed in young children, at least in their dependence on short-term memory processes. In contrast, there were no differences between children of high and low spans in performance on inhibitory tasks parsed on the basis of type of conflict, interference from previous responses (proactive interference), or interference from irrelevant stimuli (distraction).

First, the inhibitory tasks generally were intercorrelated, with adequate coherence in content among the inhibitory tasks. Therefore, there was meaningful and coherent variation in performance across inhibitory tasks, at least in this young age range, even when the influence of age was removed. This communality differs from what is typically found in adults, where performance even on executive tasks that are quite similar in format often are unrelated (e.g., Shilling, Chetwynd, & Rabbitt, 2002). Immature abilities often are considered less differentiated, which likely resulted in greater coherence in inhibitory test performance than is observed in older children and adults. This communality, however, provides support that the tasks selected measure a common construct and further substantiate the examination of performance discrepancies among tasks with differing task demands.

In contrast to children with higher spans, children with lower memory spans were less able to inhibit an internally represented rule or response set that had been previously active or were less proficient in disengaging and controlling attention, which then interfered with the child's ability to engage and implement a newly relevant response or rule. These inhibitory task performance discrepancies among children of high and low spans are consistent with those observed by Engle and colleagues (Bleckley et al., 2003; Kane & Engle, 2000, 2002, 2003) in adults, using a similar design but a different span task by which to parse groups. These findings support Diamond's (Kirkham et al., 2003) attentional inertia conceptualization, where the young child's attention is pulled away from the response set at hand by stimulus properties that are discrepant from current task demands, thereby disrupting performance. In this view, better short-term memory facilitates the child in activating of one rule or response in one context, then cognitively disengaging when the context changes and, in turn, engaging another newly salient but competing response or set. More broadly, the key to well-regulated thought may be individual differences in the ability to control attention to maintain information in an active, quickly retrievable state (Engle, 2002). Short-term memory processes, however, are composed of encoding, storage, and retrieval components. Although performance differences in children of high and low spans were more evident on the Shape School Condition C, span-related differences were capture both by naming accuracy and speed. In this vein, one might speculate that both short-term memory storage and retrieval contributed to task performance, evidenced by naming accuracy and speed measures, respectively. Such a conceptualization also is consistent with Zelazo's view (Zelazo, Müller, Frye, & Marcovitch, 2003), where short-term memory processes might facilitate the coding of stimulus-response mappings or "rules" that, in turn, facilitate more efficient task performance in a top-down manner. However, with the present design and the crude dependent measure of digit span length, it is not possible to truly determine the relative roles of short-term storage or retrieval mechanisms in this observed effect, or whether digit span represents a proxy for the influences of other variables not considered here (e.g., general verbal ability).

Of note, performance differences between children of differing spans were most evident on Shape School Condition C relative to Visual Attention. Where both tasks require attentional control in the continual selective processing of differentially relevant stimuli features, only Condition C involves active selection of the relevant mapping of a differential response to the relevant stimulus feature. In Visual Attention, there is no selection among alternative responses, in that the child always stamps the relevant stimulus. In this age range, the greater, concurrent demands to control attention in the selection of both the relevant stimulus and relevant response likely is facilitated in children with better short-term memory. Carlson and Moses (2001) found that a matching figures task loaded on the Delay factor, which was not related to working memory (Carlson, Moses, & Breton, 2002), possibly because it requires suppressing an impulsive response to carefully inspect each item where memory demands are relatively low. Greater investigation of the relative attentional control demands through systematic variation at both the stimulus and response levels would be useful to address this issue.

In contrast, on inhibitory tasks considered to require response suppression, namely Shape School Condition B, Statue, and Delayed Search, performance did not differ in children with differing digit span lengths. In the preschool age range, rather, these findings broadly support Nigg's (2000) distinction, if "behavioral" inhibition is construed as response suppression and "cognitive" inhibition as attention control, at least in the differential dependence on short-term memory processes. Wilson and Kipp (1998) argued that attentional control is utilized to operate on the contents of working memory, providing the basis for resistance to interference and engendering fluid, regulated task performance. In the case of response suppression, short-term memory processes do not appear to play a role in individual differences in task proficiencies, suggesting that the behavioral inhibition occurs at a more primary, nonmnemonic level. Such findings may not be surprising given the often noted discrepancies on tasks of motor action/impulsivity and cognitive attention in children diagnosed with attention deficit hyperactivity disorder (e.g., Bedard et al., 2003; Nigg, 2001).

These findings also parallel the noted conflict versus delay distinction of Carlson and Moses (2001), where conflict tasks in that study are similar in scope to attention control tasks labeled here, and delay to the response suppression tasks. Of note is the consistency in findings, despite the younger age range in the Carlson and Moses study. Some have argued that response suppression tasks represent a form of inhibition that matures earlier in development and that such abilities emerge earlier in life (e.g., Anderson, 1998; Welsh, Pennington, & Groisser, 1991), in 2- and 3-year-olds for example, are earlier manifestations of later attentional control (e.g., Gerardi-Caulton, 2000). The pattern of correlations observed here sheds some light on this issue. Note the weak relation among performance on Statue and Shape School Condition B across children with differing digit span lengths studied here, suggesting that these types of suppression tasks may not be isomorphic. However, the pattern of relation to Shape School Condition B and the other response suppression task, Delayed Search, across digit span lengths differed, suggesting that response suppression per se may not develop early. Rather, proficiency in resolving conflict provided through *prohibited action* is an earlier, developmentally bound manifestation of attentional control. Performance on similar prohibited action tasks (e.g., Espy et al., 2001; Kochanska et al., 1996; Reed et al., 1984) provides such evidence for this view, both in studies using cross-sectional and longitudinal designs, as well as the lack of systematic differences in difficulty level across conflict and delay tasks across age (Carlson, this issue). However, caution is required when trying to discern patterns of ability maturation from observed test performance. Psychometrically, observed test performance is constrained both by true score variance, in this case the inhibitory process of interest, and error variance that here includes test specific variance. One of the particular challenges with characterizing the maturation of inhibitory processes is that inhibition necessarily includes some other abilities (the target of the inhibition), thereby necessarily increasing nonconstruct specific variance (Freidman & Miyake, 2004). Clearly, to address this question adequately, designs that include multiple measures of the relevant inhibitory construct are necessary to reliably characterize latent ability growth.

Based on examination of the demand characteristics of the differing inhibitory tasks and child performance on these tasks, it does not appear that the distinction between conflict type (i.e., between proactive interference and resistance to distraction) is a relevant one in this age range. In one view, short-term memory processes might be important in resistance to proactive interference, more broadly. However, based on the results shown here, the influence of short-term memory processes seems to be more limited to attention control, more specifically. These findings do not support Nigg's (2000) or Wilson and Kipp's (1998) distinction of interference control and are contrary to findings in adults by Friedman and Miyake (2004), who used structural equation modeling to characterize the distinct conflict demands. Statistical modeling likely is a superior procedure due to the latent nature of conflict demands, and the findings reported here might reflect the different statistical procedures and design. Because our study was conducted in preschool children, the discrepancy in findings simply may represent relative immaturity in preschool children relative to adults, in the cognitive system that recognizes variations in conflict demands. Alternatively, both types of conflict might elicit executive processes that are indistinguishable at this young age, unlike in adults. Further cross-sectional studies in school-age children, and longitudinal investigations that track the transition from the preschool to elementary school age ranges will be important to better address this issue.

Individual variations in digit span length also were not related to task performance that differed in the type of stimulus, in keeping with the domain-general view of inhibitory processes (e.g., Engle, 2002). Contrary to prediction, performance on tasks parsed by response type differed among children of varying spans, although the effect was limited to naming, a demand that is common to digit span also. The goal here was to include tasks with a sufficient range of demands, which varied in the type of stimulus, response, and conflict. The focus on using clinically available comparison tasks, similar to Friedman and Miyake (2004), to increase generalizability also was an important consideration. The disadvantage of this approach is that control of the task demands necessarily is reduced when using commercially available tasks. Therefore, it might be that if these specific demands were varied systematically one at a time, the pattern of results would differ. For example, comparisons between administrations of computerized Shape School tasks with a manual button press versus the verbal naming response would permit further examination of the effect of response type, at least in a task-specific manner. However, this approach is not without its own disadvantages, as the common variance is magnified due to shared methodology, making it difficult to discern the relative differences due to differential task demands (Friedman & Miyake, 2004).

In summary, these findings support the unique role of short-term memory processes in attentional control tasks in preschool children. Generally, there was communality in inhibitory task demands across instruments, where relevant performance distinctions among children of varying short-term memory spans were noted on tasks that required attention control, in contrast to those that had greater demands for response suppression. It would be useful to determine whether such a distinction is supported further by inhibitory task performance differences in children with specific neurological, medical, psychiatric, and developmental disorders. Although there are many different approaches to measuring executive control in this age range, there remains comparatively few that combine careful task demand analysis with a consideration of psychometric properties and generalizability. Certainly, there is more work to be done in the efforts to translate basic cognitive neuroscience into use in the clinical context.

ACKNOWLEDGMENTS

This research was supported, in part, by Grant 1R01 MH065668 from the National Institute of Mental Health; Grant 1R01 DA014661 from the National Institute on Drug Abuse; Grant 6R01 HD038051 from the National Institute of Child Health & Development; the Pediatric Neuropsychology/Developmental Cognitive Neuroscience Award from the Rita Rudel Foundation; the Special Research Program Award from the Southern Illinois University Office of Research Development and Administration to Kimberly Andrews Espy; and grants from the Carnegie Trust and British Academy to Rebecca Bull.

We thank the participating families, undergraduates, medical students, project staff, and graduate students who assisted in various laboratory tasks associated with this study. We also thank Stephanie Carlson for her insightful comments on a previous draft of this article.

REFERENCES

Allport, A., Styles, E. A., & Hsieh, S. (1994). Shifting intentional set: Exploring the dynamic control of tasks. In C. Umilta & M. Moscovitch (Eds.), *Attention and performance XV* (pp. 421–452). Cambridge, MA: MIT Press.

Allport, A., & Wylie, G. (2000). Task switching: Positive and negative priming of task set. In G. W. Humphreys, J. Duncan, & A. Triesman (Eds.), *Attention, space, and action: Studies in cognitive neuroscience* (pp. 273–296). London: Oxford University Press.

Anderson, V. (1998). Assessing executive functions in children: Biological, psychological, and developmental considerations. *Neuropsychological Rehabilitation, 8,* 319–349.

Anderson, V., Anderson, P., Grimwood, K., & Nolan, T. (2004). Cognitive and executive functions 12 years after childhood bacterial meningitis: Effect of acute neurologic complications and age of onset. *Journal of Pediatric Psychology, 29,* 67–82.

Baddeley, A. (1996). Exploring the central executive. *Quarterly Journal of Experimental Psychology, 49A,* 5–28.

Baddeley, A. D., & Hitch, G. J. (1994). Developments in the concept of working memory. *Neuropsychology, 8,* 485–493.

Bedard, A., Ickowicz, A., Logan, G., Hogg-Johnson, S., Schachar, R., & Tannock, R. (2003). Selective inhibition in children with attention-deficit hyperactivity disorder off and on stimulant medication. *Journal of Abnormal Child Psychology, 31,* 315–327.

Bishop, D. V. M., Aamodt-Leaper, G., Creswell, C., McGurk, R., & Skuse, D. H. (2001). Individual differences in cognitive planning on the Tower of Hanoi task: Neuropsychological maturity or measurement error? *Journal of Child Psychology and Psychiatry, 42,* 551–556.

Bleckley, M. K., Durso, F., Crutchfield, J., Engle, R., & Khanna, M. (2003). Individual differences in working memory capacity predict visual attention allocation. *Psychonomic Bulletin & Review, 10,* 884–889.

Brooks, P. J., Hanauer, J. B., Padowska, B., & Rosman, H. (2003). The role of selective attention in preschoolers' rule use in a novel dimensional card sort. *Cognitive Development, 18,* 195–215.

Bull, R., & Brown, E. L. (2004). *Understanding the inhibitory processes of the Day-Night task.* Manuscript submitted for publication.

Bull, R., Johnston, R. S., & Roy, J. A. (1999). Exploring the roles of the visual-spatial sketch pad and central executive in children's arithmetical skills: Views from cognition and developmental neuropsychology. *Developmental Neuropsychology, 15,* 421–442.

Bull, R., & Scerif, G. (2001). Executive functioning as a predictor of children's mathematics ability: Inhibition, switching, and working memory. *Developmental Neuropsychology, 19,* 273–293.

Carlson, S. M. (2005/this issue). Developmentally sensitive measures of executive function in preschool children. *Developmental Neuropsychology, 28,* 595–616.

Carlson, S. M., & Moses, L. J. (2001). Individual differences in inhibitory control and children's theory of the mind. *Child Development, 72,* 1032–1053.

Carlson, S. M., Moses, L. J., & Breton, C. (2002). How specific is the relation between executive function and theory of mind? Contributions of inhibitory control and working memory. *Infant & Child Development, 11,* 73–92.

Casey, B. J., Thomas, K. M., Welsh, T. F., Badgaiyan, R., Eccard, C. H., Jennings, J., et al. (2000). Dissociation of response conflict, attentional control, and expectancy with functional magnetic resonance imaging (fMRI). *Proceedings of the National Academy of Sciences, USA, 97,* 8728–8733.

Cowan, N. (1995). *Attention and memory: An integrated framework* (Oxford Psychology Series, No. 26). Oxford, UK: Oxford University Press.

Cowan, N. (1999). The differential maturation of two processing rates related to digit span. *Journal of Experimental Child Psychology, 72,* 193–209.

Dempster, F. N. (1993). Resistance to interference: Developmental changes in a basic processing dimension. In M. L. Howe & R. Pasnak (Eds.), *Emerging themes in cognitive development. Volume I: Foundations* (pp. 3–27). New York: Springer-Verlag.

Desimone, R., & Duncan, J. (1995). Neural mechanisms of selective attention visual attention. *Annual Review of Neuroscience, 18,* 193–222.

Diamond, A. (1988). Abilities and neural mechanisms underlying AB performance. *Child Development, 59,* 523–527.

Diamond, A., Briand, L., Fossella, J., & Gehlbach, L. (2004). Genetic and neurochemical modulation of prefrontal cognitive functions in children. *American Journal of Psychiatry, 161,* 125–132.

Diamond, A., & Kirkham, N. (2005). Not quite as grown-up as we like to think: Parallels between cognition in childhood and adulthood. *Psychological Science, 16,* 291–297.

Diamond, A., Kirkham, N., & Amso, D. (2002). Conditions under which young children can hold two rules in mind and inhibit a pre-potent response. *Developmental Psychology, 38,* 352–362.

Diamond, A., Prevor, M. B., Callender, G., & Druin, D. P. (1997). Prefrontal cortex cognitive deficits in children treated early and continuously for PKU. *Monographs of the Society for Research in Child Development, 62*(4), 1–205.

Diamond, A., & Taylor, C. (1996). Development of an aspect of executive control: Development of the abilities to remember what I said and to "Do as I say, not as I do". *Developmental Psychobiology, 29,* 315–334.

Durston, S., Thomas, K., Yang, Y., Ulug, A., Zimmerman, R. & Casey, B. J. (2002). A neural basis for the development of inhibitory control. *Developmental Science, 5,* F9–F16.

Engle, R. W. (2002). Working memory capacity as executive attention. *Current Directions in Psychological Science, 11,* 19–23.

Espy, K. A. (1997). The Shape School: Assessing executive function in preschool children. *Developmental Neuropsychology, 13*, 495–499.

Espy, K. A., Bull, R. B., & Martin, J. (2005). *Measuring the development of executive control with the Shape School.* Manuscript submitted for publication.

Espy, K. A., Kaufmann, P. M., & Glisky, M. L. (1999). Neuropsychological function in toddlers exposed to cocaine in utero: A preliminary study. *Developmental Neuropsychology, 15*, 447–460.

Espy, K. A., Kaufmann, P. M., Glisky, M. L., & McDiarmid, M. D. (2001). New procedures to assess executive functions in preschool children. *Clinical Neuropsychologist, 15*, 46–58.

Espy, K. A., Kaufmann, P. M., McDiarmid, M. D., & Glisky, M. L. (1999). Executive functioning in preschool children: Performance on A-not-B and other delayed response format tasks. *Brain and Cognition, 41*, 178–199.

Espy, K. A., McDiarmid, M. D., Cwik, M. F., Senn, T. E., Hamby, A., & Stalets, M. M. (2004). The contributions of executive functions to emergent mathematic skills in preschool children. *Developmental Neuropsychology, 26*, 465–486.

Espy, K. A., Stalets, M. M., McDiarmid, M. D., Senn, T. E., Cwik, M. F., & Hamby, A. (2002). Executive functions in preschool children born preterm: Application of cognitive neuroscience paradigms. *Child Neuropsychology, 8*, 83–92.

Ewing-Cobbs, L., Prasad, M. R., Landry, S. H., Kramer, L., & DeLeon, R. (2004). Executive functions following traumatic brain injury in young children: A preliminary analysis. *Developmental Neuropsychology, 26*, 487–512.

Freidman, N. P., & Miyake, A. (2004). The relations among inhibition and interference control functions: A latent-variable analysis. *Journal of Experimental Psychology: General, 133*, 101–135.

Gathercole, S. E., & Pickering, S. J. (2000). Working memory deficits in children with low achievements in the national curriculum at 7 years of age. *British Journal of Educational Psychology, 70*, 177–194.

Gerardi-Caulton, G. (2000). Sensitivity to spatial conflict and the development of self-regulation in children 24–36 months of age. *Developmental Science, 3*, 397–404.

Gerstadt, C. L., Hong, Y. J., & Diamond A. (1994). The relationship between cognition and action: Performance of 3.5- to 7-year-olds on Stroop-like Day-Night test. *Cognition, 53*, 129–153.

Han, S-H., & Kim, M-S. (2004). Visual search does not remain efficient when executive working memory is not working. *Psychological Science, 15*, 623–628.

Harnishfeger, K. K. (1995). The development of cognitive inhibition: Theories, definitions, and research evidence. In F. N. Dempster & C. J. Brainerd (Eds.), *Interference and inhibition in cognition* (pp. 175–204). San Diego, CA: Academic.

Hughes, C. (1998a). Executive function in preschoolers: Links with theory of mind and verbal ability. *British Journal of Developmental Psychology, 16*, 233–253.

Hughes, C. (1998b). Finding your marbles: Does preschoolers' strategic behavior predict later understanding of mind. *Developmental Psychology, 34*, 1326–1339.

Hughes, C., White, A., Sharpen, J., & Dunn, J. (2000). "Hard-to-manage" preschoolers' peer problems and possible cognitive influences. *Journal of Child Psychology & Psychiatry, 41*, 169–179.

Huttenlocher, P. R., & Dabholkar, A. S. (1997). Developmental anatomy of prefrontal cortex. In N. A. Krasnegor, G. R. Lyon, & P. S. Goldman-Rakic (Eds.), *Development of the prefrontal cortex: Evolution, neurobiology, and behavior* (pp. 69–83). Baltimore: Brookes.

Isquith, P. K., Gioia, G. A., & Espy, K. A. (2004). Executive function in preschool children: Examination through everyday behavior. *Developmental Neuropsychology, 26*, 403–422.

Kane, M. J., Bleckley, M. K., Conway, A. R. A., & Engle, R. W. (2001). A controlled-attention view of working-memory capacity. *Journal of Experimental Psychology: General, 130*, 169–183.

Kane, M. J., & Engle, R. W. (2000). Working-memory capacity, proactive intereference, and divided attention: Limits on long-term memory retrieval. *Journal of Experimental Psychology; Learning, Memory, & Cognition, 26,* 336–358.

Kane, M. J., & Engle, R. W. (2002). The role of the prefrontal cortex in working memory capacity, executive attention, and general fluid intelligence: An individual differences perspective. *Psychonomic Bulletin & Review, 9,* 637–671.

Kane, M. J., & Engle, R. W. (2003). Working-memory capacity and the control of attention: The contributions of goal neglect, response competition, and task set to Stroop interference. *Journal of Experimental Psychology: General, 132,* 47–70.

Kinney, H. C., Brody, B. A., Kloman, A. S., & Gilles, F. H. (1988). Sequence of central nervous system myelination in human infancy. *Journal of Neuropathology and Experimental Neurology, 47,* 217–234.

Kirkham, N. Z., Cruess, L., & Diamond, A. (2003). Helping children apply their knowledge to their behavior on a dimension-switching task. *Developmental Science, 6,* 449–467.

Kochanska, G., Murray, K., Jacques, T., Koenig, A., & Vandegeest, K. (1996). Inhibitory control in young children and its role in emerging internalization. *Child Development, 67,* 490–507.

Korkman, M., Kirk, U., & Kemp, S. (1998). *NEPSY: A developmental neuropsychological assessment manual.* San Antonio, TX: The Psychological Corporation.

Mayr, U., & Keele, S. W. (2000). Changing internal constraints on action: The role of backward inhibition. *Journal of Experimental Psychology: General, 129,* 4–26.

Miller, E. K. (2000). The prefrontal cortex and cognitive control. *Nature Neuroscience, 1,* 59–65.

Nigg, J. T. (2000). On inhibition/disinhibition in developmental psychopathology: View from cognitive and personality psychology and a working inhibition taxonomy. *Psychological Bulletin, 126,* 220–246.

Nigg, J. T. (2001). Is ADHD a disinhibitory disorder? *Psychological Bulletin, 127,* 571–598.

O'Reilly, R. C., Noelle, D. C., Braver, T. S., & Cohen, J. D. (2002). Prefrontal cortex and dynamic categorization tasks: Representational organization and neuromodulatory control. *Cerebral Cortex, 12,* 246–257.

Pennington, B. F., & Ozonoff, S. (1996). Executive functions and developmental psychopathology. *Journal of Child Psychology & Psychiatry & Allied Disciplines, 37,* 51–87.

Perner, J., & Lang, B. (2002). What causes 3-year-olds difficulty on the Dimensional Change Card Sorting task? *Infant and Child Development, 11,* 93–105.

Perner, J., Lang, B., & Kloo, D. (2002). Theory of mind and self control: More than a common problem of inhibition. *Child Development, 73,* 752–767.

Posner, M. I., & Petersen, S. E. (1990). The attention system of the human brain. *Annual Review of Neuroscience, 13,* 25–42.

Prevor, M., & Diamond, A. (2005). Color-object interference in young children: A Stroop effect in children 3½ to 6½ years old. *Cognitive Development, 20,* 256–278.

Ready, R., Stierman, L., & Paulsen, J. S. (2001). Ecological validity of neuropsychological and personality measures of executive functions. *The Clinical Neuropsychologist, 15,* 314–323.

Reed, M. A., Pien, D. L., & Rothbart, M. K. (1984). Inhibitory self-control in pre-school children. *Merrill-Palmer Quarterly, 30,* 131–147.

Rennie, D., Bull, R., & Diamond, A. (2004). Executive functioning in preschoolers: Reducing the inhibitory demands of the Dimensional Change Card Sort task. *Developmental Neuropsychology, 26,* 423–443.

Roberts, R. J., Jr., & Pennington, B. F. (1996). An interactive framework for examining prefrontal cognitive processes. *Developmental Neuropsychology, 12,* 105–126.

Shilling, V. M., Chetwynd, A., & Rabbitt, P. M. A. (2002). Individual inconsistency across measures of inhibition: An investigation of the construct validity of inhibition in older adults. *Neuropsychologia, 40,* 605–619.

Thatcher, R. W. (1997). Human frontal lobe development: A theory of cyclical cortical eorganization. In N. A. Krasnegor, G. R. Lyon, & P. S. Goldman-Rakic (Eds.), *Development of the prefrontal cortex: Evolution, neurobiology, and behavior* (pp. 85–113). Baltimore: Brookes.

Tipper, S. P., & Cranston, M. (1985). Selective attention and priming: Inhibitory and facilitatory effects of ignored primes. *Quarterly Journal of Experimental Psychology, 37,* 591–611.

Welsh, M. C., Pennington, B. F., & Groisser, D. B. (1991). A normative-developmental study of executive function: a window on prefrontal function in children. *Developmental Neuropsychology, 7,* 131–149.

Wilson, S. P., & Kipp, K. (1998). The development of efficient inhibiton: Evidence from directed-forgetting tasks. *Developmental Review, 18,* 86–123.

Wright, I., Waterman, M., Prescott, H., & Murdoch-Eaton, D. (2003). A new stroop-like measure of inhibitory function development: Typical developmental trends. *Journal of Child Psychology & Psychiatry, 44,* 561–575.

Zelazo, P. D., Frye, D., & Rapus, T. (1996). An age-related dissociation between knowing rules and using them. *Cognitive Development, 11,* 37–63.

Zelazo, P. D., Müller, U., Frye, D., & Marcovitch, S. (2003). The development of executive function in childhood. *Monographs of the Society for Research in Child Development, 68*(3, Serial No. 274).

DEVELOPMENTAL NEUROPSYCHOLOGY, *28*(2), 689–729

Preschool Children's Performance in Task Switching on the Dimensional Change Card Sort Task: Separating the Dimensions Aids the Ability to Switch

Adele Diamond
Department of Psychiatry
University of British Columbia, Vancouver
Department of Child & Adolescent Psychiatry
BC Children's Hospital, Vancouver

Stephanie M. Carlson and Danielle M. Beck
Department of Psychology
University of Washington, Seattle

Fifty-seven children (53% female) at 3 ages (2½, 3, and 3½ years) were tested on the standard Dimensional Change Card Sort (DCCS) task with integrated stimuli (e.g., a red truck) and on a separated-dimensions version where colorless shapes were presented on a colored background (e.g., a black truck on a red background). Roughly twice as many children successfully switched sorting dimensions when color was a property of the background than when color was a property of the shape itself. Children succeeded 6 months earlier in switching sorting criteria when the dimensions were separated. When evidence of both indecision and accuracy was taken into account, a clear and rich developmental progression emerged. These results support an inhibitory control interpretation of preschoolers' problems on the DCCS task. Diamond theorized that young children can have difficulty integrating features not part of a single object and separating features of a single object so that the object can be categorized first by one attribute and then by another. Preschoolers remain stuck in thinking about objects according to the objects' initially relevant attribute (*attentional inertia*; Kirkham, Cruess, & Diamond, 2003). To switch perspectives,

---

Correspondence should be addressed to Adele Diamond, Department of Psychiatry, University of British Columbia, 2255 Wesbrook Mall, Vancouver, BC, Canada V6T 2A1. E-mail: adele.diamond@ubc.ca

the old way of thinking about the objects must be inhibited. Separating color and shape reduced the need for such inhibition; a truck was always a truck, and the background was always red.

PERCEIVING RELATIONS BETWEEN SEPARATED OBJECTS AND SEPARATING FEATURES OF A SINGLE OBJECT

Diamond has theorized that very young children have difficulty *integrating* features that are not part of a single object (e.g., relating the color of the background to the shape of an item in the foreground or relating a reward object to a stimulus object; Diamond, Churchland, Cruess, & Kirkham, 1999; Diamond, Lee, & Hayden, 2003) and, the flip side, that very young children have difficulty *separating* features of a single object (e.g., flexibly reacting to something first in terms of its being a truck and then moments later in terms of its being a red thing; Diamond & Kirkham, 2005; Kirkham, Cruess, & Diamond, 2003; Kirkham & Diamond, 2003). In this article we address the latter—separating features of a single object.

On the Dimensional Change Card Sort (DCCS) task, each card contains a simple drawing of a familiar object (such as a truck or star) in a primary color (Zelazo, Frye, & Rapus, 1996). Children 3 years of age can sort the cards flawlessly by color or shape. When asked to switch from sorting by color to sorting by shape (or vice versa), however, most 3-year-olds do not switch; they continue to sort as they had before. This is striking because the experimenter makes a point of saying that the sorting criterion has changed and before every trial either reminds the child of the sorting rules (e.g., "We are playing the color game now, and in the color game, red ones go here and blue ones go there") or asks the child where the red ones (or trucks) and where the blue ones (or stars) go, and the child points correctly. Children of 3 years thus err despite knowing and remembering the rules. This was first observed by Zelazo and colleagues (Zelazo et al., 1996) and has been observed in other laboratories in the United States (Kirkham et al., 2003; Munakata & Yerys, 2001), Austria (Kloo & Perner, 2005; Perner & Lang, 2002), Canada (Bialystok & Martin, 2004; Jacques, Zelazo, Kirkham, & Semcesen, 1999; Zelazo, Mueller, Frye, & Marcovitch, 2003), England (Riggs & Williams, 2003; Towse, Redbond, Houston-Price, & Cook, 2000), and Scotland (Rennie, Bull, & Diamond, 2004).

Diamond and Kirkham hypothesized that the difficulty 3-year-olds have in switching from sorting by color or shape to sorting by the other is a difficulty in thinking about the same thing from two different perspectives. Having thought about the primary feature of a truck being its color, it is difficult for 3-year-olds to then flip their mental focus and think about the same item ignoring its color, attending only to its shape. Diamond and Kirkham named children's tendency to continue to react to a stimulus according to its initially relevant attribute *attentional inertia* (Diamond & Kirkham, 2005; Kirkham et al., 2003; Kirkham & Diamond, 2003). Three-year-olds quickly become used to focusing on the blueness or redness of a stimulus or on its object-kind property (that it is a truck or a star) and have great difficulty switching the way they think about the stimuli. Once they have focused their attention on one dimension, their attention gets stuck there.

> It is not that they fail to realize that something can be both blue and a truck. But, having adopted the mindset that blue things go with the blue model card, they have great difficulty switching to think of a blue truck in terms of its shape and sorting it with the red-truck model card, even though they are told that the correct dimension is now shape. We posit that 3-year-old children's difficulty lies in disengaging from a mindset (a way of thinking about the stimuli) that is no longer relevant. (Kirkham et al., 2003, p. 451)

Even adults have difficulty when required to switch tasks or dimensions, as the rich literature on task switching so clearly demonstrates (e.g., Allport, Styles, & Hsieh, 1994; Mayr & Keele, 2000; Monsell & Driver, 2000; Rogers & Monsell, 1995; Waszak, Hommel, & Allport, 2003). Adults are able to switch sorting dimensions in the DCCS task, but they show the same pattern in their reaction time (RT) as 3-year-olds show in their accuracy (Diamond & Kirkham, 2005). Their inertial "stuckness" on the first dimension is evident not only in their slower RTs when the sorting criterion changes but in slower RTs on the second dimension (faster RTs on whichever dimension they started with) throughout the testing session (Diamond & Kirkham, 2005).

Evidence from a number of different domains supports the conclusion that children 3 years of age have difficulty thinking about the same thing in two different ways. For 3-year-olds, something is either A or B, but not both (e.g., an object is either a bunny or a rabbit, but not both; Perner, Stummer, Sprung, & Doherty, 2002). Many studies have illustrated this mutual exclusivity bias (Carey & Bartlett, 1978; Markman & Wachtel, 1988). Remnants of this can be seen perhaps in adults' difficulty in representing more than one interpretation at a time of an ambiguous figure (Chambers & Reisberg, 1992). For 3-year-olds the problem is more profound: Even when shown the alternatives in an ambiguous figure, many 3-year-olds are still unable to see more than one perspective in the figure (Gopnik & Rosati, 2001). Similarly on appearance-reality tasks (Flavell, Green, & Flavell, 1986), where children are shown something that appears to be one thing (e.g., a rock) but is really something else (e.g., a sponge), 3-year-olds typically say that it looks like a sponge and really is a sponge or that it looks like a rock and really is a rock, but rarely will a 3-year-old give the correct answer that it looks like a rock but really is a sponge. Children 3 years of age can conceive of it as a rock or as a sponge but not as a rock from one perspective and a sponge from another.

It is interesting that 3-year-olds *can* switch tasks if they do not have to switch the focus of their attention. When the stimuli vary along only one dimension, 3-year-olds can switch from sorting trucks with trucks and stars with stars to sorting trucks with stars and stars with trucks (Brooks, Hanauer, Padowska, & Rosman, 2003; Perner & Lang, 2002). Here, they do not have to change how they are thinking about the stimuli; a truck is always a truck and a star is always a star.

If, however, some trucks (and stars) are yellow and others blue (color varying orthogonally with the relevant dimension [shape]), children of 3 years fail the task (although color is never relevant; Brooks, Hanauer, & Rosman, 2001). Similarly, Shepp and Barrett (1991; Barrett & Shepp, 1988; Shepp, Barrett, & Kolbet, 1987) found that children 4 to 5 years of age seem unable to focus on just the relevant dimension when two dimensions are properties of the same integrated stimuli. However, they found that children could successfully focus on just one dimension, ignoring irrelevant variation in the other, when the dimensions were spatially separated. Spatial separation likewise aids adults' performance on the Stroop task. Adults find it difficult to switch between naming the ink color and reading the word of integrated Stroop stimuli (color words, such as *green*, written in the ink of another color, such as red). In that example, the incongruent ink color (red) is an attribute of the word *green*. Adults perform much better if the incongruent color, although present, is not an attribute of the word itself. Thus, adults perform better when the color and word are spatially separated (e.g., the word is written in black ink with a bar of another ink color above or below the word; Kahneman & Chajczyk, 1983; MacLeod, 1998).

There is considerable evidence that when adults attend to one aspect of an integrated stimulus, they, like children, cannot help but process its irrelevant features as well. For example, Garner and Felfoldy (1970) found facilitation with correlated dimensions and interference with orthogonal dimensions in adults when both dimensions were integral properties of all stimuli. When the dimensions were separated and properties of different stimuli, adults showed neither facilitation nor interference. Ridderinkhof, van der Molen, Band, and Bashore (1997) reported similar results in children 5 to 12 years old using a selective attention task. With integrated stimuli, responses were slowest in the correlated conditions, intermediate in neutral conditions, and fastest in orthogonal conditions. At all ages, responses were slower when the dimensions of color and orientation were integrated than when they were spatially separated. Impressively, Pratt and Hommel (2003, Exp. 4) showed that not only is an irrelevant feature (color) of an integrated stimulus processed by adults but if that irrelevant feature (the same color) then appears as part of a wholly irrelevant stimulus (an arrow), that wholly irrelevant stimulus then influences adults' performance.

In a manuscript in preparation, Diamond (2005) proposed an "all or none hypothesis"—that the brain, mind, and body initially work at a gross level and only with fine-tuning act in a more differentiated manner. One example is that it is easier to take into account *all* salient aspects of a stimulus than just its color or just its shape. That is, unbinding (rather than binding) is a problem as far as the properties of individual entities are concerned, as the studies just cited illustrate. Indeed, Schoenfeld et al. (2003) reported evidence at the neural level for rapid, automatic binding. Unbinding would require inhibiting or undoing that process.

INHIBITORY CONTROL IS NEEDED WHEN THE OLD WAY OF THINKING ABOUT THE STIMULI (WHEN ATTENTIONAL INERTIA) MUST BE SUPPRESSED

In accord with Diamond and Kirkham (2005; Kirkham et al., 2003; Kirkham & Diamond, 2003), we contend that inhibition is needed to switch from sorting by color (or shape) to sorting by the other dimension on the standard DCCS because switching sorting criteria requires that the participant flip from thinking about an object (e.g., a truck) first as a blue thing to thinking about it as a truck (or vice versa), and that requires inhibition of the initial mind-set (inhibition of the inertial tendency to continue to attend to the initially relevant attribute, to continue to think about [and react to] the stimuli in the same way one has been thinking about [and reacting to] them). If one is to flexibly switch perspectives (flexibly switch sorting criteria), one must be able to quickly and efficiently inhibit one's previous perspective and previous stimulus-response mappings.

If, however, one's old perspective does not need to be inhibited—if one never has to change how one thinks about a truck—then children should be able to succeed on the DCCS task at a younger age. Changing perspectives is required when color and shape are integral properties of the same thing. No change in perspective is required, however, if color is a property of the background rather than of the shape itself. With the dimensions separated, children would never have to think about the trucks (or stars) as anything but trucks and stars and would never have to think about the background as anything but red or blue. We therefore predicted that more 3-year-olds would successfully switch sorting dimensions if color was not an attribute of the stimulus object but instead a property of the background, even though the same colors and shapes would appear on all stimulus cards. In addition to testing our prediction that children of 3 and 3½ years would be better able to switch sorting criteria when the dimensions are separated, we also investigated whether even children of only 2½ years might be helped by the separated dimensions condition.

EARLIER REPORTS OF PRESCHOOLERS'
PERFORMANCE ON SEPARATED-DIMENSIONS
VERSIONS ON THE DCCS TASK

There is some disagreement in the literature about whether separating the dimensions only on the sorting cards or only on the model cards is sufficient to help preschoolers succeed in switching sorting dimensions. Mueller (Mueller, Dick, Gela, Overton, & Zelazo, 2004; Zelazo et al., 2003, Exp. 6) tested preschoolers with color and shape separated in a rather unusual way on the sorting cards while remaining integrated on the model cards (using standard DCCS model cards) and found that performance was no better than in the standard condition. Kloo and Perner (2005, Exp. 1) found that separating the dimensions on only the sorting cards greatly increased the number of preschoolers who successfully switched sorting dimensions. Both the Mueller studies and the Kloo and Perner studies found that separating the dimensions only on the model cards did not help; however, studies where the dimensions have been separated on the model cards by providing one model card for each value on each dimension (four model cards) have shown dramatically better switching performance in preschoolers (Rennie, Bull, & Diamond, 2004; Towse, Redbond, Houston-Price, & Cook, 2000).

Only one study, other than the one reported here, has looked at the effect on preschoolers' task switching performance of separating the sorting dimensions on both the sorting and the model cards. Simultaneously and independently, while our study was underway, Kloo and Perner (2005) tested a separated-dimensions condition where their sorting and model cards contained the outline of a colorless (white) shape on one side of a small, white card and a filled-in colored circle on the other side of each card (see Figure 1). In both a between-subjects study (Exp. 1) and a within-subjects one (Exp. 3), they found that significantly more preschoolers were able to succeed when the dimensions were separated.

Our procedure puts the prediction of better performance in the separated condition to a somewhat more rigorous test than did Kloo and Perner (2005), or at least allows certain alternative explanations to be discarded that their procedure did not. With the Kloo and Perner stimuli, children could possibly solve the task by restricting the focus of their attention to the right side of the cards when sorting by color and the left side when sorting by shape. Shape and color were spatially segregated on the cards, and each were properties of things. In our procedure, shape and color are contiguous. Shape is a property of the foreground object and color is a property of the background bordering the object on all sides. Other minor differences are that we included younger children (down to 2½ years of age), administered slightly more trials, and used a slightly more stringent criterion. We administered six trials per dimension, and our criterion for success in switching was getting at least five of the six postswitch trials correct. Kloo and Perner administered five trials per dimension and used a criterion of at least four of five correct.

Kloo & Perner Model Cards

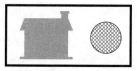   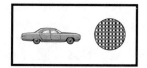

Outline of house with green circle   Outline of car with yellow circle

Kloo & Perner Sorting Cards

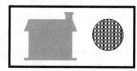   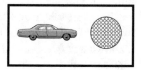

Outline of house with yellow circle   Outline of car with green circle

FIGURE 1   An illustration of the stimuli used for the separated dimensions condition by Kloo and Perner (2005) in their Experiment 3.

METHOD

Participants

A total of 57 children provided the data reported here (27 boys, 30 girls). Children in three age groups were tested: 2½-year-olds (*M* age = 32.1 months, range = 29.3–34.4 months, *SD* = 1.7), 3-year-olds (*M* age = 37.6 months, range = 35.8–40.4 months, *SD* = 1.3), and 3½-year-olds (*M* age = 43.1 months, range = 41.2–45.7 months, *SD* = 1.3). At 2½ years of age, 19 children were tested, and 63% were female. At 3 years, 24 children were tested; 46% were female. At 3½ years, 14 children were tested; 50% were female.

Half the children (29) were tested by the Carlson Lab and half (28) by the Diamond Lab. Those studied by the Carlson Lab were recruited from a database of families who expressed an interest in participating in research studies. All were tested by Danielle Beck or Stacy Underwood and were tested in a quiet testing room at the University of Washington, Seattle. Those studied by the Diamond Lab in Massachusetts were tested in a quiet testing room at the Center for Developmental Cognitive Neuroscience, Shriver Center Campus, University of Massachusetts Medical School, Waltham, MA, from a database of families who expressed interest in participating in research studies. All were tested by Aaron Baker or Adele Diamond. Those studied by the Diamond Lab in British Columbia were tested in a quiet room at the children's preschool by Adele Diamond. In all cases, approval by the relevant Human Subjects Committee was obtained prior to testing as was informed consent from a parent of each child, the rights of all study participants were protected, and each child received a small present for participating. Most were Euro-Caucasian from middle-class homes.

We attempted to test another 39 children, but their data could not be used. Five did not know their colors or understand English well enough to pass the training (4 were 2½ years old and 1 was 3 years old). Eight children of 2½ years did not meet the criterion for inclusion in the study because they failed the preswitch phase (described in the Methods section). They tended to sort all cards into the same sorting bin (5 of these children did this for both the separated and the integrated conditions, 3 did this only for the integrated dimension). Three children 3 years of age and 2 children 3½ years of age also failed the preswitch phase and so could not be included. Two children (both 3 years old), tested by the Diamond lab, got 67% or more of the knowledge questions (described in the Methods section) wrong and therefore were deemed not to show sufficient understanding of the task to be included. (The Carlson Lab included children who performed poorly on the knowledge questions and details on that appear in the Results section.) Thirteen children refused to complete testing: 8 children were 2 years old (6 refused to do the integrated condition and 2 refused the separated condition), 4 children were 3 years old, and 1 child was 3½ years old (all 5 refused the integrated condition). Finally, six sessions were unusable due to experimenter error (four sessions were with 3-year-olds and two were with 2½-year-olds).

Materials

The materials consisted of model (or target) cards and sorting cards (also called stimulus or test cards) for both integrated and separated dimensions conditions with two training cards for each, and two sorting trays. All cards were laminated, white on the reverse side, and the same size (9 × 11 cm). The back wall of each sorting tray was 28 × 13 cm, and the base was 13 × 11 cm.

The two model cards for the integrated condition depicted a red truck or a blue star on a white background. Each was mounted on the back wall of one sorting tray. The sorting cards for the integrated condition depicted a red star or blue truck on a white background. Thus the sorting cards matched the model cards on only one dimension (shape or color), and the correct answer when sorting by color (or shape) was the wrong answer when sorting by the other (see Figure 2). The integrated condition corresponds exactly to the standard DCCS testing condition, and the model and stimulus cards used here for the integrated condition are identical to those used by Kirkham et al. (2003) for their DCCS testing.

The two model cards for the separated condition depicted a black car on a green background or a black phone on a yellow background. Each was mounted on the back wall of one sorting tray. Each sorting card for the separated condition depicted a black phone on a green background or a black car on a yellow background.

Sorting Boxes With Model Cards Affixed

Red Truck   Blue Star

The Cards to be Sorted

Red Star   Blue Truck

FIGURE 2   An illustration of the stimuli used in the work reported for the integrated condition. Reprinted from Kirkham, Cruess, and Diamond (2003), with permission.

As with the integrated condition, each sorting card matched a model card on one dimension (shape or color), and the correct answer when sorting by color (or shape) was the wrong answer when sorting by the other (see Figure 3).

For the Diamond Lab's testing, the two training cards for the integrated condition for sorting by color depicted a red boat or blue bird. The corresponding train-

Sorting Boxes With Model Cards Affixed

Black Car on Green Card   Black Phone on Yellow Card

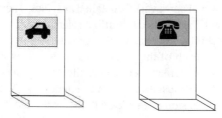

The Cards to be Sorted

Black Phone on Green Card   Black Car on Yellow Card

FIGURE 3   An illustration of the stimuli used in the work reported for the separated condition.

ing cards for the Carlson Lab depicted a red or blue bird. The two training cards for the integrated condition for sorting by shape in the Diamond Lab depicted a green truck or yellow star. For the Carlson Lab, the corresponding training cards depicted a yellow truck or star.

For the sessions conducted by the Diamond Lab, the two training cards for the separated condition for sorting by color depicted a black airplane on a yellow background or a black pumpkin on a green background. For the Carlson Lab, the corresponding training cards were a black boat on a yellow background or on a green background. The two training cards used by the Diamond Lab for the separated condition for sorting by shape depicted a black car on a blue background or a black phone on a red background. The corresponding training cards used by the Carlson Lab were a black car on a red background or a black phone on a red background. In all other respects the training cards for both labs were identical to those used for testing—the same size, color (white), and laminate.

Thus, for both labs, the training cards matched the model cards on only one dimension. Whereas in the Diamond Lab each training card contained a different color and shape, in the Carlson Lab the value on the irrelevant dimension was kept constant on the two training cards for a given Condition × Dimension practice.

Procedure

All children were tested on both conditions. Order of presentation of conditions (integrated and separated) was counterbalanced across children within each Age × Gender × Lab cell, and this was crossed with the order of presentation of the sorting dimensions (color and shape), which was also counterbalanced across children within each Age × Gender × Lab cell. All children were tested individually by an experimenter who sat at a preschool-size table with the child. All sessions were videotaped (with parental approval) for detailed analyses. The child was shown the two sorting boxes with the model cards affixed (facing the child). First the experimenter verified the child's object and color knowledge: The experimenter identified one dimension of each of the model cards (e.g., "This is a car and this is a phone."). Then the experimenter queried the child, "Can you point to the phone? to the car?" and provided enthusiastic, supportive feedback. Then the experimenter identified the other dimension of each card ("This is red and this is blue") and then queried the child, again with enthusiastic, supportive feedback.

Next the experimenter began the training for the second dimension that would be tested by saying that they could play the color (or shape) game:

In the color (shape) game, all the red ones (trucks) go here and all the blue ones (stars) go there. [Experimenter pointed to each appropriate tray] So, red ones (trucks) go in this tray, and blue ones (stars) go in this tray. [Experimenter models sort.] Okay? Can you point to where the red ones (trucks) go? And where do the blue ones (stars) go? [For each, the experimenter praised the child if correct, or corrected the child and repeated the instructions if incorrect.] Here's a red one (truck); where does this one go? Here's a blue one (star); where does this one go? [For each, the child sorted the card by placing it in a tray. The experimenter enthusiastically praised the child when correct and gently corrected the child and repeated the instructions when the child erred. If the child placed a card faceup, the experimenter praised the child for the correct sort and turned the card over so that it was facedown.]

Then the experimenter pointed out that they could also play the shape (color) game and repeated the procedure just indicated for sorting by that dimension. Note that there was only one correct answer for sorting any training card, as each card matched only one model and on only the relevant dimension. There was no conflict between the correct answer when sorting by color and the correct answer when sorting by shape.

Each child was given four training cards to sort (one card per value per dimension), and those cards could be presented a maximum of twice (allowing for one error per either value of either dimension). Children had to sort all four cards correctly (both for each dimension) to pass the training phase.

The last dimension sorted during training was always the first dimension administered for testing. Test trials started immediately and seamlessly after training. The same pseudo-random order of card presentation was used for all children. Before each trial, the child was either reminded of both rules for the current game or asked to demonstrate knowledge of both rules for the current game by pointing to the appropriate trays in answer to the experimenter's "knowledge" questions (e.g., "Where do the red ones go in the color game? Where do the blue ones go in the color game?"). On alternating trials the experimenter either reminded the child of the rules or asked the child the knowledge questions. Order of value (e.g., red or blue) mentioned first was randomly varied.

Children were given feedback both during training and on their responses to the knowledge questions during testing, but not on their sorting performance during testing. No comment or reaction of any kind was made to the child's sorts during testing. Each sorting card was left facedown in the tray so that the image depicted on the card was not visible. If a child placed a card faceup, the experimenter simply turned over the card. On the rare occasion when a child answered a knowledge question incorrectly, the experimenter reiterated the rules and asked the knowledge questions again. Immediately after the knowledge questions or the experimenter's reiteration of the rules, a sorting card was presented. The experimenter always labeled only the currently relevant dimension of the card when presenting it (e.g., "Here's a blue one. Where does it go?" or "Here's a truck. Where does it go?"), as is standard practice for DCCS testing in virtually every lab that uses this task (e.g., Kirkham et al., 2003; Kloo & Perner, 2005; Zelazo et al., 2003).

A child had to sort six cards in a row correctly by the first dimension to pass the preswitch phase. Only children who passed the preswitch were included in analyses of postswitch performance. Occasionally, a child did not quite understand the game on the first or second trial. Therefore, children were given up to eight trials to get six trials correct in a row on the first dimension. Then the experimenter announced that they were not going to play that game anymore but were going to start playing the other game instead:

> We're not going to play that game anymore! No way! Let's play the color (shape) game now. Remember, in the color (shape) game, all the blue ones (trucks) go here, and all the red ones (stars) go there. [Experimenter pointed to the appropriate trays.] Can you point and show me where the blue ones (trucks) go? Can you point and show me where the red ones (stars) go? [For each, the child pointed and received feedback.]

Testing on the second dimension then began, "Here's a blue one (truck). Where does it go?" Six trials were administered using the same procedure as just described—reiteration of the two current rules or querying of the child's knowledge of the two current rules with feedback before each trial, only the relevant dimension of each stimulus card labeled on each trial, no feedback of any kind on sorting performance, and each card left facedown in the sorting tray. Cards were not removed between testing of the first and second dimension but were left facedown where they had been placed.

After administering both dimensions of the first condition for a given session, the experimenter announced that the game was over. There was a brief break as the experimenter put away all the cards for the first condition (both the model and test cards), affixed new model cards to the back wall of the sorting trays, and retrieved a new set of sorting cards. The experimenter announced that they would now play two more games, and exactly the same procedure as just described was repeated—first verifying the child's object and shape knowledge, then providing training on both dimensions, testing one dimension, and switching to test the second dimension. For all training and testing, a child's sorting response was counted once the child placed the card in a sorting tray and let go of the card. As long as a child held onto a card, the child was allowed to change his or her mind. Indications of indecision, such as first going toward one tray and then the other, were recorded as "hesitations" and were included in descriptive analyses. The only difference between the two conditions was in the stimuli (the model and sorting cards); in all other respects the testing procedure for both conditions was identical.

RESULTS

Passing training was defined as sorting one card for each value of each dimension correctly (i.e., one yellow truck, one yellow star, one red grapes, and one blue grapes card). Most children (93%) did this in the minimum number of trials possible (four, one per each value of each dimension). Two children at 2½ years of age needed more training trials in the integrated condition; one of these children needed one additional trial and another needed two additional trials. One 3-year-old needed one additional trial to pass training in the separated condition. One 3½-year-old needed an additional trial to pass training in the integrated condition.

The vast majority of children needed only six trials to get six correct in a row on the first sorting dimension. Virtually all children (95%) in all conditions sorted all the cards correctly during the preswitch phase. Three children, one in each age group, needed one additional trial (seven total to get six in a row correct on the initial dimension)—a 2½-year-old and a 3-year-old in the integrated condition and a 3½-year-old in the separated condition.

Naturally, studies will find that children perform well on the knowledge questions even if they fail in their sorting responses if those children who fail the knowledge questions are deemed unuseable because they have not demonstrated sufficient understanding of the sorting rules. Therefore, the Carlson Lab did not eliminate any child from the analyses because of poor performance on the knowledge questions. There were three knowledge questions per each pre- and postswitch phase of each condition. Between the two labs, five children (9%) made one error on a knowledge question in the integrated condition, and four children (7%) made one error on a knowledge question in the separated condition. Two thirds of those errors (six errors) occurred during the postswitch phase (i.e., when quizzed about the rules for sorting by the second dimension). In addition, the Carlson Lab included four children who erred on 67% or more of the knowledge questions in the separated condition and three children who failed 67% or more of the knowledge questions in the integrated condition. Again, most of these errors were in the postswitch phase.

After the switch to the second dimension, 77% of the time every card was sorted correctly or every card was sorted incorrectly. In both conditions, almost all the children got either (a) five or six of six trials correct (separated condition, 35%; integrated condition, 16%) or (b) five or six of six trials wrong (separated condition, 56% [most at 2½ years]; integrated condition, 75%). In the separated condition, one child got two postswitch sorts correct, two children were correct on three postswitch trials, and two children were correct on four postswitch trials. Together these five sessions account for less than 10% of the separated-conditions data. In the integrated condition, two children got two postswitch sorts correct, three children were correct on three postswitch trials, and one child was correct on four postswitch trials. These five sessions account for less than 10% of the integrated-conditions data.

Given the lack of variance and the markedly bimodal nature of the data, analyzing the data using an analysis of variance would have been inappropriate, even with transformations of the data, such as logarithmic transforms. Binary logistic regression was used to analyze the dichotomous outcome variable "passed or failed" when looking at performance individually on the integrated or separated condition. For comparing performance between the two conditions, a nonparametric within-subject Wilcoxon signed rank test was used to compare the percentage of correct postswitch responses, the McNemar test was used to compare the percentage of children successfully switching sorting dimensions, and generalized linear mixed models (Diggle, Liang, & Zeger, 1994) for binary outcomes with repeated measures was used to compare performance on the dichotomous measure "passed or failed." These models were fit by the method of Generalized Estimating Equations with a logit link function (Fitzmaurice, 1998; Zeger, Liang, & Albert, 1988). When significant fixed main or interaction effects were found, hypotheses concerning combinations of effects were evaluated by comparing simpler models fit on subsets of the data (Fitzmaurice, 1998; Liang & Zeger, 1986; Palta & Lin, 1999; Stiratelli, Laird, & Ware, 1984; Zeger et al., 1988) by generalized linear mixed models. Models were fit using SAS Proc GENMOD (SAS Institute Inc., 1990).

All significance levels reported are for two-tailed tests, but given that we had a very clear prediction that performance would be better in the separated than in the integrated condition, one-tailed tests would certainly have been justified for all comparisons between the two conditions.

No significant differences were found by gender, order in which the conditions were tested, order in which the dimensions were tested, or the lab conducting the testing. There were no significant interactions among any of those four variables.

There was no significant difference by age in performance on integrated dimensions (the standard DCCS task). There was a significant improvement over age, however, in whether a child passed the postswitch phase when the dimensions were separated (Wald statistic [3] = 3.98, $p < .05$). Post hoc tests revealed significantly more 3½-year-old children than 2½ year olds successfully switched sorting criteria on separated dimensions (Wald statistic [2] = 4.44, $p < .04$).

Consistent with previous reports (e.g., Rennie et al., 2004; Zelazo et al., 1995, 1996), most of the children tested performed poorly on the standard DCCS task (integrated dimensions). Only 32% successfully switched dimensions. As predicted, however, performance was significantly better in the separated dimensions condition, where 62% successfully switched dimensions. The mean percentages of correct responses on the second dimension (postswitch) are portrayed in Figure 4. As is apparent from the figure, children were able to get roughly twice as many postswitch trials correct when the dimensions were separated than when the dimensions (color and shape) were properties of the same object. Wilcoxon within-subject signed pairs comparisons revealed that this dif-

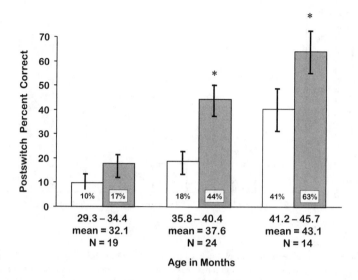

FIGURE 4   The percentage of correct sorting responses after the sorting criterion had changed by age group and condition. *Note.* The error bars show the standard error of the mean; the gray bars show the separated-dimensions condition; white bars show the integrated condition.

ference in performance on separated versus integrated dimensions was significant overall, $Z(57) = 3.75$, $p < .0001$; for both boys, $Z(27) = 2.98$, $p < .003$; and girls, $Z(30) = 2.35$, $p < .02$; for both the Diamond Lab, $Z(28) = 2.10$, $p < .04$; and the Carlson Lab, $Z(29) = 3.17$, $p < .002$; both for when switching from shape to color, $Z(28) = 3.38$, $p < .001$; and when switching from color to shape, $Z(29) = 1.98$, $p < .05$, and both for when integrated dimensions was tested first, $Z(29) = 1.91$, $p = .05$; and when segregated dimensions was tested first, $Z(28) = 3.35$, $p < .001$. The percentage of correct sorts was significantly better when the dimensions were separated versus when they were integrated for children 3½ years of age, $Z(14) = 2.26$, $p < .03$; and for children 3 years old, $Z(24) = 3.03$, $p < .002$; but not for children 2½ years of age, $Z(19) = 1.13$, *ns.*

Roughly twice as many children successfully switched to sorting by the second dimension when the dimensions were separated compared with when the dimensions were integrated, a difference significant at $p < .003$ (McNemar test [$N = 57$]; Figure 5). There was no significant difference at 2½ years, but at 3 years the separated condition was passed *three times* more often than the integrated condition ($p < .03$, $n = 24$). At 3½ years, the separated condition was passed almost twice as often as the integrated condition, but due to the small number of subjects ($n = 14$), that difference did not reach statistical significance.

Twelve children successfully switched sorting criteria when the dimensions were separated and failed when the dimensions were integrated. Only 1 child did

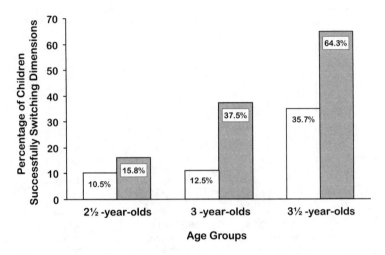

FIGURE 5   The percentage of children who successfully switched sorting criteria by age group and condition. *Note.* Criterion for success was five or more out of six responses correct postswitch; the gray bars show the separated-dimensions condition.

the reverse—successfully switched sorting criteria when the dimensions were integrated and failed when the dimensions were separated. Put another way, of the children who passed the postswitch in only one condition, 92% passed only in the separated condition, whereas 8% passed only in the integrated condition. At 3 and 3½ years of age, those percentages are 100% and 0%, respectively (i.e., all children who passed the integrated condition also passed the separated condition, whereas many children passed the separated condition but not the integrated condition).

Results of the generalized linear mixed models for binary outcomes (passed or failed on postswitch trials) with repeated measures also showed that performance in the separated condition was far superior to performance in the integrated condition, $\chi^2(1, N = 57) = 9.31$, $p < .002$. Overall, 3½-year-olds succeeded at switching sorting dimensions significantly more often than children younger: versus 3-year-olds, $\chi^2(1, N = 38) = 3.56$, $p < .05$; versus 2½-year-olds, $\chi^2(1, N = 33) = 6.66$, $p < .01$. On this binary outcome measure, the difference in performance between children of 3 years and 2½ years was not significant, although this difference is significant on the more sensitive percentage of correct responses measure described earlier. The significant effect of age was due to better performance by older children in the separated condition. There was no significant difference in performance over the ages studied on the integrated condition, but older children performed significantly better than younger ones on the separated condition, $\chi^2(1, N = 57) = 5.68$, $p = .05$. In the separated condition, children 3½ years of age performed significantly better than children of 3 years, $\chi^2(1, N = 38) = 3.80$, $p < .05$, and than children of 2½ years, $\chi^2(1, N = 33) =$

6.31, $p < .01$, although there was no significant difference between the performance of 3-year-olds and 2½-year-olds.

Most children of 2½ years and some children of 3 years were so immature in the abilities required by the DCCS task that they failed to switch sorting dimensions in both conditions and showed no awareness of error (no hesitation). Two children were so mature in this ability that they performed exquisitely on both conditions with no hesitation (no vacillation or indecision about where to sort any card). All other children (the vast majority) showed more advanced performance (more hesitation when wrong and less uncertainty when correct) with separated versus integrated dimensions, except for two children, who performed similarly on both. No child at 3 or 3½ years of age showed more advanced performance with integrated than with separated dimensions. Table 1 presents the results for this very clear progression.

DISCUSSION

Summary of Findings

As every aforementioned analysis has shown, preschoolers were significantly better at switching from sorting by color to sorting by shape (or the reverse) when color was a property of the background (i.e., colorless [black] shapes on a background of a single color) than when color was a property of the shape itself (i.e., shapes of a single color on a white background). It does not matter whether one looks at the percentage of correct responses when the sorting criterion changed, the percentage of children successfully switching sorting criteria, or the dichotomous outcome (passed/failed) in switching sorting criteria: Performance was significantly better in the separated dimensions condition. It also does not matter which subgroup one looks at—only boys, only girls, the Diamond Lab, the Carlson Lab, those who received the integrated condition first, those who received the separated condition first, those who sorted by color first, or those who sorted by shape first; postswitch performance was significantly better when color was a property of the background than when it was a property of the shape itself.

Children were able to respond correctly on roughly twice as many postswitch trials when the dimensions of color and shape were separated than when they were properties of the same object. Similarly, roughly twice as many children successfully switched to sorting by the second dimension when the dimensions were separated than when the dimensions were integrated. Twelve children successfully switched sorting criteria when the dimensions were separated and failed when the dimensions were integrated. No child 3 or 3½ years of age and only 1 child 2½ years of age did the reverse (successfully switched sorting criteria when the dimensions were integrated and failed when the dimensions were separated).

TABLE 1
Developmental Progression in the Ability to Switch Sorting Dimensions as
Indicated by Accuracy and Hesitation on Two Versions of the DCCS Task

		Number of Trials on Which the Child Hesitated in the ...	
Subject Number	*Age in Months*	*Separated Condition*	*Integrated Condition*

Those who failed to switch sorting dimensions in both conditions and showed no hesitation or awareness of their error

#A	31.5	0	0
#B	33.9	0	0
#C	36.3	0	0
#D	37.9	0	0
#E	45.1	0	0

Those who, although they failed the postswitch in both conditions, showed some hesitation when the dimensions were separated (some inkling that maybe their response was wrong), but no hesitation when the dimensions were integrated

#F	29.5	1	0
#G	33.5	1	0
#H	36.7	1	0
#I	36.9	1	0
#J	37.8	1	0
#K	37.8	1	0
#L	38.1	1	0
#M	32.8	2	0
#N	36.0	2	0
#O	38.5	2	0
#P	42.6	3	0
#Q	44.2	3	0

Those who, although they failed the postswitch in both conditions, showed some hesitation in both conditions, although usually more hesitation in the separated condition

#R	34.4	1	1
#S	43.1	2	2
#T	39.3	3	2
#U	45.7	4	3
#V	40.2	6	4

Those who successfully switched sorting criteria when the dimensions were separated, but failed when the dimensions were integrated

#W	37.5	1 (correct)	2 (wrong on both)
#X	42.5	1 (correct)	1 (wrong)
#Y	36.5	2 (correct on both)	0 (wrong)
#Z	33.9	2 (correct on both)	2 (wrong on both)
#AA	42.1	2 (correct on both)	2 (wrong on both)
#BB	41.3	0 (correct)	0 (wrong)
#CC	42.6	0 (correct)	3 (wrong on all 3; correct on next 3, no hesitation)

(continued)

TABLE 1   *(Continued)*

| | | Number of Trials on Which the Child Hesitated in the ... | |
Subject Number	Age in Months	Separated Condition	Integrated Condition
Those who successfully switched sorting criteria in both conditions, but showed more uncertainty (more hesitation) when the dimensions were integrated than when they were separated			
#DD	34.0	0	1
#EE	41.2	0	1
#FF	42.0	0	1
#GG	43.0	2	3
Those who succeeded in switching sorting criteria in both conditions without hesitation			
#HH	36.2	0	0
#II	37.0	0	0

Note. Evidence of the presence or absence of hesitation on each postswitch trial was coded only for children of 3 and 3.5 years because children of 2.5 years were so immature in the ability to switch tasks that the vast majority of them fit in the first category above (failed both conditions and showed no awareness of their error). Videotape records were unavailable for three of the children; therefore, they could not be included in the table as evidence of hesitation was coded from the videotapes. A hesitation was defined as clear behavioral evidence of uncertainty about which response to make, such as vacillating between putting a sorting card in one bin or the other.

As can be seen from Figures 4 and 5, children were about 6 months ahead in their ability to switch sorting criteria when the dimensions were separated than when they were integrated. The percentage of correct sorting responses postswitch (Figure 4) and the percentage of children who succeeded on the postswitch (Figure 5) at 3 years of age in the integrated condition was roughly comparable to those percentages for the separated condition at 2½ years. Likewise, performance at 3½ years in the integrated condition was roughly comparable to performance in the separated condition at 3 years.

At 2½ years old, a number of children could not be included in the analyses because they could not correctly sort according the first dimension (consistent with the findings of others, e.g., Zelazo et al., 1996; Zelazo & Frye, 1997). Most 2½-year-olds who could pass the preswitch phase were still so immature in the ability to switch sorting criteria that it did not matter whether the dimensions were separated or integrated. The vast majority of 2½-year-olds failed to switch sorting criteria in each condition; there was no significant difference in their performance by condition.

At 3 years of age, condition made a huge difference. *Three times* as many 3-year-olds were able to successfully switch to sorting by the second dimension when the dimensions were separated as could successfully switch when the dimensions were integrated. Viewed another way, among 3-year-olds, the percentage of postswitch responses that were correct was almost *2½ times* greater when the dimensions were separated as when the dimensions were integrated. At 3½ years of age, the difference in performance between the two conditions, although significant, was not as marked as at 3 years (percentage correct postswitch and percentage of children succeeding postswitch was roughly 1½ times greater in the separated condition than in the integrated condition).

We found no significant difference over our age range in performance when the dimensions were integrated (the standard DCCS condition). However, older children (even though all children were younger than 4) were able to perform significantly better than younger children when the dimensions of color and shape were separated (with color a property of background rather than of the shape itself). Thus, successful switching (in terms of correct responses or percentage of children responding correctly) showed a clear age-related progression under the facilitative condition (separated dimensions).

When children's hesitations and uncertainty were taken into account, and not simply whether they responded correctly, a very clear and quite rich developmental progression emerged (see Table 1). At the most immature level, children did not switch sorting criteria and showed no awareness of their error. At the next higher level, they showed some awareness in the separated condition that their postswitch responses were wrong, although they still failed to switch sorting criteria in both conditions. Next, although still failing the postswitch phase in both conditions, children showed some awareness in both conditions (not just in the separated condition) that maybe they were not responding correctly, usually showing more evidence of this in the separated than in the integrated condition. At the next higher level, children switched sorting criteria correctly when the dimensions were separated but not when they were integrated, typically showing a bit of uncertainty both about their correct responses in the separated condition and their incorrect responses in the integrated condition. Showing slightly more mature performance were those children who successfully switched sorting criteria in both conditions but were less sure about their correct answers (showed more hesitation) when the dimensions were integrated than when they were separated. Finally, children were able to successfully switch sorting criteria in both conditions with no sign of hesitation.

Different children develop at different rates, and different abilities within the same child develop at different rates. Age is at best an imperfect proxy for a child's developmental level on any given ability. As Table 1 so clearly shows, some younger children showed much more mature performance than some older children. Data on hesitation and accuracy across the two conditions used here provide a far more precise indication of a child's level of maturity on the executive function ability of being able to flexibly switch sorting criteria than does a child's age.

Our results are fully consistent with the only other study to look at separating color and shape on the model and sorting cards (Kloo & Perner, 2005). Further, we have shown that separating the dimensions helps still younger 3-year-olds than Kloo and Perner studied but does not appear to help 2½-year-olds. We demonstrated that color and shape do not have to be on separate sides of the stimulus cards. Indeed, on our stimuli, the color surrounded the shape. We have shown that simply not having color and shape be properties of the same object is critical.

Kloo and Perner (2005) reported the combined results from two different conditions (separating the dimensions on stimulus cards and attaching the dimensions to separate physical objects, instead of using cards) in reporting their within-subject results for separated versus integrated dimensions (their Exp. 3). They have kindly provided us with the raw data for just the separated and integrated dimensions on stimuli cards. Those data are provided in our Figure 6 for direct comparison with our results provided in Figure 4. Kloo and Perner found a much stronger effect than did we at their youngest age (3.33 years). That might be random variation, especially given the relatively small sample in our study and especially in theirs. The difference might be exaggerated a bit by inclusion in our study of children who might not have understood what they were supposed to do (children who had erred on over 50% of the knowledge questions in the Carlson Lab), thereby perhaps artificially depressing the success rate in our separated condition. It might be that where separated versus integrated dimensions makes the most difference is at 3.33

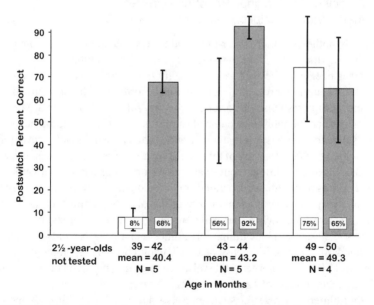

FIGURE 6   The percentage of correct sorting responses with card stimuli only after the sorting criterion had changed, by age group and condition (data from Kloo & Perner, 2005, Exp. 3). *Note.* The error bars show the standard error of the mean; the gray bars show the separated-dimensions condition.

years, rather than at 3.1 or 3.6 years (the ages we studied here). However, the most interesting possibility is that separating color and shape further in space makes it easier to shift the focus of one's attention from one to the other, especially if one can look at the relevant dimension without seeing the irrelevant one.

Most studies that have looked at separated dimensions have spatially segregated the two dimensions, as did Kloo and Perner (2005; e.g., Mueller et al., 2004). We are unaware of other studies that have separated the dimensions by putting one in the foreground and the other in the background, as we have done. Thus, this leads to some novel predictions. For example, we predict that the Stroop interference effect would be attenuated if color were a property of the background rather than of the word, even if the word is on a solid background of an incongruent color. Similarly, we predict that monkeys, which have such a difficult time in switching sorting dimensions (e.g., Moore et al., 2002), would find it much easier to switch sorting criteria if color were a property of the background rather than of the stimulus objects themselves. Implicit in these predictions is the hypothesis that young children, adults, and animals have difficulty with these tasks for similar reasons. It is primarily in the extent of the difficulty that they differ.

Consistency of Our Findings Reported Here, and Elsewhere, With an Inhibitory Account

We have hypothesized that 3-year-olds tend to stay stuck in thinking about something the way they have been thinking about it and that inhibition of their initial mind-set is needed if they are to successfully treat familiar stimuli according to new rules when the correct sorting responses according to the previous rules are the wrong sorting responses according to the new rules, and vice versa. Manipulations that reduce the inhibitory demand should therefore aid performance.

The separated-dimensions manipulation reported here did that by never requiring inhibition of the initial way of thinking about the objects pictured on the stimulus cards. Although a shift in focus of attention from foreground to background (or vice versa) was required, our separated condition did not additionally require inhibition of the initial way of thinking about the objects pictured on the stimulus cards. The star was always a star; children never had to think of it sometimes as a star and sometimes as a blue thing. Three times as many 3-year-olds succeeded as in the standard integrated-dimensions DCCS paradigm. The separated-dimensions conditions of Kloo and Perner (2005) also dramatically improved the performance of children 3 to 4 years of age.

Within-dimension reversal switching also never requires thinking about the stimuli as anything but trucks and stars (although sometimes things go with like items, as trucks with the truck model, and sometimes the rules reverse and things go with the dissimilar model, as trucks with the star model). Here, the focus of attention on shape never waivers. Both labs that have investigated this find that 3-year-olds successfully switch sorting rules on such tasks (Brooks, Hanauer, & Padowska, 2003; Perner & Lang, 2002).

Contrary to other explanations of task-switching performance (e.g., Rogers & Monsell, 1995), Diamond and Kirkham (2005; Kirkham et al., 2003; Kirkham & Diamond, 2003) have argued that *before* the stimulus appears, 3-year-olds are ready to perform correctly. They clearly have in mind both the new sorting criterion and the appropriate rules for that dimension (as their correct responses to the knowledge questions demonstrate). Then a stimulus appears that is relevant to both tasks in incompatible ways (the correct answer when sorting by color is the wrong answer when sorting by shape). That *creates* a problem for the children, triggering the mind-set they are trying to inhibit. Similarly, the familiar target cards, each with a valid value on the previously relevant dimension, serve as attractors, pulling the child to think and act according to the previously relevant rules. Children need to inhibit the pull to focus on the previously relevant dimension and the pull to act according to the previously relevant rules.

Thus, if the postswitch sorting cards are not relevant to the preswitch dimension, children would not have to inhibit the pull to think about the cards according to the preswitch mind-set, and 3-year-olds should succeed in switching sorting criteria. Indeed they do. Children 3 years of age are perfectly capable of switching from sorting red rabbits and blue boats by their color to sorting yellow flowers and green cars by their shape (Zelazo et al., 1995, Exp.3; cf Zelazo & Jacques, 1996; Zelazo et al., 2003, Studies 3 & 4).

Similarly, 3-year-olds succeed in switching sorting criteria when the model cards do not contain the previously relevant values of the previously relevant dimension or when no model cards are present at all (Kloo & Perner, 2003; Perner & Lang, 2002; Towse et al., 2000). Children of 3 years are also able to switch when there are four model cards, each containing only one dimension, so that each model card is relevant only pre- or only postswitch (not both) and the correct answers for one dimension are irrelevant when sorting by the other dimension (Rennie et al., 2004; Towse et al., 2000).

Similarly, if no sorting cards are visible and only the value on the currently relevant dimension is mentioned, 3-year-olds should also be able to switch sorting dimensions, as there is nothing to pull them back to their previous mind-set. Indeed, 3-year-olds perform almost flawlessly on the knowledge questions (Munakata & Yerys, 2001).

When inhibitory demands are essentially eliminated by using different sorting cards pre- and postswitch and by having the sorting cards match any target card on only one dimension, virtually all preschoolers succeed (96%; even those only 2 years old; Rennie et al., 2004). As no relevant values on the previously used dimension were present postswitch, attention to them did not have to be inhibited. Because there was no overlap of stimuli pre- and postswitch, no response to a stimulus had to be remapped.

Further, conditions that help children refocus their attention on the currently relevant dimension and away from the previously relevant dimension should also help preschoolers perform better. Instead of the experimenter labeling the stimulus on each trial of the standard DCCS task, Kirkham et al. (2003) had the child do the labeling, thus having the child actively redescribe the stimuli according to the postswitch dimension. This helped 3-year-olds perform better. Similarly, Towse et al. (2000) found that when they instructed 3-year-olds who had failed to switch sorting criteria to label the relevant dimension of the next sorting card, many were then able to switch correctly.

Finally, if the inhibitory interpretation is correct, then manipulations that increase the inhibitory demand should make it harder for children to succeed. Sorting the cards faceup creates a perceptual pull to continue sorting by the previous dimension and hence increases the demand on inhibition. Indeed, 4-year-olds (who usually do quite well on the standard DCCS task) are much more likely to fail to switch sorting dimensions when the cards are placed faceup in the sorting bins (Kirkham et al., 2003).

Adults also perform much better at switching tasks when there is no conflict, that is, when each stimulus or response option is relevant to only one dimension (univalent stimuli or targets; Allport & Wylie, 2000; Mayr, 2001; Meiran, 1996, 2000; Rogers & Monsell, 1995; Wylie & Allport, 2000). Adults have the same problem in task switching as do children, just in a much less extreme form. Hence, adults are helped by the same conditions that help children and, as noted in the Introduction, show a switch cost on the standard DCCS task in RT comparable to that seen in children in accuracy (Diamond & Kirkham, 2005).

At the same age that children fail to switch sorting dimensions on the standard DCCS task (3 years), they also fail an array of other tasks that similarly require holding two things in mind and inhibiting a prepotent response (Diamond, 2002). At the same age that children first *succeed* on the DCCS task (4–5 years), they likewise first succeed on those other tasks as well. This is true for (a) *appearance-reality tasks* (Flavell et al., 1986), where children must hold in mind what a thing really is as well as what it appears to be and inhibit the strong temptation to say that it looks like what it really is or that it really is what it looks like; (b) *false belief theory of mind tasks* (Perner, Leekam, & Wimmer, 1987; Wimmer & Perner, 1983), where children must hold in mind their own knowledge of the true state of affairs as well as what another person erroneously thinks to be the state of affairs and inhibit both the temptation to blurt out the true state (when asked to report the other person's false belief) and the wish for that very nice other person to find the desirous object; (c) *other false belief tasks* (Perner et al., 1987), which also involve holding in mind both a true and a false belief (the false belief was what the child had previously thought) and inhibiting the true knowledge, which they now have, when asked to say what they previously thought ("knew it all along," see Fischhoff, 1977; Fischhoff & Beyth, 1975; "hindsight bias," see Hawkins & Hastie, 1990; Hoffrage, Hertwig, & Gigerenzer, 2000); (d) *tests of spatial perspective*, where children must hold in mind two perspectives and inhibit the pull to give the perceptually salient response (their own current perspective) when asked to say what the perspective would be of someone else at a different vantage point (considered an aspect of "egocentricism," Piaget & Inhelder, 1956); (e) *ambiguous figures* (Gopnik & Rosati, 2001), where children must try to hold in mind two perspectives and inhibit one when trying to see the other; (f) *conflict tasks*, such as the Day/Night (Gerstadt, Hong, & Diamond, 1994), Tapping (Diamond & Taylor, 1996), Hands (Hughes, 1998a), and Grass/Snow (Carlson & Moses, 2001) tasks, all of which require holding two rules in mind and inhibiting a prepotent response (such as remembering to say *day* when shown a nighttime scene and to say *night* when shown a daytime scene and inhibiting saying what the pictures really represent); and (g) *liquid conservation tasks* (Piaget & Inhelder, 1941), where children must take into account both height and width and must inhibit the strong temptation to say that the beaker with the taller liquid column has more liquid even though it is narrower.

On all of these paradigms, manipulations that reduce the inhibitory demand aid children's performance. One way to reduce the demand on inhibition is to reduce the perceptual salience of the answer children are to inhibit. Thus, telling children where the object is hidden but never actually showing them makes it possible for more preschoolers to succeed on theory of mind tasks (Zaitchik, 1991). Similarly, putting a screen in front of the liquid beakers (so they cannot be seen) helps preschoolers succeed on liquid conservation tasks (Bruner, 1964). Reducing perceptual salience also aids preschoolers' performance on appearance-reality tasks (Heberle, Clune, & Kelly, 1999). Manipulations that reduce inhibitory demands in other ways also help preschoolers to succeed on these tasks. For example, pointing veridically is a well-practiced and much reinforced response in young children, and children of 3 to 4 years of age have trouble inhibiting that tendency when they should point to the false location on theory of mind tasks. Carlson, Moses, and Hix (1998) found that children performed better when given a novel response by which to indicate the false location (see also Hala & Russell, 2001).

If all these tasks have related cognitive requirements (to hold two things in mind and inhibit focusing on, and reacting to, what is most salient in the situation), then one would expect intercorrelations among performance on these tasks. Indeed, that is found. Carlson and Moses (2001) included the DCCS task in their study of the relation between inhibitory control and theory of mind in preschoolers. DCCS performance was significantly correlated with 8 of 9 other inhibition tasks. Even after controlling for age, gender, and verbal ability, DCCS performance remained significantly related to 5 of those measures and to the aggregate Inhibitory Control battery (with DCCS removed, of course). Performance on the DCCS task was most strongly related to performance on the Day/Night (Gerstadt et al., 1994), Grass/Snow (Carlson & Moses, 2001), Spatial Conflict (Simon task; Gerardi-Caulton, 2000), Bear/Dragon (Reed, Pien, & Rothbart, 1984), and Whisper (Kochanska, Murray, Jacques, Koenig, & Vandegeest, 1996) tasks. A principal components analysis of all 10 inhibition tasks confirmed that the DCCS task loaded on the same factor with these other "conflict" tasks. Carlson and Moses also found that DCCS performance was significantly related to false-belief performance, echoing findings of Frye, Zelazo, and Palfai (1995; see also Fahie & Symons, 2003). Similarly, the emergence of children's ability to accept two labels for the same thing correlates with the emergence of successful switching on the DCCS task (Stummer, 2001) and with the emergence of success on theory of mind and other false belief tasks (Doherty & Perner, 1998; Perner et al., 2002).

Having said this, we feel it is important to acknowledge that children 3 and 3½ years of age in our study, although clearly aided by the separated dimensions condition, did not perform perfectly. One reason that performance was not even better in our separated-dimensions condition may be that we did not reduce *all* the inhibition required by the task. Even though children did not have to think about the same object in two different ways, they did need to switch the focus of their attention from the foreground to the background (or vice versa). Even greater reductions in inhibitory demand should result in even better performance (as did the manipulations of Kloo & Perner, 2005, and Rennie et al., 2004). There is likely another reason that performance was not even better in our separated-dimensions condition: Although difficulty in keeping the rules in mind while inhibiting the prepotent tendency to continue to respond on the same basis as one has been responding is *part* of the problem for 3-year-olds, it is unlikely to be the whole story. For example, although 3-year-olds clearly seem able to handle higher order rules, doing so may be sufficiently difficult for them that some errors are caused by having to deal with that complexity.

Our Interpretation of Why 3-Year-Olds Perform as They Do on the DCCS Task Compared With Other Interpretations

The conceptual redescription interpretation. The redescription hypothesis offered by Kloo and Perner (2005) shares much in common with our attentional inertia hypothesis. Both have at their core the fundamental hypothesis that 3-year-olds have difficulty thinking about the same thing in two different ways; they have difficulty flipping from one perspective to another. "Having adopted the mindset that blue things go with the blue model card, they have great difficulty switching to think of a blue truck in terms of its shape and sorting it with the red-truck model card" (Kirkham et al., 2003, p. 451). Both Kloo and Perner and

Kirkham and Diamond have stated that 3-year-olds' problem is one of cognitive rigidity when it is cognitive flexibility that is required by the DCCS task.

Our interpretation differs from that of the redescription interpretation of Kloo and Perner (2005) in that we see the fundamental requirement of the DCCS task to be in having to hold information in mind and inhibit the perspective one had been using in order to switch to a different perspective. Three-year-olds' fundamental problem on the task, as we see it, is in insufficiently developed inhibitory control. Kloo and Perner (2005) saw the problem for 3-year-olds on the task to lie in an insufficiently developed conceptual ability: Children of 3 years do not yet understand

> that objects can be described in different ways … . The difference is that the re-description hypothesis sees the observed developmental progress in solving the DCCS in a conceptual change in understanding that objects can be re-described as being of a different kind without assuming any changes in executive control over these years. (p. 53)

It is too early to know which interpretation is correct, but ours appears to have an advantage in parsimony and in the diversity of phenomena for which it can account. It is more parsimonious in that we attribute the problem of adults on switch tasks, including switching dimensions on the DCCS task, to the same source as the problem for children—the difficulty of exercising sufficient inhibitory control to flexibly and readily switch mental sets. Kloo and Perner would presumably need to attribute the task-switching cost seen in adults to a different source than that for children, for adults presumably have a mature conceptual understanding of objects. Similarly, both our interpretation and that of Kloo and Perner can readily account for preschoolers' problems on theory of mind, other false belief, appearance-reality, and ambiguous figures tasks, but our interpretation can also account for why problems on measures require holding two items in mind and inhibiting a prepotent tendency that do *not* involve a conceptual redescription (e.g., the Day/Night task, Gerstadt et al., 1994) are also seen at the same ages and also resolve around the same time.

Improvements in the ability to hold information in mind, inhibiting distractors and pulls to act in ways inconsistent with that mentally represented information, and the cognitive flexibility that that affords appear to be critical for many of the cognitive advances of early childhood, such as conceptual redescription and theory of mind. Three studies have looked longitudinally at the relation between the development of executive control functions such as inhibitory control and the appearance of theory of mind understanding (Carlson, Mandell, & Williams, 2004; Flynn, O'Malley, & Wood, 2004; Hughes, 1998b). All three of these independent studies, conducted in different laboratories, found the same result: Advances in inhibitory control (specifically, inhibition plus holding information in mind) predicted theory of mind advances and not the reverse, even controlling for factors such as age and verbal ability. A cross-cultural study has also found that in China, as in the United States, individual differences in inhibitory control were significantly related to theory of mind performance (Sabbagh, Xu, Carlson, Moses, & Lee, in press). Advances in the ability to simultaneously hold information in mind and inhibit prepotent action tendencies appear to be among the necessary ingredients for cognitive advances such as a theory of mind and conceptual redescription.

Cognitive complexity and control theory.   The developers of the DCCS task (Zelazo & Frye, 1997) theorized that the key requirement for success on the task is the ability to represent a hierarchical, embedded rule structure and that 3-year-olds lack that relatively sophisticated representational ability. Their theory is called the cognitive complexity and control (CCC) theory. In the DCCS task, there are two higher order categories (color and shape), and within each are embedded two rules (e.g., "the red things go here and the blue ones there") so that if one is playing the color game, blue trucks go with a blue-star model card, but if one is playing the shape game, then blue trucks go with the red-truck model card. That is the cognitive complexity part of CCC theory. Cognitive complexity corresponds to the levels of embedding, and 3-year-olds cannot yet represent a sufficiently complex rule structure to succeed at the DCCS task according to this theory. CCC theory also claims that reflection on, and formulation of, higher order rules then makes inhibition and refocusing possible.

There is compelling evidence against CCC theory as an explanation of why 3-year-olds have difficulty switching sorting dimensions on the DCCS task. None of the manipulations that reduce the demand on inhibition and thereby aid success on the DCCS task change the complexity of the rule structure. Hence CCC theory cannot account for their efficacy. Examples include the following.

1. Within-dimension reversal tasks have the same hierarchical, embedded rule structure as does the DCCS task (in the sensible game, trucks go with trucks and stars with stars; in the silly game, stars go with trucks and trucks go with stars), yet 3-year-olds can successfully switch sorting rules on these tasks but not on the DCCS task (Brooks et al., 2003: Perner & Lang, 2002).

2. Three-year-olds easily switch sorting dimensions on the DCCS task if no target cards are used, or if the previously relevant values are no longer present on the target cards when the sorting criterion switches, although the rule structure, of course, is unchanged (Kloo & Perner, 2003; Perner & Lang, 2002; Towse et al., 2000).

3. If the values on the stimulus cards for both dimensions change when the sorting criterion changes, preschoolers can successfully switch sorting dimensions on the DCCS task (Zelazo et al., 1995, Exp. 3), yet again, this manipulation does nothing to change the embedded rule structure of the task. Sorting red rabbits and

blue boats by their color and then switching to sort yellow flowers and green cars by their shape has the same rule structure.

4. Having the children rather than the experimenter label the relevant dimension on each new sorting card helps preschoolers to perform better by helping them refocus on the currently relevant dimension (Kirkham et al., 2003; Towse et al., 2000), but it does not change the rule structure of the task or help children acquire a more sophisticated conceptual structure. Therefore it should not be effective according to CCC theory, but it is.

5. Last, as shown in the study presented here and by Kloo and Perner (2005), 3-year-olds, who fail the standard DCCS task, are able to succeed if the same color and shape values appear on the cards, but instead of being properties of the same object, they are separated. For CCC theory, this change in the stimuli should not make a difference. Indeed, Zelazo et al. (2003) explicitly stated that CCC theory predicts that children should not perform better with separated dimensions than with integrated ones because in the separated condition one must still "cross major branches of a tree-like [rule] structure" (p. 57). The embedded rule structure remains the same.

Conversely, correlational evidence has shown that performance on the DCCS task is related to performance on several executive function tasks, some of which have a simple, rather than an embedded, rule structure (Carlson & Moses, 2001), such as the Day/Night or Grass/Snow tasks. Even the false belief task, which several investigators have found to be related to the DCCS task, can be construed as having a simple rule structure (Perner, Stummer, & Lang, 1999).

In response to new data and criticisms such as those just listed, CCC theory has been revised (CCC–r; Zelazo et al., 2003). It now incorporates elements of competing interpretations, such as our attentional inertia theory, blurring distinctions between the theoretical perspectives. In so doing, CCC–r theory has lost much of the elegance and clarity of the earlier CCC theory.

In addition, the same argument concerning parsimony raised in relation to the redescription theory is also relevant here. Adults, too, show switch costs on the DCCS task (Diamond & Kirkham, 2005). We argue that those costs have their origin in having to overcome attentional inertia, in having to inhibit the previously relevant mind-set—the same origin as in preschoolers' problems in switching. Adults are capable of mentally representing embedded, hierarchical rule structures, so one might expect that proponents of CCC theory would argue that adults show switch costs for a different reason than do children. Proponents of CCC theory argue that formulating and using higher order rules is effortful; although adults are capable of doing it, it requires resources and hence produces switch costs. Higher order rules are relevant to all trials, though, yet adults are slower specifically when switching. Older adults show greater switch costs than younger adults, including on tasks similar to the DCCS task (Zelazo, Craik, &

Booth, 2004), which is due, we think, not to their greater problems with embedded, hierarchical rule structures but to their greater problems with effortful, inhibitory control.

Readers might wonder if we are really arguing that infants fail to switch where they search when a toy is hidden at a second location on the A-not-B task, frontal patients fail to switch sorting criteria on the Wisconsin Card Sort Test, and adults show task-switching costs for the same reason as many 3-year-olds fail to switch sorting dimensions on the DCCS task. The answer is basically *yes*. On the A-not-B task, babies need to hold one piece of information in mind plus inhibit a dominant tendency. The DCCS, Wisconsin Card Sorting Test, and all task-switching paradigms require holding two pieces of information in mind plus inhibiting a dominant tendency. Adults show the same problems and biases in switching as do young children, though more subtly (e.g., in relative speed rather than accuracy). If memory is more severely taxed, adults can show switch costs even in accuracy. Memory develops rapidly during infancy and then is quite robust (Diamond, 1995), although it declines noticeably beginning in early adulthood (Bialystok & Craik, in press), so memory accounts for more of the variance in infants and adults than it does in young children. Inhibitory control is one of the key challenges for young children. It shows a very slow developmental progression from 3 to 13 years (Diamond, 2002). Between those years (and likely up to age 20) we hypothesize that it accounts for more of the variance than does memory.

A negative priming interpretation.   Mueller (Mueller et al., 2004; Mueller & Zelazo, 2001) has proposed a very interesting negative priming interpretation of preschoolers' problem on the DCCS task. Negative priming refers to the cost of having to reverse inhibition (or reverse an "ignore" tag) when what had been the distractor (e.g., the irrelevant dimension on DCCS stimulus cards) then becomes the target (e.g., the relevant dimension; Milliken & Tipper, 1998; Neill, & Valdes, 1992; Neill, Valdes, & Terry, 1995; Tipper, 1985). To flexibly change the focus of one's attention, one must not only institute inhibition of what had been relevant but also reverse inhibition of what had been irrelevant. A reader might think at first that a negative priming interpretation posits just the opposite of an inhibition account, that is, overly strong inhibition (of the irrelevant dimension) rather than weak inhibition. However, there is a great deal of evidence that if it is difficult for one to inhibit something, then having instituted that inhibition, it is particularly difficult to reverse it. For example, the cost of switching from reading Stroop words to naming the color of the ink is much less than the cost of switching from naming the ink color (where the dominant response of reading the word had to be inhibited) to reading the word (because greater inhibition was initially required in the latter condition; Allport & Wylie, 1999, 2000; Wylie & Allport, 2000; Meiran, 2000). Hence, the general, well-replicated rule is that there is a greater cost in switching to doing what is easier (because more inhibition had been required to resist doing that before the switch) than to switch to doing what is more difficult.

Although Diamond and Kirkham have emphasized that children must shift their attention away from the previously relevant dimension, Mueller and Zelazo (2001) rightly pointed out that for children to shift their attention toward the currently relevant dimension they must undo their previous inhibition of that dimension. "Difficulty in exerting the required disinhibition prevents children from drawing their attention to the values of the currently relevant dimension resulting in a negative priming effect" (p. 5).

Evidence consistent with a negative priming interpretation includes that if the values of the previously relevant dimension are changed for the postswitch phase (eliminating the pull to continue to use those values to guide one's responses) but the values of the previously irrelevant dimension are left unchanged (requiring that any previous suppression of attention to them be reversed), children 3 years of age have difficulty switching sorting criteria on the DCCS task (Zelazo et al., 2003, Study 4).

Current performance is codetermined by what you are switching *from* and what you are switching *to*. The relation between the two is key. Thus, Meiran (2000) showed that if the preswitch stimuli had been relevant only to the initial task, it is easier to switch dimensions than if the preswitch stimuli had been relevant to both tasks. Hence, in 2001, Diamond made a rather strong prediction that 3-year-olds should successfully switch sorting dimensions on the DCCS task and adults should show less switch cost, if the first block has stimuli relevant only to the first dimension (e.g., colorless [black] stars and trucks on a white background when sorting by shape), even though the postswitch block would be administered *exactly* as in the standard condition (the condition that 3-year-olds fail). The only thing that would change is the context in which that postswitch block occurs. Thus, 3-year-olds should *successfully* switch from sorting red and blue blobs (by color) to sorting red and blue stars and trucks (by shape), although they *fail* to switch from sorting red and blue grapes and birds (by color) to sorting red and blue stars and trucks (by shape; Zelazo et al., 1995).

A graded memory interpretation.   Munakata (2001) and colleagues (Morton & Munakata, 2002b; Munakata, Morton, & Yerys, 2003; Munakata & Yerys, 2001), citing evidence that memory can be graded, argued that children may succeed on one measure of memory on the DCCS task (the knowledge questions) and yet not have sufficient memory to correctly switch sorting criteria on the task. Neural network models demonstrate that stronger memory representations are required for a task when greater conflict is present (Morton & Munakata, 2002a). "Children may have limited memory for a new rule, which is sufficient for tasks that do not involve conflict, but insufficient for tasks that involve conflict" (Munakata et al., 2003, p. 472). We agree, and we contend that is so precisely because a conflict situation adds an additional inhibitory requirement not present in the nonconflict situation. As we see it, in the conflict situation the conflicting information pulls the child's attention away from the rule the child knows and remembers. The child needs to inhibit the pull of the conflicting information and focus on the relevant stimulus dimension and its attendant rule.

Evidence that would appear to be inconsistent with a memory interpretation is that 3-year-olds perform better on the DCCS task when memory demands are increased (when no model cards are present; Perner & Lang, 2002; Towse et al., 2000) and fail even when memory demands are minimized, such as when the experimenter reminds the child at the outset of each trial how to sort the cards by the currently relevant dimension.

Another argument offered by Munakata et al. (2003) against our inhibitory control interpretation of problems in switching dimensions on the DCCS task, and offered by many others to account for the costs of switching tasks in general (e.g., Monsell, 2003), is that a memory interpretation alone is sufficient to account for the results. Such memory interpretations often involve enhanced activation of (or strengthened links to) the correct representation and diminished activation of (or weakened links to) the incorrect dimension (Munakata, 1998, 2001) and thus incorporate inhibition directly into the memory account. Maintaining focus on something in memory (or in visual attention) requires concentrating on what is relevant and inhibiting attention to irrelevant, compelling distractors. Switching tasks requires not only activating or retrieving the rules appropriate for the new task but also inhibiting or disengaging from the mind-set relevant to the previous task (Allport & Wylie, 1999, 2000; Mayr & Keele, 2000; Rogers & Monsell, 1995). It is an open question whether memory and inhibition can be dissociated. We tend to think they can. For example, although strengthening the activation of appropriate links causes activation of inappropriate links to decline (McClelland & Kawamoto, 1986; Waltz & Pollack, 1985), Gernsbacher and Faust (1991) found that as inappropriate links decreased in activation, appropriate links did *not* necessarily increase in activation.

Perceiving Relations Between Separated Things as the Flip Side of Separating Features of Integrated Things

We have demonstrated that a simple change in testing procedure, which involved only changing the stimuli (so that the two dimensions of color and shape were separated and not part of the same physical object, although the same colors and shapes still appeared on all cards), enabled children to switch tasks in the DCCS paradigm 6 months earlier than they are otherwise able. Diamond and colleagues (Diamond et al., 1999; Diamond et al., 2003) have demonstrated that another simple change in testing procedure *halved* the age at which infants could demonstrate the ability to deduce the abstract rule: "Choose the item that does not match (i.e., that is different from) the sample." There it was a matter of unseparating (attaching) stimulus and reward objects, where normally the reward sits just below the correct stimulus in a shallow well. Participants must deduce that reaching to the novel stimulus is always the correct response. Children cannot normally succeed on this delayed nonmatching to sample task, even at the 5-sec training delay, until they are almost 2 years old (20–21 months; Diamond, 1990; Diamond, Towle, & Boyer, 1994; Overman, 1990; Overman, Bachevalier, Turner, & Peuster, 1992). Their problem is that they do not "get" that the reward object and stimulus object are somehow related when they are not physically connected.

It turns out that infants' ability to relate the reward object to the stimulus object does *not* depend on the two objects being physically close (spatial proximity) or on the reward being received (or appearing) just after the infant acts on the stimulus (temporal proximity). Even if the stimulus is directly in front, or on top, of the reward and the reward pops up the instant the infant grasps the stimulus, infants do not understand the relation between stimulus and reward. *Physical connection* is the key: Infants of 9 or 12 months succeed if the stimulus and reward are velcroed together (Diamond et al., 1999). Indeed, they succeed even if the stimulus and reward are some *distance* apart and the reward does not appear until 5 sec *after* acting on the stimulus *if both are connected to the same piece of apparatus* (Diamond et al., 2003). Without the perception that stimulus and reward are components of a single thing, even close spatial *and* temporal proximity are insufficient. In its presence, *neither* close spatial or temporal proximity is needed (Diamond et al., 2003; Ross, Shutts, & Diamond, 2000; Shutts, Ross, Hayden, & Diamond, 2001). Even for adults, detecting a conceptual connection is aided by physical connection and may not occur in its absence. When Blaser (2003) asked adult observers to report only individual parts of a visual display, adults spontaneously encoded and learned the combinations of parts *if* the parts were physically connected.

Related findings from other paradigms include those of Rudel (1955), who found that when the reward is placed *inside* the stimuli, children 1½ to 3½ years of age learn to choose on the basis of relative size in far fewer trials than do even older children when tested with the reward *underneath* the stimuli (Alberts & Ehrenfreund, 1951; Kuene, 1946). Similarly, DeLoache and Brown (1983) found that 18- to 22-month-olds performed much better when a reward was hidden *in* a piece of furniture rather than *near* it.

DeLoache (1986) varied whether a reward was hidden in one of four distinctive containers or whether the distinctive containers were mounted on top of plain boxes into which the rewards were placed. When the boxes were scrambled, 21-month-olds were 80% correct when the rewards were *in* the distinctive containers but only 35% correct when the distinctive containers *marked* where the rewards were hidden (the reward being in the box *underneath*). "When the same distinctive visual information was a less integral aspect of the hiding location, age differences appeared" (DeLoache, 1986, p. 123).

Difficulty in seeing conceptual connections between physically unconnected things is also documented in apes and monkeys. Adult chimpanzees may take 100 trials or more to learn a color discrimination with red and blue plaques placed over shallow wells and the reward always under the blue (or red) plaque. Changing just one aspect of the testing procedure (e.g., instead of placing the peanut reward in the shallow well under the plaque, attaching the peanut to the underside of the plaque) enables chimpanzees to learn the color discrimination rule after just *one trial* (Jarvik, 1956; analogous to the velcro condition of Diamond et al., 1999).

Many studies have documented impairments in the acquisition of conditional associations in monkeys with lesions of the periarcuate region (e.g., Goldman & Rosvold, 1970; Petrides, 1982, 1985, 1986; Lawler & Cowey, 1987; Passingham, 1988). Halsband and Passingham (1982, 1985; Passingham, 1985a, 1985b) reported that monkeys with premotor lesions invading the arcuate sulcus (the periarcuate region) can learn "if blue cue, pull handle; if red, turn handle" *if* color is a property of the handle itself but not if it is a property of the background. This brings us back to the preschool period, because children of 3 years also have difficulty with such conditional discriminations. In the classic paradigm, participants first learn to always respond to one member of a pair of stimuli. After reaching a high level of accuracy, the stimuli are presented against a different background, and the reward contingencies are reversed.

When children are tested with minimal instruction and so must deduce the rules, they cannot succeed at such conditional discriminations until they are 4½ to 5½ years of age (Doan & Cooper, 1971; Gollin, 1964, 1965; Gollin & Liss, 1962; Heidbreder, 1928; Jeffrey, 1961). The work with monkeys suggests that younger children (perhaps at 3 or 3½) might succeed if color were a property of the stimuli themselves rather than of the background. Making color a property of the stimulus objects might enable 3-year-olds to see the relevance of variations in that attribute to the response rules for those stimuli. Conversely, as we have shown here, separating the attributes so that they are not properties of the same stimulus object makes it easier for 3-year-olds to switch between the two attributes when the currently correct sorting response conflicts with the previously relevant one.

ACKNOWLEDGMENTS

This research was supported by Grant R01 #DA19685–16A2 from National Institute for Drug Abuse and by Grant R01 #HD35453 from the National Institute of Child Health and Human Development NICHD to Adele Diamond.

We gratefully thank Aaron Baker and Stacy Underwood for assistance in testing the children; Stephen Baker, senior biostatistician, University of Massachusetts Medical School, for invaluable advice on the data analyses; and Daniella Kloo and

Josef Perner for generously providing a copy of their stimuli and raw data from their Experiment 3.

REFERENCES

Alberts, E., & Ehrenfreund, D. (1951). Transposition in children as a function of age. *Journal of Experimental Psychology, 41*, 30–38.

Allport, A., Styles, E. A., & Hsieh, S. (1994). Shifting intentional set: Exploring the dynamic control of tasks. In C. Umilta & M. Moscovitch (Eds.), *Attention and performance XV* (pp. 421–452). Cambridge, MA: MIT Press.

Allport, A., & Wylie, G. (1999). Task-switching: Positive and negative priming of task-set. In G. W. Humphreys, J. Duncan, & A. Treisman (Eds.), *Attention, space and action, studies in cognitive neuroscience* (pp. 273–296). London: Oxford University Press.

Allport, A. & Wylie, G. (2000). Task switching, stimulus-response bindings, and negative priming. In S. Monsell & J. Driver (Eds.), *Control of cognitive processes: Attention and performance XVII* (pp. 35–70). Cambridge, MA: MIT Press.

Barrett, S. E., & Shepp, B.E. (1988). Developmental change in attentional skills, the effect of irrelevant variations on encoding and response selection. *Journal of Experimental Psychology, 45*, 382–399.

Bialystok, E., & Craik, G. (in press). *Lifespan cognition: Mechanisms of change.* London: Oxford University Press.

Bialystok, E., & Martin, M. M. (2004). Attention and inhibition in bilingual children: Evidence from the dimensional change card sort task. *Developmental Science, 7*, 325–339.

Blaser, E. (2003, December 8). *Think locally, act globally: Color, motion, and attention.* Talk presented in the Harvard University Vision Lab Seminar Series, Cambridge, MA.

Brooks, P., Hanauer, J. B., Padowska, B., & Rosman, H. (2003). The role of selective attention in preschoolers' rule use in a novel dimensional card sort. *Cognitive Development, 117*, 1–21.

Brooks, P., Hanauer, J. B., & Rosman, H. (2001, April). *Examining the effect of stimulus complexity on preschoolers' rule use using a novel dimensional card sort.* Paper presented at the Biennial Meeting of the Society for Research in Child Development, Minneapolis, MD.

Bruner, J. S. (1964). The course of cognitive growth. *American Psychologist, 19*, 1–15.

Carey, S., & Bartlett, E. J. (1978). Acquiring a single new word. *Papers and Reports on Child Language Development, 15*, 17–29.

Carlson, S. M., Mandell, D. J., & Williams, L. (2004). Executive function and theory of mind: Stability and prediction from age 2 to 3. *Developmental Psychology, 40*, 1105–1122.

Carlson, S. M., & Moses, L. J. (2001). Individual differences in inhibitory control and children's theory of mind. *Child Development, 72*, 1032–1053.

Carlson, S. M., Moses, L. J., & Hix, H. R. (1998). The role of inhibitory control in young children's difficulties with deception and false belief. *Child Development, 69*, 672–691.

Chambers, D., & Reisberg, D. (1992). What an image depicts depends on what an image means. *Cognitive Psychology, 24*, 145–174.

DeLoache, J. S. (1986). Memory in very young children: Exploitation of cues to the location of a hidden object. *Cognitive Development, 1*, 123–137.

DeLoache, J. S., & Brown, A. L. (1983). Very young children's memory for the location of objects in a large-scale environment. *Child Development, 54*, 888–897.

Diamond, A. (1990). Rate of maturation of the hippocampus and the developmental progression of children's performance on the delayed non-matching to sample and visual paired comparison tasks. *Annals of the New York Academy of Sciences, 608*, 394–426.

Diamond, A. (1995). Evidence of robust recognition memory early in life even when assessed by reaching behavior. *Journal of Experimental Child Psychology, 59*, 419–456.

Diamond, A. (2001). *Development of cognitive functions linked to frontal lobe* [R01 research grant application submitted to National Institutes of Health].

Diamond, A. (2002). Normal development of prefrontal cortex from birth to young adulthood: Cognitive functions, anatomy, and biochemistry. In D. T. Stuss & R. T. Knight (Eds.), *The frontal lobes* (pp. 466–503). London: Oxford University Press.

Diamond, A. (2005). *An all or none hypothesis.* Manuscript in preparation.

Diamond, A., Churchland, A., Cruess, L., & Kirkham, N. Z. (1999). Early developments in the ability to understand the relation between stimulus and reward. *Developmental Psychology, 35*, 1507–1517.

Diamond, A., & Kirkham, N. Z. (2005). Not quite as grown-up as we like to think: Parallels between cognition in childhood and adulthood. *Psychological Science, 16*, 291–297.

Diamond, A., Lee, E.-Y., & Hayden, M. (2003). Early success in using the relation between stimulus and reward to deduce an abstract rule: Perceived physical connectedness is key. *Developmental Psychology, 39*, 825–847.

Diamond, A., & Taylor, C. (1996). Development of an aspect of executive control: Development of the abilities to remember what I said and to "Do as I say, not as I do". *Developmental Psychobiology, 29*, 315–334.

Diamond, A., Towle, C., & Boyer, K. (1994). Young children's performance on a task sensitive to the memory functions of the medial temporal lobe in adults, the delayed nonmatching-to-sample task, reveals problems that are due to non-memory-related task demands. *Behavioral Neuroscience, 108*, 659–680.

Diggle, P. J., Liang, K.-Y., & Zeger, S. L. (1994). *Analysis of longitudinal data.* Oxford, UK: Oxford University Press.

Doan, H. M., & Cooper, D. L. (1971). Conditional discrimination in children: Two relevant factors. *Child Development, 42*, 209–220.

Doherty, M., & Perner, J. (1998). Metalinguistic awareness and theory of mind: Just two words for the same thing? *Cognitive Development, 13*, 279–305.

Fahie, C. M., & Symons, D. K. (2003). Executive functioning and theory of mind in children clinically referred for attention and behavior problems. *Journal of Applied Developmental Psychology, 24*, 51–73.

Fischhoff, B. (1977). Perceived informativeness of facts. *Journal of Experimental Psychology: Human Perception & Performance, 3*, 349–358.

Fischhoff, B., & Beyth, R. (1975). "I knew it would happen": Remembered probabilities of once-future things. *Organizational Behavior & Human Decision Processes, 13*, 1–16.

Fitzmaurice, G. M. (1998). Regression models for discrete longitudinal data. In B. S. Everitt & G. Dunn (Eds.), *Statistical analysis of medical data: New developments* (pp. 175–201). New York: Oxford University Press.

Flavell, J. H., Green, F. L., & Flavell, E. R. (1986). Development of knowledge about the appearance-reality distinction. *Monographs of the Society for Research in Child Development, 51*, 1–87.

Flynn, E., O'Malley, C., & Wood, D. (2004). A longitudinal, microgenetic study of the emergence of false belief understanding and inhibition skills. *Developmental Science, 7*, 103–115.

Fox, E. (1995). Negative priming from ignored distractors in visual selection: A review. *Psychonomic Bulletin & Review, 2*, 145–173.

Frye, D., Zelazo, P. D., & Palfai, T. (1995). Theory of mind and rule-based reasoning. *Cognitive Development, 10*, 483–527.

Garner, W. R., & Felfoldy, G. L. (1970). Integrality of stimulus dimensions in various types of information processing. *Cognitive Psychology, 1*, 225–241.

Gerardi-Caulton, G. (2000). Sensitivity to spatial conflict and the development of self-regulation in children 24–36 months of age. *Developmental Science, 3*, 397–404.

Gernsbacher, M. A., & Faust, M. E. (1991). The mechanism of suppression: A component of general comprehension skill. *Journal of Experimental Psychology, 17*, 245–262.

Gerstadt, C. L., Hong, Y. J., & Diamond, A. (1994). The relationship between cognition and action: Performance of children 3.5–7 years old on a Stroop-like Day-Night test. *Cognition, 53*, 129–153.

Goldman, P. S., & Rosvold, H. E. (1970). Localization of function within the dorsolateral prefrontal cortex of the rhesus monkey. *Experimental Neurology, 27*, 291–304.

Gollin, E. S. (1964). Reversal learning and conditional discrimination in children. *Journal of Comparative & Physiological Psychology, 58*, 441–445.

Gollin, E. S. (1965). Factors affecting conditional discrimination in children. *Journal of Comparative and Physiological Pyschology, 60*, 422–427.

Gollin, E. S., & Liss, P. (1962). Conditional discrimination in children. *Journal of Comparative and Physiological Psychology, 55*, 850–855.

Gopnik, A., & Rosati, A. (2001). Duck or rabbit? Reversing ambiguous figures and understanding ambiguous representations. *Developmental Science, 4*, 175–183.

Hala, S., & Russell, J. (2001). Executive control within strategic deception: A window on early cognitive development? *Journal of Experimental Child Psychology, 80*, 112–141.

Halsband, U., & Passingham, R. E. (1982). The role of premotor and parietal cortex in the direction of action. *Brain Research, 240*, 368–372.

Halsband, U., & Passingham, R. E. (1985). Premotor cortex and the conditions for movement in monkeys (macaca mulatta). *Behavioural Brain Research, 18*, 269–277.

Hawkins, S. A., & Hastie, R. (1990). Hindsight: Biased judgments of past events after the outcomes are known. *Psychological Bulletin, 107*, 311–327.

Heberle, J., Clune, M., & Kelly, K. (1999, April). *Development of young children's understanding of the appearance–reality distinction.* Paper presented at the Society for Research in Child Development, Albuquerque, New Mexico.

Heidbreder, E. F. (1928). Problem solving in children and adults. *Journal of Genetic Psychology, 35*, 522–545.

Hoffrage, U., Hertwig, R., & Gigerenzer, G. (2000). Hindsight bias: A by-product of knowledge updating? *Journal of Experimental Psychology: Learning, Memory, & Cognition, 26*, 566–581.

Hughes, C. (1998a). Executive function in preschoolers: Links with theory of mind and verbal ability. *British Journal of Developmental Psychology, 16*, 233–253.

Hughes, C. (1998b). Finding your marbles: Does preschoolers' strategic behavior perdict later understanding of mind? *Developmental Psychology, 34*, 1326–1339.

Jacques, S., Zelazo, P. D., Kirkham, N. A., & Semcesen, T. K. (1999). Rule selection vs rule execution. *Developmental Psychology, 35*, 770–780.

Jarvik, M. E. (1956). Simple color discrimination in chimpanzees: Effect of varying contiguity between cue and incentive. *Journal of Comparative and Physiological Psychology, 49*, 492–495.

Jeffrey, W. E. (1961). Variables in early discrimination learning: III. Simultaneous vs. successive stimulus presentation. *Child Development, 32*, 305–310.

Kahneman, D., & Chajczyk, D. (1983). Tests of the automaticity of reading: Dilution of Stroop effects by color-irrelevant stimuli. *Journal of Experimental Psychology: Human Perception & Performance, 9*, 497–509.

Kirkham, N. Z., Cruess, L., & Diamond, A. (2003). Helping children apply their knowledge to their behavior on a dimension-switching task. *Developmental Science, 6*, 449–467.

Kirkham, N. Z. & Diamond, A. (2003). Sorting between theories of perseveration: performance in conflict tasks requires memory, attention and inhibition. *Developmental Science, 6*, 474–476.

Kloo, D., & Perner, J. (2003). Training transfer between card sorting and false belief understanding: Helping children understand conflicting descriptions. *Child Development, 74*, 1823–1839.

Kloo, D., & Perner, J. (2005). Disentangling dimensions in the dimensional change card sorting task. *Developmental Science, 8*, 44–56.

Kochanska, G., Murray, K. T., Jacques, T. Y., Koenig, A. L., & Vandegeest, K. A. (1996). Inhibitory control in young children and its role in emerging internalization. *Child Development, 67*, 490–507.

Kuene, M. (1946). Experimental investigation of the relation of language to transposition behavior in young children. *Journal of Experimental Psychology, 36*, 471–486.

Lawler, K. A., & Cowey, A. (1987). On the role of posterior parietal and prefrontal cortex in visuo-spatial perception and attention. *Experimental Brain Research, 65*, 695–698.

Liang, K.-Y., & Zeger, S. L. (1986). Longitudinal data analysis using generalized linear models. *Biometrika, 73,* 13–22.

Llamas, C., & Diamond, A. (1991). Development of frontal cortex abilities in children between 3–8 years of age. *Abstracts of the Society for Research in Child Development, 8*, 347.

MacLeod, C. M. (1998). Training on integrated versus separated Stroop tasks: The progression of interference and facilitation. *Memory & Cognition, 26*, 201–211.

Markman, E. M., & Wachtel, G. F. (1988). Children's use of mutual exclusivity to constrain the meanings of words. *Cognitive Psychology, 20*, 121–157.

Mayr, U. (2001). Age differences in the selection of mental sets: The role of inhibition, stimulus ambiguity, and response-set overlap. *Psychology and Aging, 16*, 96–109.

Mayr, U., & Keele, S. W. (2000). Changing internal constraints on action: The role of backward inhibition. *Journal of Experimental Psychology: General, 129*, 4–26.

McClelland, J. L., & Kawamoto, A. H. (1986). Mechanisms of sentence processing: Assigning roles to constituents of sentences. In J. L. McClelland & D. E. Rumelhart (Ed.), *Parallel distributed processing: Exploration in the microstructure of cognition. Volume 1: Foundations* (pp. 272–325). Cambridge, MA: MIT Press.

Meiran, N. (1996). Reconfiguration of processing mode prior to task performance. *Journal of Experimental Psychology: Learning, Memory, and Cognition, 22*, 1423–1442.

Meiran, N. (2000). Reconfiguration of stimulus task-sets and response task-sets during task-switching. In S. Monsell & J. Driver (Eds.), *Control of cognitive processes: Attention and performance XVIII* (pp. 377–400). Cambridge, MA: MIT Press.

Milliken, B., & Tipper, S. P. (1998). Attention and inhibition. In H. Pashler (Ed.), *Attention* (pp. 191–221). Hove, UK: Psychology Press.

Monsell, S. (2003). Task switching. *Trends in Cognitive Sciences, 7*, 134–140.

Monsell, S., & Driver, J. (Eds.). (2000). *Control of cognitive processes: Attention and performance XVIII.* Cambridge, MA: MIT Press.

Moore, T., Killiany, R., Rosene, D., Prusty, S., Hollander, W., & Moss, M. (2002). Impairment of executive function induced by hypertension in the rhesus money (*macaca mulatta*). *Behavioral Neuroscience, 116*, 387–396.

Morton, J. B., & Munakata, Y. (2002a). Active versus latent representations: A neural network model of perseveration and dissociation in early childhood. *Developmental Psychobiology, 40*, 255–265.

Morton, J. B., & Munakata, Y. (2002b). Are you listening? Exploring a developmental knowledge action dissociation in a speech interpretation task. *Developmental Science, 5*, 435–440.

Mueller, U., Dick, A. S., Gela, K., Overton, W. F., & Zelazo, P. D. (2004). *The role of negative priming in the Dimensional Change Card Sort task.* Manuscript submitted for publication.

Mueller, U., & Zelazo, P. D. (2001, October 26–27). *The role of selective attention and negative priming in the DCCS.* Paper presented at the Second Biennial Meeting of the Cognitive Development Society, Virginia Beach, VA.

Mueller, U., Zelazo, P. D., & Imrisek, S. (2004). *What is the best predictor of the understanding of false belief? Gauging the impact of executive function, representational understanding, and propositional negation.* Manuscript submitted for publication.

Munakata, Y. (1998). Infant perseveration: Rethinking data, theory, and the role of modelling. *Developmental Science, 1,* 205–211.

Munakata, Y. (2001). Graded representations in behavioral dissociations. *Trends in Cognitive Sciences, 5*, 309–315.

Munakata, Y., Morton, J. B., & Yerys, B. E. (2003). Children's perseveration: attentional inertia and alternative accounts. *Developmental Science, 6*, 471–473.

Munakata, Y., & Yerys, B. E. (2001). All together now: When dissociations between knowledge and action disappear. *Psychological Science, 12*, 335–337.

Neill, W. T., & Valdes, L. A. (1992). Persistence of negative priming: Steady state of decay? *Journal of Experimental Psychology: Learning, Memory, and Cognition, 18*, 565–576.

Neill, W. T., Valdes, L. A., & Terry, K. M. (1995). Selective attention and the inhibitory control of cognition. In F. N. Dempster & C. J. Brainerd (Eds.), *Interference and inhibition in cognition* (pp. 207–261). New York: Academic.

Overman, W. H. (1990). Performance on traditional match-to-sample, nonmatch-to-sample, and object discrimination tasks by 12 to 32 month-old children: A developmental progression. *Annals of the New York Academy of Sciences, 608*, 365–393.

Overman, W. H., Bachevalier, J., Turner, M., & Peuster, A. (1992). Object recognition versus object discrimination: Comparison between human infants and infant monkeys. *Behavioral Neuroscience, 106*, 15–29.

Palta, M., & Lin, C.-Y. (1999). Latent variables, measurement error and methods for analyzing longitudinal binary and ordinal data. *Statistics in Medicine, 18,* 385–396.

Passingham, R. E. (1985a). Cortical mechanisms and cues for action. *Philosophical Transactions of the Royal Society (London) Series B, 308,* 101–111.

Passingham, R. E. (1985b). Premotor cortex: Sensory cues and movement. *Behavioural Brain Research, 18,*175–185.

Passingham, R. E. (1988). Premotor cortex and preparation for movement. *Experimental Brain Research, 70,* 590–596.

Perner, J., & Lang, B. (2002). What causes 3-year olds' difficulty on the dimensional change card sorting task? *Infant & Child Development, 11*, 93–105.

Perner, J., Leekam, S. R., & Wimmer, H. (1987). Three-year-olds' difficulty with false belief: The case for a conceptual deficit. *British Journal of Developmental Psychology, 5,* 125–137.

Perner, J., Stummer, S., & Lang, B. (1999). Theory of mind finds its piagetian perspective: Why alternative naming comes with understanding belief. *Cognitive Development, 17,* 1451–1472.

Perner, J., Stummer, S., Sprung, M., & Doherty, M. (2002). Theory of mind finds its Piagetian perspective: Why alternative naming comes with understanding belief. *Cognitive Development, 17,* 1451–1472.

Petrides, M. (1982). Motor conditional associative-learning after selective prefrontal lesions in the monkey. *Behavioural Brain Research, 5*, 407–413.

Petrides, M. (1985). Deficits in non-spatial conditional associative learning after periarcuate lesions in the monkey. *Behavioural Brain Research, 16*, 95–101.

Petrides, M. (1986). The effect of periarcuate lesions in the monkey on the performance of symmetrically and asymmetrically reinforced visual and auditory go, no-go tasks. *Journal of Neuroscience, 6*, 2054–2063.

Piaget, J., & Inhelder, B. (1941). *Le développement des quantités physiques chez l'enfant* [The development of physical quantities in the child]. Neuchâtel, Switzerland: Delachaux.

Piaget, J., & Inhelder, B. (1956). *The child's conception of space*. London: Routledge & Kegan Paul.

Pratt, J., & Hommel, B. (2003). Symbolic control of visual attention: The role of working memory and attentional control settings. *Journal of Experimental Psychology: Human Learning and Performance, 2,* 835–845.

Reed, M., Pien, D. L., & Rothbart, M. K. (1984). Inhibitory self-control in preschool children. *Merrill Palmer Quarterly, 30,* 131–147.

Rennie, D., Bull, R., & Diamond, A. (2004). Executive functioning in preschoolers: Reducing the inhibitory demands of the dimensional change card sort task. *Developmental Neuropsychology, 26,* 423–443.

Ridderinkhof, K. R., van der Molen, M. W., Band, G. P. H., & Bashore, T. R. (1997). Sources of interference from irrelevant information: A developmental study. *Journal of Experimental Child Psychology, 65,* 315–341.

Riggs, K. J., & Williams, O. (2003). *Rule following and inhibition in the dimensional change card sorting task.* Unpublished manuscript, London Metropolitan University, England.

Rogers, R. D., & Monsell, S. (1995). Costs of a predictable switch between simple cognitive tasks. *Journal of Experimental Psychology, 124,* 207–231.

Ross, E., Shutts, K., & Diamond, A. (2000). *Spatial or temporal contiguity: Factors underlying infants' understanding of the relation between stimulus and reward.* Paper presented at the New England Mini-Conference on Infant Studies, Worcester, MA.

Rudel, R. G. (1955). *A re-evaluation of the dichotomy of absolute and relative responses in transposition.* Unpublished doctoral dissertation, New York University, New York.

Sabbagh, M. A., Xu, F., Carlson, S. M., Moses, L. J., & Lee, K. (in press). The development of executive functioning and theory of mind: A comparison of Chinese and U.S. preschoolers. *Psychological Science.*

SAS Institute Inc. (1990). *The SAS System.* Cary, NC: Author.

Schoenfeld, M. A., Tempelmann, C., Martinez, A., Hopf, J.-M., Sattler, C., Heinze, H.-J., et al. (2003). From the cover: Dynamics of feature binding during object-selective attention. *Proceedings of the National Academy of Sciences, USA, 100,* 11806–11811.

Shepp, B. E., & Barrett, S. E. (1991). The development of perceived structure and attention: Evidence from divided and selective attention tasks. *Expermental Child Psychology, 51,* 434–458.

Shepp, B. E., Barrett, S. E., & Kolbet, L. L. (1987). The development of selective attention: Holistic perception versus resource allocation. *Journal of Experimental Child Psychology, 43,* 159–180.

Shutts, K., Ross, E., Hayden, M., & Diamond, A. (2001). *Grasping that one thing is related to another: Contributions of spatial contiguity, temporal proximity, and physical connection.* Paper presented at the biennial meeting of the Society for Research in Child Development, Minneapolis, MN.

Stiratelli, R., Laird, N. M., & Ware, J. H. (1984). Random-effects models for serial observations with binary response. *Biometrics, 40,* 961–971.

Stummer, S. (2001). *Sag es anders—ToM! Von einem metalinguistischen Bewusstsein zu alternativen Erklärungsansätzen.* Unpublished doctoral dissertation, University of Salzburg, Austria.

Tipper, S. P. (1985). The negative priming effect: Inhibitory priming by ignored objects. *Quarterly Journal of Experimental Psychology: Human Experimental Psychology, 37A,* 571–590.

Towse, J. N., Redbond, J., Houston-Price, C. M. T., & Cook, S. (2000). Understanding the dimensional change card sort: Perspectives from task success and failure. *Cognitive Development, 15,* 347–365.

Waltz, D. L., & Pollack, J. B. (1985). Massively parallel parsing: A strongly interactive model of natural language interpretation. *Cognitive Science, 9,* 51–74.

Waszak, F., Hommel, B., & Allport, A. (2003). Task-switching and long-term priming: Role of episodic stimulus-task bindings in task-shift costs. *Cognitive Psychology, 46,* 361–413.

Wimmer, H., & Perner, J. (1983). Beliefs about beliefs: Representation and constraining function of wrong beliefs in young children's understanding of deception. *Cognition, 13,* 103–128.

Wylie, G., & Allport, A. (2000). Task switching and the measurement of "switch costs". *Psychology Research, 63,* 212–233.

Zaitchik, D. (1991). Is only seeing really believing? Sources of true belief in the false belief task. *Cognitive Development, 6,* 91–103.

Zeger, S. L., Liang, K.-Y., & Albert, P. S. (1988). Models for longitudinal data: A generalized estimating equation approach. *Biometrics, 44,* 1049–1060.

Zelazo, P. D., Craik, F. I. M., & Booth, L. (2004). Executive function across the life span. *Acta Psychologica, 115,* 167–184.

Zelazo, P. D., & Frye, D. (1997). Cognitive complexity and control: A theory of the development of deliberate reasoning and intentional action. In M. Stamenov (Ed.), *Language structure, discourse, and the access to consciousness* (pp. 113–153). Amsterdam: Benjamins.

Zelazo, P. D., Frye, D., & Rapus, T. (1996). An age-related dissociation between knowing rules and using them. *Cognitive Development, 11,* 37–63.

Zelazo, P. D., Frye, D., Reznick, J. S., Schuster, B. V., & Argitis, G. (1995). *Age-related changes in the execution of explicit rules.* Unpublished manuscript.

Zelazo, P. D., & Jacques, S. (1996). Children's rule use: Representation, reflection and cognitive control. *Annals of Child Development, 12,* 119–176.

Zelazo, P. D., Mueller, U., Frye, D., & Marcovitch, S. (2003). The development of executive function in early childhood. *Monographs of the Society for Research in Child Development, 68*(3, Serial No. 274).

Zelazo, P. D., Reznick, J. S., & Piñon, D. E. (1995). Response control and the execution of verbal rules. *Developmental Psychology, 31,* 508–517.

2005 SUBSCRIPTION ORDER FORM

DEVELOPMENTAL NEUROPSYCHOLOGY
AN INTERNATIONAL JOURNAL OF LIFE-SPAN ISSUES IN NEUROPSYCHOLOGY
Volumes 27 & 28, 2005, 6 Issues — ISSN 8756-5641/Online 1532-6942

SUBSCRIPTION PRICES PER VOLUME:

Please ❑ enter ❑ renew my subscription:

Category:	Access Type:	Price: (U.S.-Canada/All Other Countries)
❑ Individual	Online & Print	$100.00/$145.00

Subscriptions are entered on a calendar-year basis only and must be paid in advance in U.S. currency—check, credit card, or money order. Prices for subscriptions include postage and handling. **Journal prices expire 12/31/05. NOTE:** Institutions must pay institutional rates. Individual subscription orders are welcome if prepaid by credit card or personal check. **Please note:** A $20.00 penalty will be charged against customers providing checks that must be returned for payment. This assessment will be made only in instances when problems in collecting funds are directly attributable to customer error.

❑ Check Enclosed (U.S. Currency Only)   **Total Amount Enclosed $**_____

❑ Charge My: ❑ VISA   ❑ MasterCard   ❑ AMEX   ❑ Discover

Card Number _____ Exp. Date____/_____

Signature _____
(Credit card orders cannot be processed without your signature.)
PRINT CLEARLY for proper delivery. STREET ADDRESS/SUITE/ROOM # REQUIRED FOR DELIVERY.

Name _____

Address _____

City/State/Zip+4 _____

Daytime Phone # _____ E-mail address _____
Prices are subject to change without notice. **Direct all inquiries and orders to the address below.**

For information about online journal access, visit our online journal portal at: www.LEAonline.com

LIBRARY RECOMMENDATION FORM

DEVELOPMENTAL NEUROPSYCHOLOGY
AN INTERNATIONAL JOURNAL OF LIFE-SPAN ISSUES IN NEUROPSYCHOLOGY
Volumes 27 & 28, 2005, 6 Issues — ISSN 8756-5641/Online 1532-6942

Category:	Access Type:	Price: (U.S.-Canada/All Other Countries)
❑ Institutional	Online & Print	$850.00/$895.00
❑ Institutional	Online Only	$765.00/$765.00
❑ Institutional	Print Only	$810.00/$855.00

Name _____Title_____

Institution/Department _____

Delivery Address _____

E-mail Address _____
Complete and forward to your librarian. Librarians, please send your orders directly to LEA or contact your subscription agent.

DIRECT ALL SUBSCRIPTION ORDERS TO:
Lawrence Erlbaum Associates, Inc.,
Journal Subscription Department; 10 Industrial Avenue, Mahwah, NJ 07430
(201) 258–2200; FAX (201) 760–3735; journals@erlbaum.com

LAWRENCE ERLBAUM ASSOCIATES

LEA *Online*
WWW.LEAONLINE.COM

Building Object Categories
in Developmental Time

Edited by
Lisa Gershkoff-Stowe • David H. Rakison

BUILDING OBJECT CATEGORIES IN DEVELOPMENTAL TIME

Edited by
LISA GERSHKOFF-STOWE
Indiana University at Bloomington
DAVID H. RAKISON
Carnegie Mellon University

A VOLUME IN CARNEGIE MELLON'S SYMPOSIA ON COGNITION

The study of object category development is a central concern in the field of cognitive science. Researchers investigating visual and auditory perception, cognition, language acquisition, semantics, neuroscience, and modeling have begun to tackle a number of different but centrally related questions concerning the representations and processes that underlie categorization and its development. This book covers a broad range of current research topics in category development. Its aim is to understand the perceptual and cognitive mechanisms that underlie category formation and how they change in developmental time.

The chapters in this book are organized around three interrelated themes: (1) the fundamental process by which infants recognize and remember objects and their properties, (2) the contribution of language in selecting relevant features for object categorization, and (3) the higher-level cognitive processes that guide the formation of semantic systems. The volume is appropriate for researchers, educators, and advanced graduate students.

0-8058-4490-2 [cloth] / 2005 / 480pp. / $99.95
0-8058-4491-0 [paper] / 2005 / 480pp. / $49.95
Prices are subject to change without notice.

LAWRENCE
ERLBAUM
ASSOCIATES
www.erlbaum.com

Toll-Free: 1-800-926-6579 ◇ E-mail: orders@erlbaum.com ◇ Fax: 201-760-37.

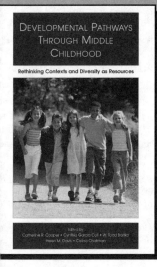

DEVELOPMENTAL PATHWAYS THROUGH MIDDLE CHILDHOOD

Rethinking Contexts and Diversity as Resources

Edited by
Catherine R. Cooper • Cynthia García Coll • W. Todd Bartko
Helen M. Davis • Celina Chatman

DEVELOPMENTAL PATHWAYS THROUGH MIDDLE CHILDHOOD
Rethinking Context and Diversity as Resources

Edited by
Catherine R. Cooper, *University of Californa at Santa Cruz*
Cynthia T. García Coll, *Brown University*
W. Todd Bartko, *University of Michigan/Ann Arbor*
Helen M. Davis, *University of California at Los Angeles*
Celina Chatman, *University of Chicago*

When can contexts and diversity be resources, rather than risks, for children's developmental pathways? Scholars, policy makers, and practitioners increasingly realize that middle childhood matters as a time when children's pathways diverge, as they meet new and overlapping contexts they must navigate on their way to adolescence and adulthood. This volume shines new light on this important transition by tracing how these contexts-cultural, economic, historical, political, and social-can support or indermine children's pathways, and how children's own actions and the actions of those around them shape these pathways. With a focus on demographic changes taking place in the U.S., the volume also maps how experiences of diversity-reflecting culture, ethnicity, gender, and social class-matter for children's life contexts and options.

Chapters by a team of social scientists in the MacArthur Foundation Research Network on Successful Pathways through Middle Childhood present the fruits of ten years of research on these issues with diverse cultural and ethnic communities across the U.S. These include:

> a set of models and measures that trace how contexts and diversity evolve and interact over time, with an epilogue that aligns and compares them;

> surprising new findings, quantitative and qualitative, with cases showing how children and families shape and are affected by their individual, recreational, institutional, and cultural experiences; and

> applications to policy and practice for diverse children and families.

The importance of these new models, methods, findings, and applications is the topic of commentaries by distinguished scholars with both U.S. and international perspectives.

The book is intended for researchers, practitioners, and policy makers, as well as students in psychology, sociology, and education.
-8058-5199-2 [cloth] / 2005 / 368pp. / $69.95
Special Discount Price! $36.00
Applies if payment accompanies order or for course adoption orders of 5 or more copies. **No further discounts apply.**
Prices are subject to change without notice.

LAWRENCE
ERLBAUM
ASSOCIATES
www.erlbaum.com

Toll-Free: 1-800-926-6579 ◇ E-mail: orders@erlbaum.com ◇ Fax: 201-760-3735

AUTISM SPECTRUM DISORDERS

Identification, Education, and Treatment, Third Edition

Edited by
DIANNE ZAGER, *Pace University*

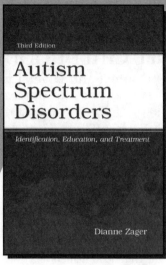

The field of autism has been growing at an unprecedented rate in recent years. In addition to an actual rise in the number of classic DSM-IV cases, broadened diagnostic criteria have uncovered a wider range of autistic behaviors and ability levels. The third edition of this well-known text continues the mission of its predecessors—to present a comprehensive, readable, up-to-date overview of the field of autism, one that links research, theory, and practice in ways that are accessible to both practitioners and parents. Key features include:

› **Expanded Coverage**—To accommodate the recent explosion of research, the book has been expanded from 11 to 14 chapters that examine the impact of autism on the individual and the family from infancy through adulthood.
› **Expertise**—Internationally recognized experts offer cutting-edge treatment and educational information on topics such as early diagnosis, medical treatment, assessment, educational methods, language development, behavior regulation, and family support.
› **Neurobiological Research**—Comprehensive medical research and treatment chapters provide an understandable overview of neurobiological research and current treatments including when and how medication can be employed as part of a treatment plan.
› **Focus on Early Years**—Old sections I and III have been combined and a new 3-chapter section on early identification and intervention added.
› **Focus on Parents and Families**—In addition to a chapter on the evolving role of families, a new chapter addresses family needs during the preschool years.
› **Integration of Assessment and Intervention**—The chapters on assessment and intervention have been reorganized and more closely integrated in keeping with current thinking about their inter-relatedness.
› **Future Directions**—Two chapters discuss emerging directions in this exploding field and how to make informed decisions among a variety of approaches.

This book is appropriate for anyone—students, practitioners or parents—who must provide care for an autistic child.

0-8058-4578-X [cloth] / 2005 / 608pp. / $135.00
0-8058-4579-8 [paper] / 2005 / 608pp. / $59.95
Prices are subject to change without notice.

LEA LAWRENCE ERLBAUM ASSOCIATES
www.erlbaum.com

Toll-Free: 1-800-926-6579 ◇ E-mail: orders@erlbaum.com ◇ Fax: 201-760-37

THE DEVELOPMENT
OF JUDGMENT
AND DECISION MAKING
IN CHILDREN AND ADOLESCENTS

Edited by
Janis E. Jacobs • Paul A. Klaczynski

THE DEVELOPMENT OF JUDGMENT AND DECISION MAKING IN CHILDREN AND ADOLESCENTS

Edited by

JANIS E. JACOBS,

PAUL A. KLACZYNSKI

Pennsylvania State University

In recent years, newspaper articles, television specials, and other media events have focused on the numerous hard decisions faced by today's youth, often pointing to teen pregnancy, drug use, and delinquency as evidence of faulty judgment. Over the past 10 years, many groups—including parents, educators, policymakers, and researchers—have become concerned about the decision-making abilities of children and adolescents, asking why they make risky choices, how they can be taught to be better decision makers, and what types of age-related changes occur in decision making. This book serves as a starting point for those interested in considering new ways of thinking about the development of these issues. The purpose is to bring together the voices of several authors who are conducting cutting-edge research and developing new theoretical perspectives related to the development of judgment and decision making.

The Development of Judgment and Decision Making in Children and Adolescents is divided into three parts:
 › Part I presents three distinctive developmental models that offer different explanations of "what develops" and the relative importance of different cognitive components and experiential components that may be important for developing judgment and decision-making skills.
 › Part II emphasizes the emotional, cultural, and social aspects of decision making—three topics that have been influential in the adult literature on judgment and decision making but are just beginning to be explored in the developmental area.
 › Part III provides three examples of research that applies developmental and decision-making models to practical research questions.

This book is intended for the professional market or for graduate courses on decision making or cognitive or social development.

-8058-4256-X [cloth] / 2005 / 384pp. / $99.95

Special Discount Price! $39.95
Applies if payment accompanies order or for course adoption orders of *or more copies.***No further discounts apply.**
Prices are subject to change without notice.

LEA LAWRENCE
ERLBAUM
ASSOCIATES
www.erlbaum.com

Toll-Free: 1-800-926-6579 ◇ **E-mail: orders@erlbaum.com** ◇ **Fax: 201-760-3735**